HOMEWATERS

Homewaters

A HUMAN AND NATURAL
HISTORY OF PUGET SOUND

David B. Williams

UNIVERSITY OF WASHINGTON PRESS

Seattle

A MICHAEL J. REPASS BOOK

Homewaters was made possible in part by a grant from the Michael J. Repass Fund for Northwest Writers.

Additional support was provided by a generous gift from Claudia Skelton.

Copyright © 2021 by the University of Washington Press

Composed in Charis SIL, based on Charter, designed by Matthew Carter
Display type set in Soria, designed by Daniel Iglesias Arreal,
and Trade Gothic, designed by Jackson Burke
Maps by Pease Press Cartography, https://peasepress.com

25 24 23 22 21   5 4 3 2 1

Printed and bound in the United States of America

UNIVERSITY OF WASHINGTON PRESS
uwapress.uw.edu

LIBRARY OF CONGRESS CATALOGING-IN-PUBLICATION DATA
Names: Williams, David B., 1965– author.
Title: Homewaters : a human and natural history of Puget Sound / David B. Williams.
Description: Seattle : University of Washington Press, [2021] | Includes bibliographical references and index.
Identifiers: LCCN 2020045928 (print) | LCCN 2020045929 (ebook) |
    ISBN 9780295748603 (hardcover) | ISBN 9780295748610 (ebook)
Subjects: LCSH: Human ecology—Washington (State)—Puget Sound Region. | Natural history—Washington (State)—Puget Sound Region. | Nature—Effect of human beings on—Washington (State)—Puget Sound Region. | Puget Sound Region (Wash.)—Environmental conditions | Puget Sound Region (Wash.)—History, Local.
Classification: LCC GF504.W2 W55 2021 (print) | LCC GF504.W2 (ebook) |
    DDC 304.209164/32—dc23
LC record available at https://lccn.loc.gov/2020045928
LC ebook record available at https://lccn.loc.gov/2020045929

To Marjorie

You are my rock, always supportive,

willing to listen, offer advice,

and share a shot of good whiskey.

CONTENTS

PREFACE

In the summer of 2018, I grieved, with millions of people around the world. Our collective sadness focused on a twenty-year-old mother, Tahlequah, one of a dwindling number of orca who regularly visit Puget Sound. On July 24, Tahlequah had given birth to her second child, a daughter, who died within thirty minutes. For the next seventeen days, she carried the six-foot-long body of her dead offspring on a journey of more than one thousand miles. Finally, Tahlequah let her calf go. Our hearts broke.

Then, two years later, on September 6, 2020, it was with much joy that whale researchers announced Tahlequah had given birth two days earlier. The healthy and precocious boy calf, dubbed J57, was born in the Strait of Juan de Fuca, after an eighteen-month gestation. Researchers have high hopes the baby will survive. To paraphrase Emily Dickinson, "Hope is a baby orca in Puget Sound."

Mourning the loss of a child is a natural response for humans and orca: both species are smart, self-aware, and deeply connected to their families. Clearly Tahlequah, like us, had loved her daughter and did not want to part from her. And, as we learned, her extended family tried to help by providing food for the grieving mother. Ecologists suggested that they might also have been mourning with her.

Tahlequah and her family are members of a group of more than seventy orca known as the southern resident killer whales. (Orca are not actually whales; they are in the dolphin family.) These animals, which have evolved a culture and community unique to their home in Puget Sound, travel together, hunt together, and communicate using their own distinctive dialect. Solidifying their cultural affinity, the southern residents also rely on the collective knowledge of their elders, particularly the matriarchs, who act as guides and teachers to their family members. Why shouldn't they also love and grieve together?

And why shouldn't we also love and grieve with Tahlequah? Few animals are as sacred and iconic to Puget Sound residents as orca, or in more dire straits. Habitat loss, disturbance from noise and boat traffic, exposure to an ever-increasing toxic mixture of pollutants, and over-fishing of their favorite food, salmon, have pushed the southern resident population to the point where their very survival in Puget Sound is in doubt. For many who followed Tahlequah, their grief for her was compounded by their grief for the environment of Puget Sound and the way its degradation affects orca and humans. If Tahlequah and her calf couldn't thrive, what did it mean for us?

More than any other story, Tahlequah's loss crystallized the central environmental challenges of Puget Sound. The orca are suffering. The salmon are suffering. We are responsible.

I had been working on this book for two years when Tahlequah and her baby became globally known emblems of Puget Sound. Their story came at a critical moment. In the past few decades, restoration efforts have created a Puget Sound healthy enough to support the majority of its species, yet not healthy enough to fully support iconic species such as salmon and orca. The human residents have to decide how to act: Will we continue working to restore the ecological health of Puget Sound or allow it to suffer from our actions?

What prompted me to begin this book was my longtime fascination with exploring the past to better understand the present. For the most part, my earlier books focused on local stories, as in *Too High and Too Steep: Reshaping Seattle's Topography*, where I had a simple pair of questions: How did the early settlers in Seattle reshape the landscape to suit their needs, and how do those changes still influence the city, its residents, and its development? I hoped that by answering those questions I would help people develop deeper relationships and stronger connections to their home landscape, as well as an awareness of how we affect the natural world around us.

For most of my life, I have lived within a few miles of Puget Sound, the narrow inland sea between the Cascade and Olympic Mountains. (As chapter 1 shows, though, the geography is more complicated than this basic definition.) I knew that I lived by troubled waters but I did not fully grasp the magnitude of the crisis that had been rising around me, like the tide submerging a low island. Although I saw myself as someone deeply aware of my natural surroundings, I realized I simply hadn't paid close enough attention to a place I love and where I intend to reside for the rest of my life. I needed to ask the same questions about Puget Sound that I had asked about Seattle. I needed to take heed of all the people who have lived here, how they have related to the landscape over the millennia, and how their stories could provide a better understanding of the conditions now shaping the lives of modern residents.

Furthermore, as a writer who has generally focused on stories about the land, I had not fully appreciated the water and those who dwell in it. Standing on the shoreline or riding a ferry and seeing only the surface of the water, which tends to appear untainted and beautiful, I had long failed to see the interconnected lives of the plants and animals beneath, and to understand how they sustain and breathe life, both metaphorically and literally, into Puget Sound. The effects of human activity—overfishing, pollution, and climate change—reach deep beneath the surface. Our actions, their lives, our lives: we cannot cut one strand without unraveling the many connections that link us.

This book, then, is my way to rectify my lack of understanding of the cultural and ecological history of my homewaters and to provide a resource for others. The more of us who know and care about this place, the more momentum we can build to change our ways. We have reached a critical confluence for the waters of Puget Sound. Paraphrasing Wallace Stegner, is this a native home of hope where we can create a society to match its scenery, or will we succumb to baser values?

As I learned of the origins, complexity, and connections of Puget Sound, I realized that the stories began to tell a biography of place. In the introduction to her book *The Presidio*, the geographer Lisa Benton-Short writes: "Simply defined, a biography is a written account of a life. In this case, the life is that of a place. . . . What follows is a biography . . . that represents my interpretation of a unique set of circumstances and opportunities; it is just one of many stories that could be written."[1] A biography of a human being tells of the interactions between the protagonist and others, be they family, friends, coworkers, or enemies. A biography of a place tells the stories of interactions among the more-than-human inhabitants as well as between the people and landscape, the people and the flora and fauna, and the long-term residents and newcomers.

Many stories could be written about Puget Sound. In this biography of my homewaters, I have chosen stories that distill the essence of this place. Some have previously been overlooked, such as warfare and Native peoples' struggles over thousands of years to protect their homes; the stories of the kelp and herring, the Sound's most ecologically important plant and animal species; and the history of the mosquito fleet, the poetically named vessels that presaged the modern transportation network. Others are more iconic narratives, including those of the salmon and orca and their unique adaptations to the Sound. Collectively, these stories help us understand how the human and more-than-human residents made their homes in this landscape.

My stories also tell how people have inhabited this home, used its natural resources, traveled through its landscape, and defended the place they cherished. These stories focus on both non-Native and Coast Salish peoples, the latter of whom have resided in the Puget Sound region for millennia. Throughout this book, I use the terms *Coast Salish*, *Native*, and *Indigenous* to refer to the Native peoples of Puget Sound. *Coast Salish* more broadly refers to Indigenous peoples in the United States and Canada who speak one among the family of languages known as Coast Salish, which is spoken from northern Oregon to the northern tip of Vancouver Island. Within Puget Sound, two of the many distinct languages and dialects in this family are Lushootseed, which is spoken more widely, and Twana, used primarily around Hood Canal. In including Native stories and voices, I certainly make no claim to be authoritative or to speak for anyone else. I simply hope that I have been respectful of the culture, the history, and the knowledge embodied in them.

For my stories of natural history, I have focused on lesser-known but key species, including geoduck (arguably better known than understood), rockfish, and Olympia oysters. Their stories illustrate the complexities of the ecosystem and accentuate how the actions of residents have direct effects on the health of Puget Sound. They show why it is imperative that we act now to address threats to these species' survival. These accounts share many themes with the stories of salmon and orca: habitat degradation, overconsumption of resources, inadequate science, poor decision-making, and human arrogance. By looking across the ecosystem and seeing the connections that bind it together, we can understand better what habitat restoration looks like and make wiser choices for recovery of the entire Puget Sound ecological community.

Many of my stories required getting out in the field, and I was privileged during my work on this book to tag along with biologists who regularly fish, dive in, and dredge deep into Puget Sound. I have been struck by their passion and knowledge, as well as their desire to share both with the general public. The snapshots of those adventures included throughout the book are a way to provide further appreciation of the astonishing life that inhabits the Sound.

• • •

Despite the challenges that face the Puget Sound ecosystem, it is in far better health now than it has been for much of its recent history, primarily because scientists, citizens, and government officials have worked together to clean the water, curtail industrial pollution, and reduce resource extraction. As one ecologist told me, "You have to wonder if orca and salmon would exist if we hadn't already begun to change what we do." The improvements that have occurred certainly do not mean that all is well; recent events such as the loss of Tahlequah's calf remind us that although the overall health of Puget Sound has improved, many species still struggle for existence.

One of my intentions in blending human and ecological stories is to highlight what I consider the most significant change in the human history of Puget Sound: how the European settler mindset of land ownership and resource extraction has begun to evolve toward a relationship to the waterway based on connection and respect, and how that shift in turn has fostered the ecological improvements. By this I mean that modern-day residents of the Sound are less likely to view the water and surrounding land from an economic perspective, which tends to be (though is not always) exploitative, than from the perspective of recreation, science, and stewardship, which are more likely to generate connections to a place based on appreciation and responsibility. This change in viewpoint has occurred in part because resource-extraction jobs (such as commercial fishing and logging) have been replaced by jobs in areas such as technology, service, retail, and health care, particularly in the large cities that now dominate the population and politics of Puget Sound. It has also taken place as scientists have started to conduct more studies and to learn more about the ecology of the waterway and how it has suffered by past and present actions.

If policymakers and residents are to fashion an enlightened plan for how to act in the future, they need to work toward a more interwoven and nuanced consideration of the nature and culture of the waterway. Adopting such a new way of thinking has the benefit of greatly expanding the potential to create a thriving Puget Sound hospitable and accommodating to all forms of life.

One challenge, though, is that many residents know little about the health and history of Puget Sound, have a limited emotional connection to it, and don't see an urgency to work on cleaning and restoring it. And most scientists I spoke to expressed a need for more studies and better monitoring of the plants, animals, land, and water. But they also noted that we already have enough knowledge and commitment to work toward a better Puget Sound.

By taking these actions, the people of Puget Sound can inspire others around the world. In the words of my friend Lynda Mapes, whose stories about Tahlequah for the *Seattle Times* captivated readers, we are in a unique situation in Puget Sound where we have a convergence of people who want to protect the ecosystem, the knowledge of what we need to do to meet this goal, the funds to pay to do it, and governments willing to explore how to do it. If trying to restore a damaged ecosystem cannot happen here, then where can it occur?

Since I began writing *Homewaters*, my own enhanced appreciation and understanding of Puget Sound's incredible diversity, beauty, and potential for recovery have led me to believe that the most valuable assets of Puget Sound are not the resources we have long extracted but the relationships that residents can make with this place. Learning from the past is central to forging and nurturing these relationships and to creating a positive future for Puget Sound and all its inhabitants.

By taking this journey, I feel I gained an extra dimension of sight. Now when I look out over the surface of the Sound, I can see deep into its history and the peopling of the landscape, its residents' travels by canoe, steamer, and ferry, their endeavors to carve out a living, and their fears of invaders. I can see deep underwater to lush forests of exquisite beauty and complexity, to corpulent clams that can outlive people, and to fish whose annual spawning creates a spasm of desire attracting uncountable numbers. I can also see into a future where I have hope. If the residents of Puget Sound hold this place to be special and unique, as I think we do, then we will recognize our responsibilities not only to this generation but to the generations to come, human and more-than-human.

HOMEWATERS

1

Birth of a Name

"On Puget Sound alone, there seem to have been in the neighborhood of ten thousand proper names," wrote the ethnographer T. T. Waterman in 1922. "I have secured about half of this number, the remainder having passed out of memory."[1] This is a fundamental truth about place names. Like the natural world, they are constantly changing to reflect how different peoples relate to the land. This change is evident in Puget Sound place names, which reflect choices made by Indigenous, colonist, settler, and later inhabitants. Exploring how and why each group has chosen particular place names to define locations in and around Puget Sound provides essential insights into those groups and their relationship with the landscape.

Consider the oldest place name we know of—x̌ʷəlč—often written in English as *Whulge*. The word comes from Lushootseed and means a stretch of saltwater. It is an onomatopoeic word: the verb form refers to the noise that waves make as they come up on the beach. But x̌ʷəlč is more of a concept than a defined location, more of a way to delineate a relationship to place for the waterway's Coast Salish people. In another of Waterman's works, *Puget Sound Geography*, he wrote that Puget Sound dwellers considered those who lived far up the rivers and in the mountains as greenhorns.[2] People who lived on saltwater were better bred and wealthier and had access to better resources. This distinction was reflected in their vocabulary. As Waterman's informants told him: "If a child behaved unbecomingly, or exhibited bad taste, or bad breeding, he was told: 'Similar thou art to that fellow from yonder Issaquah.'" When someone used the word x̌ʷəlč, they did so in part to distinguish themselves from those who lived in less desirable locations.[3]

The use of x̌ʷəlč also reflects the Coast Salish inhabitants' relationship to the landscape. "We were and are part of this place. We were caretakers. We didn't have the perspective of ownership. That's why you won't find specific names for places, such as Puget Sound," says Warren King George Jr., oral historian for the Muckleshoot Indian Tribe.[4] Instead, place names reflected features of the environment that affected daily life. For example, of the 605 place names that Waterman collected describing parts of x̌ʷəlč, 202 were descriptive terms, and another 126 referenced food, human activities, plants, and animals.[5] "If your worldview is from a canoe, it is very different from that of an explorer, who had a top-down view," says Dennis Lewarch, historic preservation officer for the Suquamish Tribe.[6]

In contrast, many of the prominent place names that now appear on maps of the region reflect the ideas of a single man, George Vancouver, the British explorer who led the first known European expedition into the x̌ʷəlč. Sailing aboard the HMS *Discovery*, he left England in 1791 and arrived in the x̌ʷəlč in May 1792. Like many Royal Navy explorers, Vancouver frequently named geographical features in honor of a colleague or patron. For instance, on June 3, 1792, Vancouver named the Gulf of Georgia in honor of King George III; the preposition *of* implies ownership. That same day he also named Possession Sound, the place where he claimed formal ownership of the lands he was exploring "in the name of, and for his Britannic Majesty, his heirs and successors."[7]

If he had asked, Vancouver could have learned that the Lushootseed names for places around his Possession Sound referred to birds, canoes, plants, and topography. Vancouver, however, did not record any Lushootseed names he might have heard, even in corrupted form. Considering how often expedition members' journals mention interaction with residents, it seems highly likely that Vancouver and his men must have picked up some place names. But to have adopted Indigenous names would have acknowledged that others already inhabited the place.

Nowhere was this naming practice better illustrated than on May 29, 1792, when Vancouver made his most significant naming decision and one that continues to influence how people describe that landscape. Referring to a weeklong exploration south of modern-day Seattle by his lieutenant, Peter Puget, Vancouver wrote in his journal: "Thus by our joint efforts, we had completely explored every turning of this extensive inlet; and to commemorate Mr. Puget's exertions, the south extremity of it I named Puget's Sound."[8] Vancouver's use of the possessive form illustrates a naming convention typical of British explorers: it was another way to signal that the location had been claimed. (As with many similar names, the possessive 's was later dropped.) The precedent had been set: a newcomer's name would replace the name used by the Indigenous people.

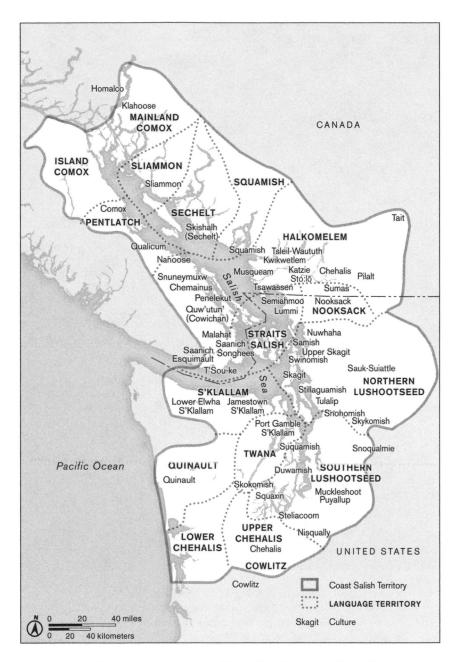

Coast Salish peoples and languages. (Adapted from Brotherton, *S'abadeb*)

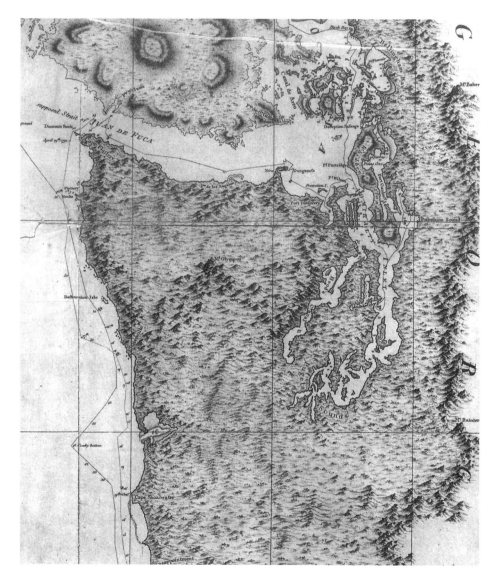

Detail of Captain Vancouver's 1792 map of the Northwest Coast, the first European map to show Puget Sound. On this map, what Vancouver named "Puget's Sound" refers only to the southernmost part of the waterbody, while Admiralty Inlet extends into what is now known as Puget Sound. (Courtesy of the Library of Congress)

Vancouver's choice of the term *sound* was unusual: the more common *bay* and *gulf* could both have been applied to the waterway. (A gulf is defined as a portion of the sea partially enclosed by land; a bay is a small gulf.) *Sound* comes from both Old English *sund*, meaning water or sea, and Old Norse *sund*, meaning swimming or strait. It was a term favored by Vancouver and his former commander, James Cook, who bestowed it on many features they encountered in their journeys, including King George III's Sound in Australia, Queen Charlotte's Sound in New Zealand, and Prince William's Sound in Alaska.

Vancouver's original description limited his lieutenant's name only to the waters south of what is now called the Tacoma Narrows; all the water north, as far as what Vancouver called Point Wilson, near Port Townsend, he named Admiralty Inlet. Neither of the narrowly specific definitions for these locations survived long. Today Admiralty Inlet refers only to the passage between Port Townsend and Whidbey Island, whereas Puget Sound has "grown" to seventy times its original area. Not that the shoreline has changed; people have simply altered their nomenclature to suit their needs.

Puget Sound's greatest official expansion occurred in 1987, at the hands of the Puget Sound Water Quality Authority, established by the Washington State legislature in 1985 to evaluate pollution-related threats to the Sound's marine life and human health. In its first comprehensive management plan, the agency defined its authority as encompassing "Puget Sound south of Admiralty Inlet (including Hood Canal and Saratoga Passage); the waters north to the Canadian border . . . extending westward to Cape Flattery; and all the land draining into these waters."[9] One way to think of the state's definition is as "greater Puget Sound," whereas the water south of Admiralty Inlet is known by some as "Puget Sound proper."

By the state's definition, Puget Sound comprised not only the inland sea but also its watershed—every inch of land where precipitation fell and flowed into a creek or stream or river that emptied into the Sound. This included the 14,411-foot summit of Mount Rainier, whose north side drains into the Puyallup River and Tacoma's Commencement Bay. To the west, it extended as far as Beach Creek, at the northwest corner of the Olympic Peninsula, more than 170 miles from Mount Rainier.

With this definition, the authority sought to emphasize that what people do on land has a direct impact on the health of Puget Sound, whether it's farmers using pesticides in the Skagit River valley, residents dumping pharmaceuticals down their toilets in Seattle, industries washing toxic substances into creeks, or hatcheries treating fish with antibiotics. Restoring, maintaining, and sustaining a functioning Puget

Sound ecosystem requires not only clean, healthy saltwater but also clean, healthy freshwater flowing into it.

This definition of the Sound reflects the priorities of those who created it—in this case, a state agency with the mandate to assess the health of the "unique and unparalleled resource" of Puget Sound.[10] The authority needed a definition that was useful, practical, and manageable, as well as boundaries that could be clearly designated, so that the legislature could see if progress was being made. Over time, and in part because of the imprimatur of the state legislature, the area defined by the authority has become part of the regulatory framework that guides federal, tribal, and state agencies.

•   •   •

Recently, another name has come into use, one that explicitly recognizes the Coast Salish inhabitants on both sides of the international border. Many people have started to refer to the waterway south of Admiralty Inlet as the southern part of the Salish Sea, a term coined in 1988 and adopted by the state in 2009. The Salish Sea encompasses Puget Sound proper, the Strait of Juan de Fuca, and the Strait of Georgia, which runs along the east side of Vancouver Island. A principal goal of adopting this name was to recognize that the inland waters of Washington and British Columbia form a single, integrated estuarine ecosystem, irrespective of the legal boundary between the United States and Canada. This understanding is particularly important to Native peoples, who traded, traveled, intermarried, and fought across this waterway for generations.

The two names offer two logical ways to view the geography: *Salish Sea* highlights modern ecological, cultural, and political issues, while *Puget Sound proper* reflects the way many residents envision the Sound and the issues that affect it. This narrower definition is the one I adopt throughout this book. I fully embrace the term *Salish Sea* as a necessary and valuable way to acknowledge the complex cultural and natural connections between Washington and British Columbia. I know that many stories, as well as human and more-than-human inhabitants of the region, cross and recross arbitrary geographic and international boundaries. Nor do these boundaries constrain my stories: when necessary, I wander into the San Juan Islands and the Strait of Juan de Fuca, as well as occasionally into Canada. In this book, however, I focus on the waterway, people, flora, and fauna south of Admiralty Inlet and the essential strands of life that form the Sound's unique stories.

2

Birth of a Place

I know of no better view of the full extent and awe-inspiring beauty of Puget Sound than from the summit of Mount Townsend on a clear summer day. I first accessed the peak via a relatively steep trail on the northeast corner of the Olympic Peninsula, about thirty-five miles west of Seattle. The trail begins in a forest of Douglas fir, western hemlock, and Pacific rhododendron and climbs into a subalpine zone of silver firs before ascending a set of switchbacks where the horizon keeps expanding with every turn. At the top of the switchbacks, it's a short walk north, on a ridge above the treeline, to the basalt-strewn summit, 6,280 feet above Puget Sound.

Across the water to the east rise the Cascade Mountains and the state's five volcanoes. Farthest north shimmers Mount Baker, named "La gran montana del Carmelo" by Spanish explorers in 1790. South of it and farther east, distant and faint, sits Glacier Peak, the last of the state's volcanoes to be recognized as such. Then comes "The Mountain," Mount Rainier, known in Lushootseed as teqʷuʔbeʔ (pronounced Takobah, Tahoma, or Tacoma), meaning "mother of waters." To the south of Rainier is Mount Adams, Rainier's little sibling—though geologists say it is bulkier and a greater lava producer than its better-known neighbor. And still farther south rises the barely perceptible, flat-topped summit of Mount St. Helens.

Each of these volcanoes formed through violent blasts of ash, gas, and rock—or, less dramatically, as flows of molten rock, all of which built up layer atop layer on a previous range of mountains that had mostly eroded away. None of these modern peaks is more than 600,000 years old, and geologists consider all five to be active volcanoes.[1] Each has erupted relatively recently: Baker 6,600 years ago; Glacier about 5,000; Rainier around 2,200; Adams 3,800 years ago; and St. Helens sporadically since May 18, 1980. I still remember being mesmerized as

I watched the mountain's incredible 1980 eruption and its aftermath on our black-and-white television.

The Olympic Mountains, which rise to the west and south of me, have a less violent and far earlier origin. Located on the edge of an active region of plate tectonics, much of Washington State consists of slivers of rock known as terranes that rammed into and attached themselves to North America. The most recent of the terranes accreted to the continent between fifty-five and fifty million years ago. Composed of basalt that erupted out of deep ocean vents and sediment that accumulated on the ocean bottom, this terrane forms Mount Townsend, as well as the rest of the Olympics.

Before the arrival of white loggers, the mountain slopes were mantled in forests of enormous trees. Foremost were the lower elevation Douglas fir, western red cedar, and western hemlock, the biggest specimens of which were more than three hundred feet tall, with circumferences greater than seventy feet. Underneath the tall conifers were tangles of salal, sword fern, trillium, Oregon grape, red huckleberry, and other understory plants. These lowland forests were interspersed with bogs, where large trees were scarce, and prairies, rimmed by Garry oaks and carpeted in camas, grasses, and bracken ferns. Red alder and bigleaf maple grew on unstable slopes and recently altered areas, such as fire scars.

When the timber companies began to arrive in the early 1850s, they quickly established more than two dozen sawmills along the shores of the Sound. Most of the lumber ended up in San Francisco; the city's rapid expansion after the California gold rush had created a bottomless demand for wood. The lumber trade was so extensive and unregulated that travelers in Puget Sound noted seeing and smelling the smoke from the mills long before they reached them.

Despite the historical logging, from the top of Mount Townsend I could still see tens of thousands of acres of forest below me, their bright green fading to dark on the islands and in the lowland and turning to dusty blue in the eastern foothills. Although less widespread, less diverse, and less ecologically productive than the old-growth forests, the modern forests still contain the same trinity of cedars, hemlocks, and Douglas firs and remain important to the health of Puget Sound.

From my summit I could also see the glacier- and river-etched landscape that wraps the Sound in accordion folds of valleys and ridges. Most of the estimated 2,800 streams and rivers of the Puget Sound watershed are small, but a few stood out. The largest and most prominent is the Skagit River, which contributes one-third to one-half of the freshwater that enters Puget Sound, followed by the Snohomish, Nooksack, and

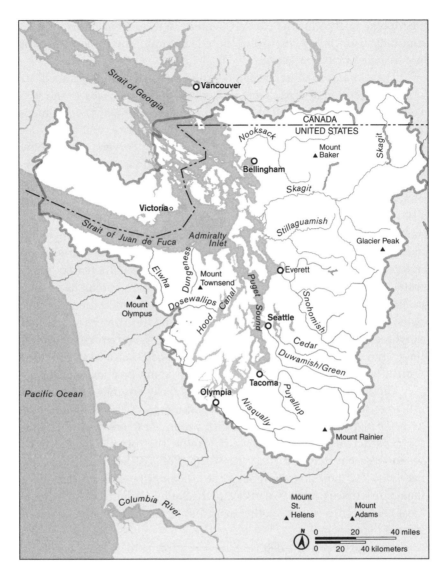

Greater Puget Sound watershed. (Adapted from PugetSoundPartnership)

Puyallup Rivers. If Puget Sound were emptied, the volume of water from these rivers would refill it in about five years.

The Skagit, like all rivers draining to the Sound, has been heavily altered over time. Its delta, which was the most visible feature from my viewpoint, has been diked, diverted, and drained. Through its midsection, municipalities extract water for drinking, development degrades its floodplain, and pollutants regularly enter the river from farms, homes, and industry. Upriver, its natural flow is disrupted by three dams that provide electricity for Seattle.

These changes reflect one of modern humans' most significant effects on the Puget Sound ecosystem: alterations to the hydrology. The 436 dams on the Sound's various waterways starve them of the sediment that nourishes life both in the water and on floodplains, make it harder for salmon to return upstream to spawn, change the rivers' natural flow regimes, and create reservoirs of warm water ideal for salmon predators. Cutting down forests and replacing them with impervious surfaces has eliminated the dead trees that once created valuable logjam habitat; it has further altered seasonal river flows, leading to higher fall, winter, and early spring flows and lowered summer flows. (Climate change also alters the flows by causing more rain than snow to fall, particularly in late autumn and early winter.) Land cover change has led to increased storm-water runoff contaminated by the effluents of modern human lives, such as fertilizers, motor oil, PCBs, and caffeine. Delta degradation has eliminated wetlands, emergent marshes, mudflats, and freshwater swamps that provided shelter and food for fish, filtered runoff, and protected shorelines from storms and waves. These wetlands could also have provided protection from future sea-level rise brought about by climate change.

The loss of delta ecosystems is particularly troubling. Deltas are estuaries, areas where salt- and freshwater merge. Rich with plants and animals adapted to protected, brackish water, these are critical ecosystems, particularly for salmon, which exploit the mix of salt and fresh to undergo the physiological transformation (called smoltification) necessary for their migration out to sea. Ecologists estimate that more than ninety miles (about 56 percent) of the Sound's original delta habitats have been destroyed, yet another contributing factor to the depletion of salmon populations.

What survives of the delta habitat is rewarding to observe. For many summers, I and a group of friends have paddled down the Skagit to a sandbar exposed at low tide in the delta. We sit on the sand watching bald eagles, harbor seals, flounders, sandpipers, and stickleback fish. One year we found a six-foot sturgeon trapped in a pool in the middle of the sandbar. When the tide submerges the bar, we leave and head back upriver, propelled by the advancing water.

Ecologists describe the entire Puget Sound ecosystem as an estuary, fed by the river of tidal water that floods in twice a day through Admiralty Inlet. The saltwater carries nutrients, sediments, and plankton more than a hundred miles down the waterway to Olympia. Along the way, the water washes up on 1,332 miles of shoreline. Because of this daily flux, the Sound is phenomenally productive and diverse, with more than two hundred fish species, almost two hundred types of birds, more than thirty-five species of mammals, and several thousand invertebrate species.

• • •

In choosing to focus this book on Puget Sound proper, the area south of Admiralty Inlet, I drew on my discussions with oceanographers and geologists who separate Puget Sound from the Strait of Juan de Fuca because of a geologic structure called a sill. A sill is a natural rise of hard rock in the seafloor between two basins. The sill at Admiralty Inlet is eighteen miles long from north to south and has two high points, like a camel's humps. Another sill at the Tacoma Narrows, which separates what oceanographers call the Main, or Central, Basin from the South Sound (that is, Vancouver's original Puget's Sound), is half the length of the one at Admiralty. A third prominent sill lies at the entrance to Hood Canal. The Sound's fourth basin, the Whidbey Basin, lacks a boundary sill.[2]

The sills exist because of how the Sound was formed. Puget Sound is a fjord, or a deep, glacially carved coastal inlet. At least seven times in the past two million years, massive ice sheets advanced from Canada into the lowland. The most recent of these ice ages began around 17,600 years ago, when glacial ice began to extend a finger south between the foothills of the Olympic Mountains and the Cascades. At its maximum extent, around 16,850 years ago, this great glacier, known as the Puget lobe of the Cordilleran ice sheet, was a mile thick at Bellingham, the height of five Space Needles when it passed through Seattle, and perhaps 750 feet high at Olympia, its southernmost point.

As the Puget lobe advanced, rivers of sediment-rich water flowed under the ice and cut deep into the land below, carving the depressions now filled by Puget Sound, Lake Washington, and Lake Sammamish. The Duwamish River Valley formed at this time, too, but it has been partially filled by epic debris flows resulting from Mount Rainier's eruptions. Gouging out these depressions was not a straightforward process. In areas composed of softer underlying material, the water cut deeper. For example, Puget Sound's deepest spot—off Point Jefferson, across the water from the northern boundary of Seattle—bottoms out at a depth of 938 feet, compared with the Sound's average depth of 230 feet. This is more than ten times the average depth of San Francisco Bay and Chesapeake Bay; Puget Sound's volume is also twice that of Chesapeake Bay despite the latter's surface area being four times that of Puget Sound's.

In areas of harder rock, which resisted glacial erosion, sills formed and created restrictions that impede the flow of tidal water. The Strait of Juan de Fuca, in contrast, has less variation in depth, and cold, dense ocean water enters and mostly stays along the bottom. Flowing in the opposite direction is a surface layer of river-supplied, fresher water, generally warmer than the ocean in summer and colder in winter. These two currents only partly mix, which results in two distinct layers of water.

Although the same basic pattern of incoming ocean water and outflowing freshwater occurs in the Sound, the sills complicate the flow patterns. "The sills in the main part of the Sound are basically Mixmasters," says Richard Strickland, a retired University of Washington oceanographer and author of *The Fertile Fjord: Plankton in Puget Sound*.[3] During the flood tide, a river of cold ocean water, twenty to thirty times the volume of all freshwater entering Puget Sound, travels in from the deep of the Strait of Juan de Fuca and over the camel-hump sill at Admiralty Inlet. Because of the uneven bulges, water flows at different rates and generates turbulence that mixes the incoming saltwater and outgoing freshwater.[4]

According to Richard, this mixing in the Main Basin is beneficial. "It means you don't get anoxic conditions. The mixing forces oxygen from the outgoing freshwater down into the deeper water flowing landward." The sill at Admiralty Inlet, however, creates an ecological problem. Outgoing surface water doesn't flow freely out of the Main Basin into the strait. Instead, two-thirds of the freshwater gets mixed back in with the inflowing saltwater and remains in the basin. Known as reflux, this phenomenon affects the Sound in two ways. On the positive side, reflux restricts the movement of fish and invertebrate larvae, which translates to more nutrients and greater productivity (as well as an evolutionary issue that I address in chapter 8). "The bad news is that pollutants remain in the Main Basin longer because of the sills. Two-thirds of the pollutants come back to you during tidal movement," says Richard. Some oceanographers refer to the effects of reflux as the long-term memory of Puget Sound because microscopic particles that enter the waterway tend to persist in the Sound, a reminder of past actions and the ways they still influence the present.

Hood Canal and Whidbey Basin have different flow patterns from the other basins. Because of the large volume and length of the Hood Canal basin, water mixes less and has a longer residence time (the amount of time it takes to flush water and replace it). This results in stagnant, deep water in the basin. It is one of the main reasons why Hood Canal experiences low oxygen levels, or hypoxia, at depth most years in autumn.

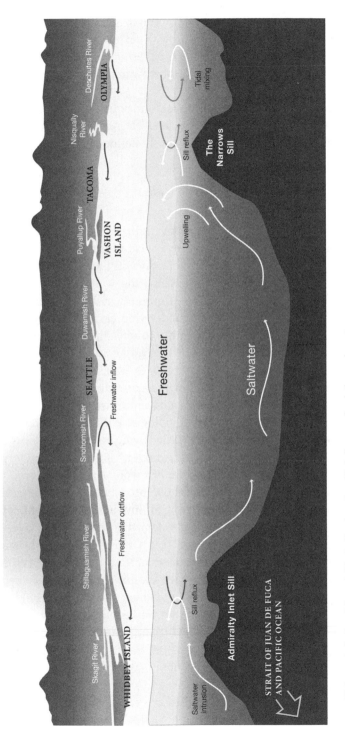

Water cycle in Puget Sound, illustrating how the sills influence circulation and create reflux. (Courtesy of Su Kim, Northwest Fisheries Science Center/NOAA Fisheries)

Hypoxia can lead to reduction in density and diversity of bottom-dwelling invertebrates, force bottom-dwelling fish up toward the surface, and make animals more susceptible to parasites and diseases. In Whidbey Basin, because of the high volume of freshwater from the Skagit River, the water is more stratified.

Ultimately, says Richard, the circulation patterns that are key to the ecology of Puget Sound depend on the sill at Admiralty Inlet. "It's the valve that controls the flow. That's why we define Puget Sound as south of Admiralty Inlet."

• • •

The Puget lobe had two additional topographic effects. It left behind beds of clay topped by sand and capped by a sheet of silt, sand, cobbles, and boulders. This three-tiered layer cake makes up the hills that challenge urban drivers and the bluffs that envelop the waterway. A secondary effect of the layered sediments is that groundwater percolates through the sand but cannot penetrate the underlying clay, which results in a saturated zone of weakness susceptible to landslides. The ice sheet is also responsible for sculpting the land into ridges and troughs. These can be felt by anyone traveling east or west in Seattle, as they roller-coaster over the hills and valleys that align with the southward ice movement.

Historical place names in Hood Canal appear to reference this glacial past. In the 1930s and 1940s, the ethnologist William Elmendorf interviewed Twana people (Skokomish Nation) who referred to places with names that meant "large rock" and "was a river."[5] Elmendorf's informants told him that the rock was the daughter of a woman in "myth times" who did not wish the Skokomish River to flow into what is now Oakland Bay in Puget Sound. Instead, she wanted it to flow into Hood Canal, which it now does. The daughter rock is the dam that rerouted the river and left behind a dry channel known as "was a river." Trevor Contreras, a geologist with the Washington Department of Natural Resources (WDNR), told me that this story could reference the time during glacial retreat when water flowed from Hood Canal into Puget Sound. As the Puget lobe continued to melt and a northern outlet was established, this route was cut off, leaving behind the abandoned ice-age channel.

From the summit of Mount Townsend, the other glacial features that stand out are the bluffs that make up about 40 percent of the shoreline of the Sound. Most of the bluffs are covered in Douglas fir, bigleaf maple, and red alder, but I can also see long ribbons of bare tan walls of sediment along the west side of Whidbey Island and north of Seattle. The bluffs are generally higher and more prominent in the north than the south.

Puget Sound's bluffs, up to three hundred feet high, result from relentless wave action pounding and gnawing at the glacial sediments. On average, erosion occurs at a rate of about one foot per decade. Occasionally, though, bluffs collapse catastrophically. During one of these "change events," as geologists call them, tons of sediment and vegetation crash to the beach. Triggers of these collapses include big rainstorms, especially in areas where people have denuded the bluffs and altered drainage routes.

Few features of the landscape better illustrate the relationship between modern Puget Sound residents and place than bluffs. To protect the bluffs from wave erosion, we have armored our shorelines with concrete, boulders, wood, tires, and sheet metal. Armoring was first practiced by farmers and industrialists, but since the 1970s, the practice has been most widespread among private landowners seeking to protect their beachside homes. Initially seen as relatively benign, the seven hundred miles of bulkheads and seawalls in Puget Sound—enough to armor the entire ocean shoreline of Washington and Oregon—have become more of an "in your face" environmental issue, says Hugh Shipman, a retired Washington Department of Ecology shoreline geologist.[6] Armoring shrinks beaches by changing wave dynamics and preventing the inland movement of the shoreline. The consequent reduction of space and burial of the upper beach leads to reduced accumulation of drift logs and beach wrack (tide-deposited debris), which provide habitat for insects, worms, and amphipods. In addition, studies show that armored beaches are less hospitable to fish that deposit their eggs in the sand, and create one more obstacle for salmon by changing the nearshore habitat that juvenile fish prefer. Armored bluffs are also more vulnerable to storm damage and erosion from sea level rise. Reducing bluff erosion is further problematic because gradual, natural changes in the shape of the bluffs create feeding, roosting, and nesting habitat for birds. Ultimately, says Hugh, a loss of the natural connection between land and water has few benefits in the long run.

Not all the news is bad, says Hugh, who has studied armoring for more than three decades. "When I began, most people were unaware of the potential problems with bulkheads, nor were they aware that the eroding shoreline is an important element of the coastal ecosystem. Today, property owners are increasingly interested in environmental stewardship, and there's a lot more information on how to build sustainably on the shoreline."

Seahurst Park in 2008 exemplified how shoreline armoring narrowed the beach and degraded habitat. A concrete wall is a typical armoring technique, also called a bulkhead or seawall. (Courtesy of Hugh Shipman)

Government thinking on the issue has also changed. One of the best places to see this shift, says Hugh, is at Seahurst Park, about eight miles southwest of downtown Seattle. In the 1970s, planners dumped thousands of cubic yards of fill and built a 2,900-foot seawall along the shoreline. "At the time, the goal was to provide the public with easy and direct access to the water's edge. You could drive to the beach, park at the seawall, and watch the sunset without getting out of your car. The view from the beach had become more important than the beach itself," he says. By the early years of the twenty-first century, attitudes were starting to change as ecologists and public officials began to recognize the adverse effects of armored shorelines. In 2005 and 2015, officials removed the Seahurst seawall and made the shoreline more natural.

Light rain fell the day Hugh and I visited Seahurst in May 2019. Because the old wall and the accompanying steep drop-off created by erosion were gone, we had easy access to the gravel, sand, and logs that now make up the beach. Behind us grew ocean spray, red alder, beaked hazelnut, and salmonberry.

Seahurst Park in 2015 after removal of armoring, resulting in a wide beach, additional habitat, and debris such as logs. (Courtesy of Hugh Shipman)

For Hugh, the multiyear restoration at Seahurst demonstrates the potential of removing armoring along Puget Sound shorelines. Reconnecting the terrestrial and marine environments, and removing artificial barriers that straitjacket creeks has led to a natural shoreline that provides more and better habitat, as well as a dynamic ecosystem better adapted to storms and rising sea levels.

Seahurst also reconnects people with the beach, says Hugh. Earlier in the day, he and I had visited Saltwater State Park, a few miles south, where a long, ragged wall of boulders separates the beach from a lawn with picnic tables. Although Seahurst and Saltwater have virtually the same original environment—a stream washing out of a ravine and forming a little estuarine beach—the riprap wall at Saltwater made beach access challenging, and few people ventured onto it. The restoration at Seahurst not only breathed life into the ecosystem but also opened up the park to people. As a consequence of this project and widespread education about armoring, Hugh has found that more people are now thinking about removing it, not simply because it is the right thing to do for the environment but also because it results in better access to the beach, a more attractive shoreline, and higher property values.

Tides, currents, and reflux. Subduction, uplift, and erosion. Rivers, forests, and bluffs. Freshwater, saltwater, and estuary. Tallying the physical descriptions and understanding the geological forces that shape an environment are the first steps in considering the foundations of place. The next step is equally important: connecting the human story to its surroundings. In a place like Puget Sound, ecology and geology are the catalysts of every aspect of residents' lives, from what drives the economy to where people live and what inspires them. In this beautiful inland sea, that human story began on a lakeshore more than 12,500 years ago, when a group of people gathered to fashion hunting tools out of the local rocks.

3

Peopling Puget Sound

Standing on the Bear Creek Trail in Redmond, Washington, between two major roads, I find it hard to imagine what this area looked like when people first began to inhabit Puget Sound soon after the last ice age. Fortunately, I am with the archaeologist Bob Kopperl, who helped lead a multifaceted excavation of the land between us and the creek to the south. During a routine archaeological survey in 2009 for a project to restore salmon habitat in Bear Creek, Bob and other archaeologists uncovered several artifacts. Digging deeper, they excavated a foot-thick mat of reddish-brown peat. Because the peat contained organic materials, it could be carbon dated. Tests showed that the peat might be as much as ten thousand years old. More exciting to Bob, within what he called "judiciously placed" trenches, archaeologists found more stone artifacts under the peat. Any artifact located under the organic-rich peat layer had to predate its deposition.

Bob and his team eventually unearthed several thousand artifacts at the Bear Creek site, which he describes as the oldest evidence of human existence in Puget Sound so far. The archaeologists concluded that the area's first human residents arrived at least 12,500 years ago, making Puget Sound one of the longest continuously inhabited landscapes in the lower forty-eight states. People appear to have come to this location to take advantage of abundant and diverse food sources and a wide variety of rock types that could be hewn into exquisite stone tools.[1]

I find it amazing to think about humanity's first forays into Puget Sound, of people arriving on land where no humans had ever walked or hunted or made tools or camped. In the waters of a proto–Puget Sound, they would have found aquatic newcomers but nothing like the modern diversity. It would have been a startling place.

During the initial glacial retreat around 16,850 years ago, large freshwater lakes formed south of the melting glacier and covered most of the lowland between the Olympic and Cascade Mountains. Within a few hundred years, the ice had retreated far enough to the north that ocean water could flow from the Strait of Juan de Fuca into the central and northern lowland, changing those lakes, including the depression now filled by Lake Washington, into saltwater. As the ice continued its retreat, the land began to rise, a result of the glacier's great mass no longer pushing it down. Geologists call this process *glacial* (or *isostatic*) *rebound*. The land rose high enough to separate Lake Washington from saltwater, and the lake reverted to freshwater.

Pollen studies show that Puget Sound's first human inhabitants would have found an open habitat of bogs, wetlands, and ponds interspersed with pine and minimal amounts of spruce, Douglas fir, and true fir. The savannah-like habitat was ideal territory for hunting the great beasts that had moved into the post-glacial landscape, including mastodon, giant sloth, bison, and short-faced bear.[2] Evidence suggestive of a hunting lifestyle comes from two locations. Between 1977 and 1979, at the Manis Mastodon site in Sequim on the Strait of Juan de Fuca, archaeologists excavated the nearly complete skeleton of a male mastodon. Embedded in one of his ribs was a pointed fragment of a bone point. Based on recent laboratory analysis, some researchers hypothesize that 13,960 years ago someone threw or thrust a spear into the mastodon and the point broke off, causing the animal's death.

Around the same time, hunters may have butchered a bison—an extinct behemoth about twice the size of the modern species—on Orcas Island. In 2003, workers digging a trench discovered the bison's remains and unearthed almost one hundred bone fragments. On the basis of new analysis, archaeologists recently concluded that the fracture patterns of the bones could be explained only by the presence of tool-using humans. However, because both Manis and Orcas Island lack evidence of stone tools, not all archaeologists agree that the dead animals offer proof of human presence in Puget Sound.

Unfortunately for archaeologists, the Redmond site does not include any mammal bones. It does offer rich evidence of stone tools, such as projectile points, knives, scrapers, and hammerstones, made primarily from local rock. Based on the assortment of implements and rock types found, Bob hypothesizes that the location was a procurement site, a place where people came to collect rock that could be worked to fashion a wide array of tools. The site could have been a base camp as well, but without any additional signs of human use, such as a hearth, Bob cannot say

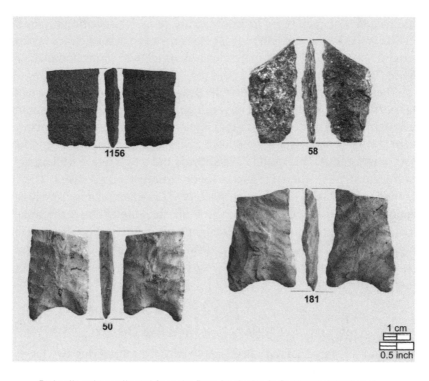

Projectile points collected from the Bear Creek site, in Redmond, Washington. Point 1156 is made from chert, a sedimentary rock. Point 58 is made from fine-grained volcanic material, either dacite or basalt. Point 181 is made from rhyolite, a volcanic rock. Point 50 is a fine-grained metasedimentary rock. (SWCA Consulting Inc. Courtesy of the Muckleshoot Indian Tribe)

conclusively whether Bear Creak was a permanent settlement. This lack of hearths does not surprise him, because these features are uncommon among other sites of this age in North America.

Even if the tools do not provide evidence of settlement, they do provide indirect evidence of hunting. On one of the stone tools, analyses indicated protein residue from bear, deer, bison, salmon, and sheep. These findings suggest that the Bear Creek people used the tool for some sort of subsistence activity, but Bob and his team concluded that "this analysis should be viewed as hypothetical unless additional lines of evidence can be found."[3]

The diversity of artifacts at the site implies a deep connection between the people who made the tools and the landscape they inhabited, says Bob. They knew where to find the raw materials they needed, and most likely they traveled to gather them. They knew how to make use of different rock types to manufacture tools for specific purposes. "These were people who had an intimate knowledge of subsistence across several habitats. They knew where to stop, find good stone, and make a living," he says.[4]

Researchers hypothesized that the Bear Creek denizens were a "small task-oriented group," part of a larger, highly mobile residential community of several extended families that hunted, fished, and gathered plants together. They most likely would have traveled longer distances by some sort of watercraft. This would have allowed them to interact with others in the Salish Sea, where perhaps a thousand other people lived. Then, around ten thousand years ago, the waters of Lake Sammamish rose high enough to inundate the site and render it uninhabitable. Where the stone tool makers went is unknown. They might have moved a short distance to higher ground, but because there is no archaeological evidence for that possibility, the story of the Bear Creek people ends when rising water forced them to move.

•   •   •

I cannot leave Puget Sound's first people without considering two facets of their lives and the landscape they inhabited. The first centers on one of the smallest and rarest artifacts discovered in the Bear Creek dig: a salmon bone, the only bone found at the Redmond site. It is brownish-gray from heating, cracked in half, and smaller than a raisin. Because the bone was burned, no DNA remains by which to identify the species it came from, though sockeye, which makes use of lakes, seems the most likely.

The bone and the salmon protein residue found on the Bear Creek tool may be the earliest evidence for people eating salmon in Puget Sound. No sooner had our species arrived here than we discovered what is arguably the most defining and sustaining food of the region. Part of what makes this idea intriguing is that salmon themselves had only recently arrived in this newly formed waterway. (Based on fossil evidence, paleontologists conclude that salmon have inhabited Puget Sound for at least a million years, cycling in and out during glacial advance and retreat.)

Five species of salmon occur in Puget Sound at present: Chinook (king), chum (dog), coho (silver), pink (humpy), and sockeye (red). A landlocked variety of sockeye, known as kokanee, is considered by some to be the most flavorful salmon. All are in the genus *Oncorhynchus* (meaning "hooked snout"), which also includes steelhead and cutthroat trout. Some ecologists give the steelhead (but not the cutthroat) honorary status as Pacific salmon. When I use the term *salmon*, I am generally referring to the classic five. None of these species is doing well relative to their historical numbers. /

How and when salmon reached Puget Sound is open to debate. Some biologists hypothesize that salmon returned before Puget Sound had a saltwater connection to the open ocean, by swimming up the Chehalis River into the south end of the glacial depression. Others theorize that after the connection to the Strait of Juan de Fuca was reestablished, salmon swam in from the north. Recent research showing a close genetic relationship between Puget Sound salmon and those found off the Olympic Peninsula and Vancouver Island suggests that the northern route might be the more likely, though different species might have used each route. Steelhead genetics, for example, shows overlaps between populations found in the Chehalis River and Puget Sound.

There are other explanations for the arrival of salmon. The Puyallup elder John Xot told the anthropologist Arthur Ballard in the 1910s that Moon, the Transformer, was responsible for salmon in the Sound. Traveling up a river, Moon created Dog Salmon, whom he told: "The new generation is coming now, and you shall be food for the people, O Dog Salmon." Initially, Moon told Dog Salmon to go downstream but then realized that this was not the best decision and made Dog Salmon run upstream as well, thus creating the migration cycle that provides food for the people. After his transformation of people into animals such as sandpipers, mallards, and clams, Moon explained to the new generation of people that "fish shall run up these rivers: they shall belong to each people on its own river."[5]

For their first seven thousand to eight thousand years in the Sound, the salmon survived on marginal spawning habitat, at least on the Skagit and Stillaguamish Rivers. The rapid erosion of glacially deposited sediment at the river mouths made the slopes of the rivers and their tributaries steeper than optimal for salmon. Eruptions of Glacier Peak generated mudflows that also choked the riparian habitat. Whether similar conditions occurred on other waterways that flowed into Puget Sound is unclear, but erosion and eruptions on the Skagit and Stillaguamish compromised the habitat for salmon and made it difficult for them to thrive until about five thousand years ago.[6]

Archaeological studies throughout Puget Sound and the Northwest Coast confirm that people caught salmon consistently but not intensively up to around four thousand years ago. From this time forward, as salmon numbers started to rise and the fish became a keystone species of the marine ecosystem, they became more and more tightly integrated into the lives of the humans who inhabited and still live in Puget Sound.

A Salishan man named William We-ah-lup smoking salmon and salmon eggs on the Tulalip Indian Reservation, 1906. Photograph by Norman Edson. (Courtesy of UW Special Collections, Image NA709)

The second intriguing facet of human existence in this area has to do with geology. The early generations of Puget Sound residents lived at a time when the landscape was reshaping itself more rapidly and dramatically than at any time since. Consider the local volcanoes. Between fourteen thousand and twelve thousand years ago, Mount St. Helens was in a short-lived but intense phase of volcanism. Unstable volcanic domes produced by lava regularly collapsed and sent flows of intensely hot rocks, gas, and ash down the mountain. During this phase, several eruptions produced plumes of rock fragments (tephra) and gas similar to those observed during the mountain's 1980 eruption. At the north end of the state, eruptions of Mount Baker were also sending ash and rock thousands of feet into the sky. Even more dramatic were the eruptions at Glacier Peak, a mountain now quiescent but which erupted nine times around thirteen thousand years ago. The biggest of these blasts ejected more than five times as much tephra as Mount St. Helens did in 1980 and sent mudflows with the consistency of liquid concrete cascading down mountain valleys at forty-five miles an hour out to Puget Sound. At Arlington, more than sixty miles from Glacier Peak's summit, these rivers of mud and rocks carried plants and animals down, burying them in deposits seven feet deep.

Arguably, however, the most consequential geologic event in greater Puget Sound was occurring much more slowly. In the postglacial era, when people were beginning to enter the region, isostatic rebound caused the land to rise at the rate of three to four inches per year. Over the course of a lifetime, human observers might have noticed that shoreline travel corridors once accessible only at low tide were now always above water, saltwater ponds next to the sea had changed to freshwater, and former islands were now connected to the land. As the water receded, sacred shoreline sites might have lost their connection to their water-based origin stories.

Isostatic rebound slowed substantially between ten thousand and nine thousand years ago. It was then outpaced by sea level rise, a process that had begun at the end of the ice age with the melting of glaciers to the north. The sea began a rapid reclamation of the land, rising more than 350 feet from the end of the ice age until about five thousand years ago, when sea level was within a couple of dozen feet below its present elevation. Sea level rise then slowed dramatically, though climate change has now pushed us into a new regime with a high potential for rapid rise.

Landscape change on this scale must have dramatically influenced settlement patterns around Puget Sound. Initially the rising land could have facilitated travel and opened up new territories for exploration. When the sea began to rise, people could have taken to the water and traveled by boat. But both circumstances might have made people hesitant to establish more permanent dwelling sites along shorelines. In fact, archaeological evidence suggests that more permanent habitation sites began to develop only about five thousand years ago, when sea level stabilized—although this picture may be incomplete because older structures may have been submerged.

We have no idea what people thought during this time of geologic upheaval. Change on a scale that we consider catastrophic might not have appeared to be odd to them. It might have been normal to see the land expand steadily year by year and then eventually for the sea to reclaim its lost territory. It must have been a very exciting, and terrifying, time to inhabit Puget Sound.

In the past few decades, people in Puget Sound have been reminded that they live in one of the country's most active geologic regions, most notably by the eruption of Mount St. Helens in the 1980s and from 2004 to 2008. Geologists have recently developed a better understanding of what lies beneath the urban centers around the Sound; they will eventually experience either a very deep or a very shallow earthquake because of interaction between the North American Plate and the smaller Juan de Fuca Plate, which sits to the west and is diving under, or subducting, North America. The last large-scale, shallow quake at this boundary, on January 26, 1700, had a magnitude between 8.7 and 9.2 and generated a tsunami that struck the coast of Japan. Seattle and Tacoma are both built on another type of shallow quake zone: one of the faults under Seattle cracked about 1,100 years ago and raised the ground as much as twenty-three feet in places. Geologists are working to better determine the recurrence intervals of these types of earthquakes, but they have already acquired enough data to know that life-changing earthquakes could strike Puget Sound anytime.

These threats have led to billions of dollars of expenditures to make urban areas more resilient. Modifications include seismically retrofitting older structures, building a new seawall in Seattle, and taking down the elevated State Route 99 viaduct along Seattle's waterfront and putting the road through a tunnel. The threats have also translated to a less measurable, equally important change. From schoolchildren practicing duck-and-cover earthquake drills to articles in the newspapers listing emergency earthquake supplies to government agencies exhorting residents to be ready for "the Big One," the active geologic nature of this place has permeated the collective psyche of the region. Residents are proud of and thrilled by Puget Sound's geology but they are also unnerved by it. Yet the geology is what makes this such a beautiful place to live, even if it has the potential to inflict catastrophic damage.

· · ·

Although evidence for land use at Redmond ends at around ten thousand years ago, other local sites show that the sheltered body of water continued to attract people. Until around seven thousand years ago, there were still small, highly mobile groups of hunters and gatherers living in an environment far different from what we know at present. The climate was hotter and drier; the ecosystem was savannah-like with vast open spaces and big vistas, amply populated with oaks. Great herds of deer and elk would have roamed the land and fed on nutritious acorns. Archaeological evidence suggests that these ungulates were such easy prey that human hunters had little need for aquatic food sources, though they did harvest small quantities of harbor seals and shellfish.

Most of the archaeological sites from this period are located on river and lake terraces; those along the marine shoreline would have been inundated by the rising sea. They lack evidence of habitation structures but are rich in stone tools. Bob Kopperl notes that the artifact assemblages from these locations changed very little over several thousand years, suggesting a continuity in how people lived on the land. Beginning around seven thousand years ago, though, the Puget Sound climate gradually grew cooler and moister, becoming comparable to the area's current climate by about five thousand years ago. The new conditions led to the development of closed-canopy forest of the kind familiar to present-day residents of Puget Sound, with conifers towering over a nearly impenetrable understory. In addition, the slowing of sea level rise improved salmon habitat and stabilized nearshore communities rich in marine invertebrates.

The new habitat led to new ways of human living. Elk and deer—far less prevalent in the closed forest—were replaced as food sources by salmon and shellfish, supplemented with a broad range of plants and animals. (Salmon, in particular, benefited from the denser, coniferous forests because downed trees formed logjams in streams, creating more favorable spawning habitat.) One comprehensive study of the archaeological record found that people ate food from 23 mammal families, 27 bird families, 24 marine and freshwater invertebrate families, and 24 fish families, as well as dozens of species of roots and berries.[7] This diet has persisted for thousands of years, with both seasonal and local variation. Of equal importance, cedar became central to people's material lives around five thousand years ago. Ropes, cradles, and canoes, homes, hats, baskets, and masks, bowls and diapers—all were made from the wood and bark of what was and is called the tree of life.

Over time, the people of Puget Sound developed a culture based on coexistence with the region's abundant natural resources. Extended family groups established winter villages, which were the home base and heart of social and ceremonial life. At other times of year they moved to seasonal camps to acquire useful plants and animals. They continuously modified their technologies and strategies to increase their food harvests.[8] In doing so, they created a sustainable and resilient lifestyle based on reciprocity between bands of people inhabiting different watersheds, which persisted up to the time of contact with Europeans.

Two events in the last quarter of the eighteenth century forever changed the lives and culture of Puget Sound's Indigenous residents. The first was the arrival of smallpox around 1781–82, which led to the deaths of a catastrophically high number of Coast Salish people. The second was the arrival of Europeans, the first of whom sailed into the Strait of Juan de Fuca in 1788. That "discovery" of the strait ultimately led to George Vancouver's sailing into x̌ʷəlč four years later.

How did smallpox reach the Sound before Europeans did? The Portland State University historian Robert Boyd believes it was introduced

Summer residence ca. 1912 on the Skokomish River, which empties into Hood Canal. Those who lived around Hood Canal spoke Twana, a Coast Salish dialect. Photograph by Edward Curtis, from his monumental twenty-volume *The North American Indian*. (Courtesy of Seattle Public Library, spl_nai_09_032)

via a shipwreck on the Oregon coast. A second theory holds that Spanish explorers could have brought the disease during their journeys to Nootka Sound on the west side of Vancouver Island in the late 1770s. Cole Harris, a retired University of British Columbia geographer, believes that Native people carried the smallpox virus from the Great Plains to the Columbia River and finally north into Puget Sound via trade networks. After initial contact, the disease then spread through Coast Salish populations.

For thousands of years, smallpox was one of the world's most devastating diseases, particularly deadly to populations that had never before experienced it. Spread by exhaled droplets or physical contact, the *Variola* virus typically incubated in the human body for about two weeks before causing high fever and aches. Soon a rash appeared on the tongue, radiated within the mouth, and changed to sores that broke open and further spread the virus. Within twenty-four hours, the rash traveled across the face and down the limbs and torso before festering into oozy, itchy, foul-smelling pustules that crusted and scabbed. Eventually the scabs dropped off, leaving those who recovered with scarred, pitted skin; some lost an eye. About 30 percent of those who caught the disease typically died, though the percentage was sometimes significantly higher./

The earliest written records of smallpox in Puget Sound come from the Vancouver expedition, at least ten years after the disease had reached the Pacific Northwest. Vancouver and his men noted "a great many deserted Villages . . . capable of holding many hundred Inhabitants" and "vestiges of the human body . . . promiscuously scattered about the beach, in great numbers" near Port Discovery.[9] In Hood Canal, Vancouver wrote that his men recognized a man they had seen earlier who "suffered very much from the small pox. This deplorable disease is not only common, but it is greatly to be apprehended is very fatal amongst them, as its indelible marks were seen on many; and several had lost the sight of one eye . . . owing most likely to the virulent effects of this baneful disorder."[10]

Although we may never know exactly how smallpox reached Puget Sound, we understand how it enabled postcontact settlers to wrest control of the land. "The eventual result, everywhere," wrote Harris, "was severe depopulation at precisely the time that changing technologies of transportation and communication brought more and more of the resources of the northwestern corner of North America within reach of the capitalist world economy. Here was an empty land, so it seemed, for the taking, and the means of developing and transporting many of its resources."[11]

• • •

To understand the second transformative event for Puget Sound—the arrival of Europeans—requires a side trip to Venice, Italy, to a meeting between the English merchant Michael Lok and Apostolos Valerianos, a Greek pilot and mariner, in April 1596. Lok had sought out Valerianos, better known as Juan de Fuca, to learn of a voyage the mariner had taken in 1592. Lok later recorded the substance of their meeting. Employed by the viceroy of Mexico, Juan de Fuca had commanded "a small Caravela, and a Pinnace, armed with Mariners onely," and sailed north from Acapulco.[12] The Greek had been sent to find the Straits of Anian, which had first appeared on maps as a shortcut between Asia and North America thirty years earlier and had quickly become the object of explorers' quests.

Juan de Fuca said that he had sailed north until he reached a latitude between 47 and 48 degrees and come to a "broad Inlet of Sea" marked at its entrance by "an exceeding high Pinacle . . . like a piller thereupon." After turning east into the inlet, he had sailed more than twenty days and landed at "divers places" where the land was very productive and abounding in precious metals and pearl. Feeling he had "done the thing which he was sent to doe," that is, find the Straits of Anian, Juan de Fuca returned to Acapulco.

Tantalizing with its details and its suggestion of riches, and its account of possibly discovering the much-sought-after shortcut, this first description of what we now call the Strait of Juan de Fuca became well-known to mariners and explorers, though more as a curiosity or fable than as fact. Indeed, although most historians have concluded that Juan de Fuca's story was false, his tale was enticing enough that nearly every explorer who roamed the north Pacific Ocean for the next two centuries mentioned it, even if simply to discredit him. For example, after James Cook, accompanied by a young George Vancouver, sailed by the strait in 1778 and failed to see the opening, Cook wrote in his journal: "It is in the very latitude we were now in where geographers have placed the pretended *Strait of Juan de Fuca* but we saw nothing like it; nor is there the least probability that iver any such thing exhisted."[13]

Nine years later, Cook was proved wrong. In July 1787, the British fur trader Charles William Barkley sailed south from Nootka Sound and to his "great astonishment . . . arrived off a great opening," wrote his wife, Frances, in her journal of the trip. "[My] husband immediately recognized [it] as the long lost strait of Juan de Fuca."[14] The following year another British fur seeker, Charles Duncan, confirmed Barkley's observation and remarked on a key element noted by Juan de Fuca, the pillar on the coast. Duncan drew a map of the opening to the strait and made it available to the influential geographer Alexander Dalrymple, who published it in January 1790.

Now that the strait had been marked on maps, Britain's rivals attempted to exert their own influence. Ambitious traders out of Boston—whose arrival led to the label *Bostons* for subsequent arrivals from the recently established United States of America—came in search of sea otter pelts but made little headway into the strait because of bad weather. (For the rest of the chapter, I use *Bostons, Americans,* and *settlers* interchangeably to refer to non-Native and non-British people who moved into the Puget Sound region.) More successful were the Spanish, who had first arrived on the Pacific Northwest coast in 1774 and had returned regularly to explore, claim new territory, and perhaps unwittingly introduce smallpox. In 1789, they claimed Nootka Sound to preempt Russian explorers from the north and the British from the south, and now sought to map nearby territory that fell under what they perceived to be their jurisdiction.

To do so they sent Manuel Quimper on May 31, 1790, in the sixty-ton sloop *Princesa Real.* He and his crew spent the first month exploring, naming, and claiming the north side of the strait, then repeated the process on the south side. Like Vancouver, Quimper was distinctly possessive in his choice of names: Ensenada (bay) de Caamaño was named for a fellow ship captain (whose name, minus the double *a,* was also bestowed on a nearby island in 1847 by the British geographer Henry Kellett); Puerto de Bodega y Quadra (later Discovery Bay) for the commandant at Nootka; and Canal de Lopez de Haro (Haro Strait) for Quimper's second-in-command. Two additional Spanish explorations followed in 1791 and 1792; in the latter year they circumnavigated Vancouver Island.

Considering how rarely Spanish exploration makes it into Pacific Northwest history books, it's surprising that so many Spanish names dot the landscape: Fidalgo, Guemes, Lopez, Orcas, Quimper, Rosario, San Juan, and more. Many additional Spanish names were replaced by later explorations. But the Spanish *were* the first Europeans to thoroughly survey the Strait of Juan de Fuca and the Strait of Georgia and circumnavigate Vancouver Island. The Spanish dream of imperial expansion was fading, however, particularly so far from their well-defended colonial possessions to the south, and Britain's was rising. In 1794, British and Spanish diplomats signed the Convention for the Mutual Abandonment at Nootka, and both nations left Nootka Sound. The Spanish eventually ceded the territory they claimed on the Pacific Northwest coast. With the Adams-Onis Treaty of 1819, Spain renounced claims to all territory north of the forty-second parallel, the modern Oregon-California border.

With the circumnavigation of Vancouver Island, the Spanish had finally ended any speculation that Juan de Fuca had found the Northwest Passage. Yet his tale launched the proverbial thousand ships and ultimately led to the European exploration of Puget Sound.

Although the Spanish had been the first Europeans to arrive in the Strait of Juan de Fuca, it was George Vancouver's expedition that explored the inlet to the south. Their presence resulted from equal parts geopolitics and hubris. On March 1, 1791, Vancouver had received orders from the British Admiralty to sail to Nootka Sound and address the territorial dispute between Spain and Britain. Vancouver was also to acquire "information with respect to the nature and extent of any water communication which may tend, in any considerable degree, to facilitate an intercourse for the purpose of commerce, between the north-west coast and countries upon the opposite side of the continent."[15] In other words, the Admiralty had said, find the Northwest Passage and see if there's a way for us to make money through it.

Thirty-four years old when he sailed into the Sound, Vancouver had entered the Royal Navy at the age of thirteen and been fortunate a year later to join James Cook's second great voyage of exploration. One year after leaving England in April 1791, Vancouver arrived on the Pacific Coast with more than 125 men in the ninety-six-foot, three-masted sloop-of-war HMS *Discovery*. (The biggest ferries that run on Puget Sound today are ninety feet wide.) After the mutiny on the HMS *Bounty* (its captain, William Bligh, and Vancouver had sailed together on Cook's third voyage), all British naval expeditions had to consist of at least two ships. Accompanying the *Discovery* was the eighty-foot armed tender HMS *Chatham*, captained by William Broughton. The officers and crew of the expedition included men who are remembered now only through the places to which their names were assigned: Peter Puget, Joseph Baker, Joseph Whidbey, and James Vashon, who had all previously sailed with Vancouver. On April 30, 1792, they entered the Strait of Juan de Fuca.

Following his orders, Vancouver took the *Discovery* and *Chatham* into the strait to see how far east it extended. On May 19, he sent the *Chatham* to explore the San Juan Islands and turned his boat south into what Puget called the "great SE Inlet."[16] They continued south and anchored off what is now known as Bainbridge Island, at what Vancouver christened Restoration Point in honor of "that memorable event," the restoration of Charles II to the British monarchy in 1660.[17] The Lushootseed name for the point translates to "place of squeaking," in reference to the wind, though the island itself had no name.

While stopped at this location, the expedition's naturalist, Archibald Menzies, made some of the first European observations of Indigenous life in the Sound. "Several of the women were digging on the Point, which excited my curiosity." They were harvesting a "little bulbous root of a liliaceous plant," which he described as new to science, along with salmonberries and barnacles. They also harvested bulrushes for mats.[18] After trading copper sheeting for deer, which the locals had "ensnard," Menzies and several men tried to hunt a deer themselves. They were not successful. Nor did they succeed in their attempt to emulate another practice Menzies had witnessed: using a seine, or net, to catch salmon. "Tried a haul of the Seine with very little success, only one Salmon trout," he wrote in his journal, despite having been told that "there were plenty [salmon] up a river."[19]

During their short stay at the place of squeaking, Vancouver concluded that between eighty and one hundred people lived there. He described their lodging as "constructed something after the fashion of a soldier's tent."[20] This was most likely a seasonal site, used primarily for harvesting the edible lilies. Later visitors to Puget Sound described more permanent villages, which were inhabited in the winter. Each consisted of one or more longhouses made of cedar planks, logs, and shingles. The biggest residences were up to ninety feet long and housed up to thirty or forty members of an extended family. The historian David Buerge estimates that several thousand people lived around what is now Seattle when Vancouver arrived.

Because the *Discovery* was too large for a detailed survey of inland waters, Vancouver sent two small boats south. Peter Puget was in charge of the launch, twenty feet long with two removable masts, and ten oarsmen. It carried guns, food, beads, medals, surveying and navigational equipment, and trinkets for trade. Joseph Whidbey commanded the slightly smaller cutter. Joining the two leaders and other crewmen was Menzies, subsequently best known as the first scientist to describe Douglas fir (*Pseudotsuga menziesii*). In Vancouver's words, duty in the open, unprotected boats would be "extremely laborious, and expose those so employed to numerous dangers and unpleasant situations."[21]

Born in London in 1765 of French Huguenot ancestry, Puget had been at sea since the age of twelve, when he became a midshipman, a sort of officer in training. The position often indicated a family of some financial means. Over the next dozen years he sailed the North Sea, the Caribbean, and the Indian Ocean. With his appointment to the *Discovery*, he was commissioned as a lieutenant. Puget remained a naval officer for the rest of his life, becoming a rear admiral in 1821. He died in Bath, England, the following year.

Puget, Whidbey, and their men left the *Discovery* before sunrise on May 20. Puget's crew spent a week rowing through the Sound to survey the farthest reaches of the waterway and trade with the local people. The weather ranged from "extremely sultry" to a "perfect deluge of rain" to fog so thick Puget and Whidbey couldn't leave their camp.[22] They traveled as far south as what are now Budd, Eld, and Totten Inlets and reached the endpoints of Case, Hammersley, and Carr Inlets.[23]

When the explorers returned to the *Discovery* on May 26, they found that Vancouver, feeling the expedition had "no time to spare," had departed two days earlier in the *Discovery*'s yawl (a twenty-six-foot, three-masted, eight-oared vessel) to explore the waterway east of Puget's route. This took him by what is now Commencement Bay and the Nisqually River delta.[24] Vancouver returned to the *Discovery* on May 29 and, learning of the thoroughness of Puget's efforts, decided to honor his lieutenant.

During their month of exploration in the waterway, the British came away with two distinct impressions. Their disparaging descriptions of Indigenous people were typical of European explorers of the time. One village was the "most lowly and meanest of its kind" and the people "ill made" and of "pilfering dispositions."[25] And yet the explorers observed that the Native residents had abundant and varied food, including salmon, deer, clams, and "a small well tasted wild onion." They were also willing to share their knowledge of the geography and to help free a British boat stuck in the mud. Vancouver further wrote of "several tribes of Indians, whose behavior had been uniformly civil, courteous, and friendly."[26]

The British were much more complimentary about the landscape. Menzies wrote of towering ferns, bountiful oysters, thick forests, and "salubrious & vivifying air."[27] Near what would become Everett was a "fine rich Country abounding with luxuriant lawns, cropt with the finest verdure & excessive prospects teeming with the softer beauties of nature."[28] The climate was "exceeding favorable," Mount Rainier "most charming," and the surrounding scenery "harmoniously blended in majestic grandeur."[29] Puget added that the flowers were "by no Means unpleasant to the Eye."[30]

Vancouver summed up their thoughts. "To describe the beauties of this region, will, on some future occasion, be a very grateful task to the pen of a skilful panegyrist," he wrote. Keeping in mind the imperial objectives of the nation that had sent him, he added: "The serenity of the climate, the innumerable pleasing landscapes, and the abundant fertility that unassisted nature puts forth, require only to be enriched by the industry of man with villages, mansions, cottages, and other buildings, to render it the most lovely country that can be imagined."[31]

The British reaction to the people and landscape of Puget Sound at the time of first contact makes sense in context. It was an encounter of groups with two completely different worldviews. In a land of abundance, the Coast Salish people had thrived for thousands of years with relatively little negative impact on the area's natural resources; they hunted, fished, gathered, traded, and traveled according to the seasons. Their major worries had been warfare and raids from other Salish Sea inhabitants. Just as they probably found it hard to grasp the motives and culture of the British explorers, the explorers struggled to understand a culture without any form of industry they recognized. Britain at this time was in the midst of the Industrial Revolution; progress and success were signaled by steam, brick, and metal, not hook and line or bow and arrow. There was virtually no chance that men who represented this new world of industrialization could have responded positively to the peoples and cultures they encountered in Puget Sound. And, clearly they made little effort to learn from, understand, or respect the people they met.

MOUNT RAINIER, from the South part of ADMIRALTY INLET.

First European illustration of Mount Rainier, drawn by W. Alexander from a sketch made by John Sykes, midshipman on the Vancouver expedition, 1792. The pole was used for netting ducks. (Courtesy of UW Special Collections, Image NA3985)

• • •

The next Britons to reach Puget Sound had a different mindset. Instead of pursuing imperial expansion, they came in search of trade. They also came by a much different route, traveling overland from the south. The first to do so, forty or so men on an exploratory trip for the Hudson's Bay Company (HBC), reached present-day Eld Inlet, at the southernmost end of Puget Sound, on December 5, 1824. Established in 1670 and initially focused on the fur trade in what is now eastern Canada, the HBC had recently merged with its rival the North West Company and was working to expand its presence in British-claimed land in western North America.

This group had started seventeen days earlier at the Company's Fort George outpost (now Astoria, Oregon). Drenched by days of what the clerk John Work called "weighty rain," the men had sailed three boats holding six weeks' worth of supplies across the Columbia River, portaged to Willapa Bay, lined the boats in ocean surf to Gray's Harbor, and finally wrestled up the Chehalis and Black Rivers to the southern tip of Puget Sound. They then sailed north for twelve days, reached their goal in Canada, turned around, and passed south out of Puget Sound on Christmas Day.[32]

Although the HBC men found the route favorable, the land bountiful, and the Coast Salish people friendly, nine more years passed before the

HBC arrived to stay.[33] In that time they had established Fort Vancouver on the north side of the Columbia River and Fort Langley near the mouth of the Fraser River, and now they hoped to extend their reach into Puget Sound. The company's goals were farming and trading for furs. The HBC had also begun to establish a new travel route connecting its forts, which went up the Cowlitz River from its confluence with the Columbia River to about modern-day Toledo, then overland to the mouth of the Nisqually River. This route would eventually become a northern offshoot of the Oregon Trail and one of the most important transportation corridors into Puget Sound.

In the spring of 1833, the company started erecting Fort Nisqually in an open space about twelve miles east of modern-day Olympia. "The most conspicuous object was a store half finished, next a rude hut of cedar boards, lastly a number of Indian lodges constructed of mats hung on poles," wrote William Fraser Tolmie about the fort on May 30, 1833.[34] A twenty-one-year-old Scotsman and new recruit for the HBC, Tolmie had recently arrived from Fort Vancouver along with HBC's chief trader, Archibald MacDonald; four unnamed Hawaiian, or Kanaka, paddlers; oxen and horses; and a load of potatoes and garden seeds. (Kanaka working in the fur trade played an often-overlooked role in early Puget Sound.)

By October, houses, a store with space for trading, and sheds had been built. Eventually a wall of upright logs with corner bastions encircled the compound. Out on the grassy plains, cattle roamed, and fields plowed with the oxen grew cabbages, carrots, corn, peas, potatoes, radishes, and turnips.[35] Coast Salish people from as far away as the Strait of Juan de Fuca arrived daily by horse and canoe, bringing otter and beaver pelts for the British traders. In return for pelts from 1,450 beavers, 700 muskrats, 190 raccoons, 340 river otters, 46 bears, and 80 minks in 1834, the Native suppliers received ammunition, blankets, clothing, fabric, guns, and tobacco.[36]

With their desire for pelts, the HBC introduced a relationship to place fundamentally different from that practiced by the Coast Salish residents for thousands of years. The HBC saw the landscape in terms of economic gain, not as a place to sustain. They came to "reap all the advantage we can for ourselves . . . scour the country wherever Beaver can be found," as George Simpson, the HBC governor, wrote to his colleague John McLoughlin. Simpson later wrote McLoughlin that "we therefore entreat that no exertions be spared to explore and Trap every part of the country." The company's goal was not only to maximize profit but also to prevent the advance of American interests: Simpson wrote that "if the country becomes exhausted in Fur bearing animals they [the American government] can have not inducement to proceed hither."[37]

This onslaught on the environment had drastic effects, particularly with regard to salmon. Beavers' stream engineering had long benefited salmon by enhancing wetlands, regulating stream flows, attenuating the effects of droughts and floods, increasing the retention of sediments and organic materials, and creating a diverse mosaic of vegetation. Within a few years of the HBC's arrival, the rapid removal of beavers from the watersheds that emptied into Puget Sound began the long-term ecosystem changes that continue to plague salmon.

The establishment of Fort Nisqually marked another new era in Puget Sound. For the first time, Coast Salish people and "King George men," as the locals called the British arrivals, had a chance to live and work together. Whether they were involved in trade, religion, medicine, or conflict, both sides "developed ways of dealing with each other that usually worked to all parties' perceived advantage," according to the historian Alexandra Harmon.[38]

The British harbored negative stereotypes, attempted to proselytize, and exploited Native resources, but they also learned to respect the trading and hunting skills of the people who visited the forts, recognizing that their own survival depended on good relations with the Indigenous people. In Harmon's view, the Native residents may have seen the new arrivals as unclean, bad-mannered, and ignorant of basic survival skills, but interaction with the King George men could increase prestige and lead to better relations with other Coast Salish people long considered to be enemies.

Unfortunately, the mostly positive initial relations between newcomers and longtime residents did not last. Whereas the British had built their relationship on "lucrative trade and coexistence," wrote Harmon, the "United States was a nation that had limited citizenship to 'whites' and defined itself largely in opposition to 'Indians.'"[39]

The US government began to consider Puget Sound as American territory in 1846, after Britain and the United States signed the Oregon Treaty. Disputes over the location of the border and who had the best claim to the land had percolated for decades, with Spain, Russia, Britain, and the United States each asserting their prerogative. Spain was the first to drop out, followed by Russia, after treaties established the border between Russian and British territories at latitude 54°40'. Aggressive American expansionists would have preferred to retain this northern border, particularly as immigration to the West Coast swelled, but negotiations ultimately led to the present boundary between the United States and Canada at the Forty-Ninth Parallel.

Five years prior to the establishment of the border, American explorers had made their initial voyage into Puget Sound under Captain Charles Wilkes and the United States Exploring Expedition. On May 6, 1841, three years into a voyage of science and surveying that had taken him and his crew to Chile, Australia, and Antarctica, Wilkes, who was now despised by most of the men under his command, led the USS *Vincennes* and USS *Porpoise* south of Admiralty Inlet. For the next three months, they surveyed the waterway, named what they saw, and collected plants and animals—including the first scientific specimen of a banana slug ("the body is large and corpulent").[40]

Wilkes had an insatiable need to name. Inlets and islands, passages and points, bluffs and bays—no feature appears to have been too small for him to label. More than 260 of his names have survived, though some of his more colorful choices, such as Bung Bluff, and Ned and Tom, for two islets he also dubbed Pepper Corns, no longer appear on maps. Like most explorers, Wilkes named geographic features for his crewmen, such as Lieutenant Overton Carr (Carr Inlet), ship's artist Alfred Agate (Agate Passage), and the surgeon John Lawrence Fox (Fox Island). We do not know which of the three Elliotts on the expedition gave his name to Elliott Bay, where Seattle is now located.

A handful of the names Wilkes assigned, including Toandos Peninsula and Tekiu Point, are Twana. The Suquamish tribal historic preservation officer Dennis Lewarch believes that this unusual choice could have been connected with Wilkes's mission. He had come, in part, to figure out who the Native groups would side with if the United States had to fight Great Britain, which meant that he and his crew had to get to know, or at least try to converse with, the Native inhabitants. Lieutenant Augustus Case, who mapped Hood Canal, the region where the expedition assigned the most numerous Twana-language names, made clear in his notes that he encountered and talked with several different groups of Indigenous people.

The place names assigned by the Wilkes expedition were a boon to later arrivals who used them as reference points for land claims. More than anyone else, Wilkes is responsible for the names used today to describe the geography of Puget Sound—except for the town names, which came shortly afterward.

The first town to be named was New Market, at the falls on the Deschutes River, where it enters Budd Inlet. Among its first settlers were the families of Michael Simmons and George Washington Bush, who had

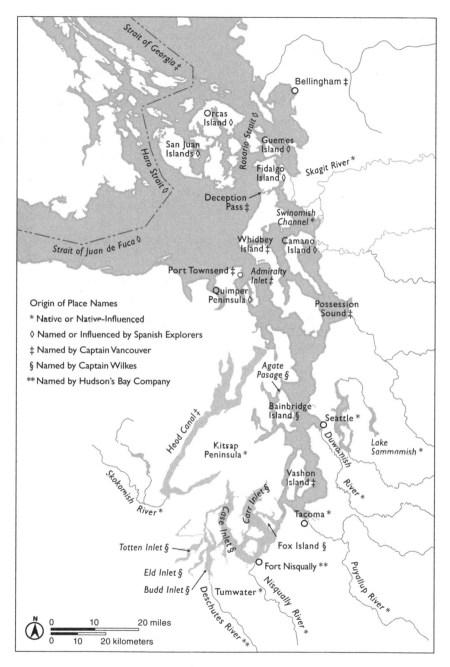

Origin of Place Names

* Native or Native-Influenced

◊ Named or Influenced by Spanish Explorers

‡ Named by Captain Vancouver

§ Named by Captain Wilkes

** Named by Hudson's Bay Company

Origin of some Puget Sound place names

traveled together from Missouri. They had originally planned to settle in Oregon, but the Territory's racist laws excluded people of color, such as Bush, from living there, so they headed north across the Columbia River and reached the Deschutes in November 1845. The thirty-one settlers of New Market immediately began farming the land. Although they had some success, they could not have survived without Native knowledge and assistance in obtaining local foods.

Both the Simmons and Bush families ending up staying in the area. Simmons became an Indian agent under the territory's first governor, Isaac I. Stevens. Bush and his family learned Lushootseed, befriended many of their Native neighbors, and became generally well known and well liked. These good relations ultimately worked to their benefit. When the new territory of Washington was created, lawmakers intended to apply the same racist laws as Oregon, which prevented African Americans from owning land. Several friends of the Bush family, however, were territorial legislators, who urged the US Congress to pass a special resolution that confirmed the family's land title. The resolution was passed in 1855, and the Bush family kept their land and later expanded it. After George Washington Bush died in 1863, his descendants retained ownership of parts of the family property until the 1960s.

Of longer-lasting importance than the new town name, which survived only a few years before being changed to Tumwater—the Chinook Jargon place name—Bush, Simmons, and the other settlers built a gristmill and sawmill, the first on Puget Sound. On October 27, 1848, the Puget Sound Milling Company delivered 12,993 board feet of lumber to the Hudson's Bay Company at Fort Nisqually.[41]

Most of the wood from this first sale of lumber ended up in Hawaii, but within a year, the local lumber was headed for the new, rapidly expanding San Francisco market, for which Puget Sound offered the best, most easily accessible source of wood on the West Coast. Demand from California would control the destiny of local lumber, as well as the development of small towns around the Sound, for many decades. By the mid-1850s, more than two dozen mills had opened, including ones at Seattle and Port Orchard, and the largest of all, Andrew Pope and William Talbot's Puget Mill Company at Port Gamble. By 1858, mills in Kitsap County were producing 174,000 board feet a day.

With the mills came town development. In the words of the historian Robert E. Ficken, "The sawmill sat next to the wharf on the shorefront. Straggling up the muddy bluff were the buildings of the town: store, manager's house, cottages for married workers, and the hotel for single employees and visitors. Most towns also had a schoolhouse, a church, a saloon, and a field for baseball."[42] The mills also solidified the relation-ship to place established by the HBC. To J. Ross Browne, a special agent to the United States Treasury who had been sent in 1854 to evaluate the commercial prospects of Puget Sound, the territory was "a good country for coarse lumber, and nothing more."[43]

When the new arrivals did start to cut the trees, they didn't concern themselves about deforestation. As one early resident wrote, the forests "will only be exhausted when the mountains and valleys surrounding the Sound are destroyed by some great calamity of nature."[44] But, as with the trapping of beaver but on a far greater scale, the environmen-tal effects of logging were disastrous for salmon. Not only did cutting trees open up habitat and raise stream temperatures, but it also meant that trees no longer stabilized stream banks or fell into rivers to cre-ate logjams, which had enhanced the riparian ecosystem by moderating water velocity and sediment movement. Transporting the massive logs to riverbanks and mills via skid roads and logging roads led to gullying, landslides, and culverts that blocked fish movement. Loggers built splash dams that backed up river water in order to flush huge accumulations of wood downstream in a destructive deluge of water, logs, and debris. They improved their riparian log highways by blasting rocks, removing obstructions, and blocking side channels, all of which further degraded salmon habitat. At the mill, inefficient cutting generated piles of sawdust that washed into streams and smothered salmon eggs, clogged the gills of fish, and sucked the oxygen out of the water as it decomposed. As the environmental historian Jim Lichatowich wrote, "Within a matter of decades, these destructive practices shattered the natural economics of watersheds that had been evolving for 4,000 to 5,000 years."[45]

• • •

By 1853, as the logging industry thrived, the population of Bostons in the counties bordering Puget Sound had increased to 2,058. In contrast, the number of Indigenous people had plummeted because of the introduction of smallpox, measles, influenza, and syphilis. Cole Harris and Robert Boyd estimate that in the hundred years after Europeans arrived, diseases led to a population decline that exceeded 30 percent and may have been as high as 80 to 90 percent.[46]

As the Native population shrank and the number of settlers grew, the pressures on the environment made conflict inevitable. The forests that grew to the water's edge around Puget Sound were some of the densest on Earth and limited settlement to the edges of waterways, quiet bays, or the few open prairies, some of which Coast Salish people had burned for generations to keep them clear for deer hunting and camas bulb cultivation.

The new arrivals brought with them a fundamentally different attitude than had prevailed for thousands of years in Puget Sound. An individual Coast Salish family might retain the right, or privilege, to fish or harvest shellfish from a particular location, but that spot was not owned by the family in the sense that settlers understood ownership, whereby one could claim exclusive use of it and transfer that right to other people. Indigenous people's relationship to land and natural resources focused (and still focuses) more on maintaining the productivity of living resources and the relationships between those who controlled access to these resources and those allowed to use them. This control equated to wealth and the ability to give away goods. These relationships centered on sharing access and building connections and reciprocity: they involved stewardship rather than outright ownership.

In contrast, to the newcomers, private land ownership in the American sense was a source of status and power. The Bostons believed that ownership was their natural right and their destiny; they were supposed to own the land from sea to shining sea. They did not see Indigenous people as rightful or legitimate owners of the land. Their sense of entitlement to the land was backed up by the US government. In 1850, Congress had passed the Oregon Donation Land Act, which allowed a husband and wife to claim up to 640 acres of land for free, regardless of the fact that no treaties had been signed that gave the United States formal possession of the land. The act resulted in 529 claims for land bordering greater Puget Sound.[47]

Tensions over land increased after Washington separated from Oregon and became Washington Territory. Its first governor, Isaac Ingalls Stevens, had graduated first in his class at the United States Military Academy at West Point, fought in the Mexican-American War, and obtained his position by backing Franklin Pierce for president. In 1853, Pierce rewarded Stevens with the governorship as well as the title of superintendent of Indian affairs for Washington Territory. He arrived in Olympia on November 25, 1853.

Two months later Stevens traveled around Puget Sound and claimed that he "saw nearly all the Indians."[48] By the summer of 1854, Stevens had begun to consider how to address the struggles between settlers and residents. He sought the advice of the ethnologist George Gibbs, who favored placing Natives in reservations of one square mile where they could "raise their vegetables and bury their dead," and Michael

Simmons, one of the founders of Tumwater.[49] Despite his debt to the Indigenous people who had helped him when he arrived, Simmons not only failed to acknowledge their skills and experiences but illustrated the narrow-minded views of his day when he wrote that "they are filthy, cowardly, lazy, treacherous, drunken, avaricious, and much given to stealing."[50]

Stevens held his first treaty signing at Medicine Creek, where it empties into Puget Sound near the Nisqually River. *Negotiation* is often the word associated with a treaty, but, as J. Ross Browne wrote in an 1858 report, "none of the so-called treaties with the Indians are anything more than forced agreements, which the stronger power can violate or reject at pleasure."[51] On Christmas Eve, 1854, between six hundred and seven hundred delegates from the Nisqually, Puyallup, Squaxin Island, and other bands and groups living around southern Puget Sound listened as Stevens's men translated the treaty into Chinook Jargon, which lacked words for the central principles of the document. The next day, sixty-three Indigenous leaders signed it.

Two more treaties quickly followed. Late in January 1855, Stevens met at Point Elliott (Mukilteo) with more than two thousand Coast Salish people from northeast Puget Sound, including those designated as Stillaguamish, Snohomish, Skopahmish, Skagit, Lummi, and Duwamish. One week later, the third treaty was signed at Point No Point, covering the territory around Hood Canal and the Strait of Juan de Fuca.

Each treaty contained similar language whereby the tribes agreed to "cede, relinquish, and convey to the United States all their right, title, and interest in and to the lands and country occupied by them." In exchange, the tribes would receive money, be permitted to live on reservations a tiny fraction of the size of their traditional lands, and retain the right to fish, gather, and hunt at their "usual and accustomed grounds and stations." In return for giving up their claim to 2.5 million acres, the Medicine Creek tribes received three 1,280-acre-reservations and $32,500, to be paid over thirteen years.

One of the critical changes foisted upon the Coast Salish groups in the treaty process was the creation of tribes and chiefs. Neither of these concepts had existed before in Puget Sound. A "chief," wrote the Indian agent E. A. Starling to Stevens, was "any one who has riches (in their sense of the word blankets & slaves) and is the head of a family."[52] According to Starling, the chief had limited authority outside his own family group, which most likely centered on a winter village. The residents of a village, though, were not a tribe. In a nuanced analysis of the differences between Natives and non-Natives in early Puget Sound,

Alexandra Harmon wrote that a Coast Salish person might say she was from a certain village, but kinship relations usually crossed boundaries of geography and language, knitting diverse groups into a "roughly woven regional social fabric [that] had multiple affiliations, multiple loyalties, and multiple ways [for individuals] to identify themselves to others."[53]

As they had done across the continent, however, US authorities sought to impose specific structures of social hierarchy and land ownership on Native peoples in order to take their land. From the US point of view, it would be far "easier to exact a land cession from a few purported tribal chiefs than hundreds of families," wrote Russel Lawrence Barsh, a lawyer and ecologist, in a 2008 analysis of the treaties. "What is more, a tribe was considered civilized enough to sell its land but not civilized enough to assert the right to keep its land for itself."[54]

• • •

The treaty signings were the most significant steps in a process that had begun with George Vancouver and his men. When the British first arrived, they had "claimed" the land around Puget Sound for King George III. These gestures had little practical meaning, as they consisted primarily of naming features on the landscape after themselves and discharging the royal salute.

Nor had settler actions during the years 1792–1853 had much official or permanent effect, except for the horrible spread of disease. Though HBC employees had moved into the area, their claims to the land were only slightly less tenuous than Vancouver's, and only the King George men inhabited the HBC land in 1846, when Britain ceded its claims to the United States. Few believed that this new American claim meant much either. On November 4, 1846, the chief factors of HBC at Fort Vancouver, James Douglas and Peter Skene Ogden, wrote to William Tolmie at Fort Nisqually, "Business will of course go on as usual, as the treaty will not take effect on us for many years to come."[55]

By 1853, though, the Americans had begun to establish a new reality in Puget Sound. With the signing of the treaties, the Bostons, or at least the federal government, now owned nearly all the land around Puget Sound. The new arrivals had begun to develop towns and to extract natural resources, often at rates that far exceeded the environment's capacity to replenish them. Their population grew from 4,928 in 1860 to 180,812 in 1890.[56]

The Coast Salish people certainly were not gone. Many of them had been shunted to reservations with drastically reduced access to the lands that had sustained them, but they still retained and practiced many of their cultural traditions. They maintained complex kinship relations over long distances. They fished, collected shellfish, harvested roots and berries, and hunted marine mammals at the "usual and accustomed places" guaranteed by the treaties. They also found employment in Puget Sound's nascent towns, providing key labor in many logging communities. Despite numerous attempts to eliminate the Native people of Puget Sound, they survived.

In essence, the treaties created two distinct ways of relating to the land in Puget Sound. Gone was the stewardship of the past 12,500 years. Plants and animals were now products to be acquired, processed, and sold. In the view of the waves of newcomers, the land was there to be owned and used, water a dumping ground. At the same time, the treaties codified Native people's rights to hunting, fishing, and gathering, which preserved, albeit on the margins, a traditional way of life. The paradigm established by the treaties is still shaping the relationship to place of the residents of Puget Sound.

4

Defending Puget Sound

On the morning of May 8, 1792, Peter Puget was fetching fresh water on a small island near what is now Port Townsend when he encountered a "Sight so truly horrid, that it awakened all New Ideas . . . of the Savage Customs and Manners of the Indians who inhabit these extensive countries." Standing upright on the beach were three poles, each topped by a human skull, the hair and skin still relatively fresh. Unable to determine why the three had merited their unhappy fate, Puget hypothesized that they might have been lawbreakers or enemies and ultimately concluded that "the Effect was judged without a Knowledge of the Cause." Exhibiting a rare display of objectivity for an eighteenth-century European explorer, he realized that what he was seeing had been happening for centuries in London, where traitors' and enemies' heads were placed for all to see at places such as London Bridge (which had a Keeper of Heads). "I have heard & read of this mode of Punishment in England, for very Capital Offenses . . . that it should have the public Exposal to deter others from falling into the same Snare."[1]

Although we don't know the origin of the heads Puget saw, post-battle displays of victims' heads were not unusual on the Pacific Northwest coast, including Puget Sound. In 1847 the artist Paul Kane described a battle in which the Makah triumphed over the Klallam. Upon their return to Cape Flattery, at the entrance to the Strait of Juan de Fuca, the victors placed their enemies' heads on poles "in front of the lodge of the warriors who had killed them as trophies."[2]

The rationale for this practice has long been debated among ethnographers and anthropologists. Edward Curtis wrote in 1915 that the point of war was "the winning of gory trophies," particularly for more northern groups, such as the Kwakiutl. (*Kwakiutl* was a term generically applied by Europeans to groups of people who refer to themselves as

Kwakwaka'wakw, meaning those who speak Kwak'wala. I use the term *Kwakwaka'wakw* instead of *Kwakiutl*.)[3] More recent work by the anthropologist Brian Ferguson argues that headhunting was an incidental part of battles but served the purpose of conveying "a real message to potential adversaries."[4]

Such a warning would have been widely understood, because warfare had an important cultural role in the Pacific Northwest. The earliest evidence for combat in the region comes from three-thousand-year-old bones and artifacts found at Prince Rupert Harbor, about thirty miles south of the southern tip of the Alaska Panhandle. A high ratio of male to female bones, combined with an extraordinary amount of trauma to the bones (particularly forearm and skull injuries), along with numerous bone and stone clubs and slate daggers, led archaeologists to conclude that the remains resulted from hand-to-hand battles.

Ferguson defines warfare as "organized, purposeful group action, directed against another group that may or may not be organized for similar actions, involving the actual or potential application of lethal force."[5] He speculates that productive but patchy resources were a main reason for warfare on the northern Pacific Coast. Abundant food allowed for the development of large, settled villages and a political hierarchy. It was the leaders of these villages who spurred violence between groups. "If the bounty of their village was unpredictable, they needed to find new sources of food in times of need," says Ferguson. This led to fighting between rival groups.[6]

Although warfare developed very early to the north, Puget Sound was different, he says, because of the less intimidating terrain. Up north the mountains come right down to the sea, creating some areas that offered easy access to a safe, well-protected harbor and good salmon streams and other areas where bad weather was more likely to disrupt food supplies. Puget Sound's relatively sheltered shoreline and diverse foods may have meant less competition for resources.

Other archaeologists argue that food scarcity is too simplistic an explanation for the variety of fortifications, the long-term evidence of warfare, and the adoption of new technology such as the bow and arrow, firearms, and armor. Nor, they assert, does competition for food resources explain the many different political, economic, and social changes that occurred through the thousands of years that people battled in the Pacific Northwest. Instead, they ascribe regional warfare to motives such as revenge, gaining prestige, and acquiring territory.

Despite decades of studying warfare in the north, researchers have only lately begun to study it in the Puget Sound region. The anthropologist

Bill Angelbeck has written that the southern Coast Salish were "often portrayed not as warriors, but, rather, as victims, subject to the preying of northern raiders."[7] He rejects this characterization. Work by Angelbeck and others has shown that Coast Salish people actively engaged intruders who attacked them. Beginning around 1,500 years ago, they began to construct trench embankments that exploited the local topography, such as peninsular spits, high bluffs, and rocky headlands. The trenches were dug two to three yards deep and sometimes more than five yards wide with the sediment mounded into an embankment on the protected side, resulting in a moat-like structure. Further protection included a wooden palisade on the embankment and sharp wooden stakes concealed by turf in the trench. The greatest density of these trenches occurs at the southern end of Vancouver Island, with another concentration on Whidbey Island, around Penn Cove.

In the early 1950s, the archaeologist Alan Bryan described several Penn Cove trenches and included a report of an interview between an early settler and Goliah, a Skagit leader who signed the Treaty of Point Elliott in 1855. Goliah described how, when he was younger, a lookout on the west side of Whidbey Island had spotted "northern Indians" in their canoes. "The lookout ran back to the village to give warning. The local warriors, including himself, advanced to the center of the island, where they met the invaders. A short skirmish ensued, and the defenders retreated rapidly to the enclosed area of the entrenchment. Pointed stakes had been placed upright in the bottom of the trench. . . . The invaders charged into the area, expecting to push the defenders over the cliff, but instead fell through the camouflage and were impaled on the sticks. The defenders then dispatched all of their enemies in proper order."[8]

Puget Sound people protected themselves in many other ways, writes Angelbeck. Located at high-elevation spots with extended views, lookouts were the first line of defense. One on the Fraser River was known as Alámex, meaning "babysit." One lookout on Hood Canal was reached by a tunnel through a bluff that emerged at a hole hidden by brush. Angelbeck records an account from the warrior who built the lookout tunnel; he claimed to have sighted Skagit raiders on the beach below and killed or enslaved most of them by himself. The Snoqualmie also employed lookouts from which they could use "smoke signals, foot runners, and reflections of sunlight" to alert others of raiding parties.[9]

Capturing women and children was common practice in warfare. If the attackers couldn't be stopped, noncombatants could attempt to survive by retreating into the woods, where they might hide in the dense foliage or take refuge in a cave or an excavated shelter. Bryan described

Illustration of what a Coast Salish trench embankment might have looked like. Note the steep, protective bluffs and how the trench isolates the village from land-based invaders. Drawn by Gordan Friesen. (Courtesy of the Friends of Beacon Hill Park)

one of these underground hideouts behind a village at Penn Cove: an informant noted that the "pits were quite deep, and were covered by planks and underbrush."[10] Other refuges or shelters throughout greater Puget Sound included one in north Seattle and a cave under a large fallen rock on the Skagit River.[11]

Those who were captured could become enslaved, providing labor for food production and collecting fuel and water. Slavery was widespread throughout the Pacific Northwest from Alaska to the Columbia River. Most groups considered slaves to be the lowest class of people, with virtually no rights and subject to the needs of their owner, though several contemporary tribal members I spoke with said that slaves in Puget Sound were more like indentured servants than stereotypical slaves. And no one who has researched slavery in the region equates the treatment of slaves among Native peoples in the Pacific Northwest to the atrocities of slavery in the American South.

For their owners, slaves represented status and wealth, particularly after the establishment of trading ventures, such as the Hudson's Bay Company. The anthropologist Donald Mitchell has described how slaves captured in a raid were traded to other Indigenous groups for furs, which were then exchanged at an HBC fort for goods later given away at a potlatch. In Mitchell's view, that potlatch and the status and prestige it afforded were possible because of slaves and their new value as a commodity.[12]

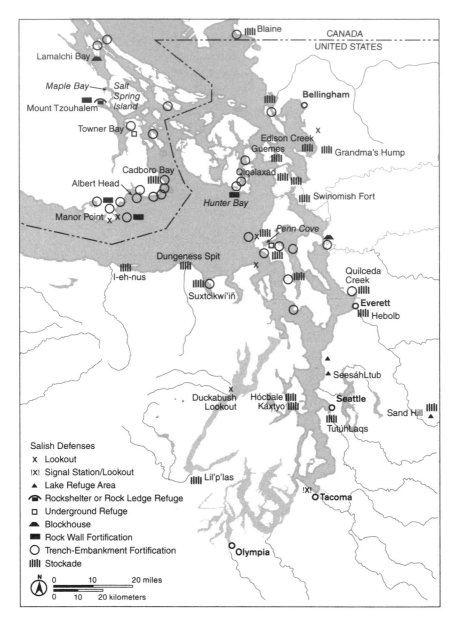

Coast Salish defensive sites, 1,600 years before present to 1880 CE. (Adapted from a map by Bill Angelbeck)

As a result of this monetization of slaves, warfare began to change, too. Prior to contact, according to Ferguson, battles were either "highly ceremonialized, involving a great deal of bluster but few casualties" or, in the words of another historian, "complex maneuvers featuring multiple forces and mixed arms . . . in both stealthy attacks and siege battles."[13] In both situations, slaves were typically the by-product of a successful attack rather than the central reason for battle. After the arrival of the HBC, people began to make war explicitly to acquire slaves. Not only were northerners raiding Puget Sound, but in neighboring Sound villages "slave-raids became so prevalent that up-river peoples were afraid to make the trips to the salt water sites which had always been part of their annual subsistence quest," wrote the ethnographer June McCormick Collins, based on her interviews with Stillaguamish, Samish, Swinomish, and Skagit people.[14]

European contact changed warfare in other ways as well. Northern Indigenous groups suffered less from the disease epidemics that devastated the south, which meant they had more fighters. Northerners also acquired guns earlier. Explorers such as Archibald Menzies regularly noted muskets of Spanish and unknown origin, clearly not English—at Nootka Sound and Queen Charlotte Sound. But ownership of guns was uncommon: an HBC census in 1838–39 found that only 3.4 percent of the Native people in Puget Sound had guns.[15] Some scholars contend that muskets were "notoriously unreliable and inaccurate" and therefore their effect on warfare has been overrated.[16] When Vancouver and his men fired their muskets, the Native people "heard [the shots] without any apparent surprise, and exclaimed *poo!* after every report."[17]

A primary response to the new tactics of slave raiding was the construction of stockades, or palisades of erect logs. Angelbeck lists more than thirty on the shores of the Salish Sea, including Kitsap Peninsula, Seattle, and Guemes Island. Generally built on unprotected sites such as bays and river banks—in contrast to trench embankments, which were located on defensible landforms—stockades could surround individual structures or entire villages. Charles Wilkes described a stockade at Penn Cove that "has all the aspect of a fortress." Four hundred feet long and constructed from thirty-foot-high pickets made of thick planks embedded in the ground, it was "impregnable to any Indian force." As Wilkes observed, the stockades were built to protect villages from "more northern tribes" who came to capture slaves.[18] Numerous other ethnographers and nineteenth-century visitors to Puget Sound also noted the local people's fear of northern tribes. As the ethnologist Marian Smith wrote, the northern warriors were "a constant menace to life and property."[19]

Stockaded village on Whidbey Island, drawn by Joseph Drayton, an artist on the Wilkes expedition, 1841. (Courtesy of the Oregon Historical Society, OrHi 962)

These changes transformed life in Puget Sound. For thousands of years, warfare had typically been waged on a small scale between people who shared similar values and responses to conflict. Over the span of a few generations, new invaders shattered the relative peace and safety of Puget Sound and created a corridor of potential death and enslavement. Will Bill Jr., cultural programs director for the Muckleshoot Indian Tribe, told me that the great size and speed of the northern war canoes prompted his ancestors to develop much speedier and more maneuverable canoes than they had previously used.[20]

Native Puget Sound residents also had to contend with the coming of Europeans. None of the initial arrivals, such as Vancouver, the Hudson's Bay Company, and Wilkes, posed a military threat or were overly aggressive; they had come primarily for exploration and trade. The HBC, in particular, led to both positive and negative changes. The company did provide the guns, which gave the northern groups more power, and the goods, which made the northerners more envious of southerners, but its trading forts also brought together people from all around greater Puget Sound. In August 1833, only months after the opening of Fort Nisqually, the HBC Journal of Occurrences refers to hundreds of people arriving at the fort, including Klallam, Makah, Nisqually, Puyallup, Snohomish,

Skagit, and Suquamish. Longtime enemies, or at least rivals, had to get along in order to trade with the HBC. As Alexandra Harmon wrote, "The desire to trade regularly with the King George's men was a compelling motive for making friends with the HBC's other patrons."[21]

But the incursions by groups from outside this region, often in search of slaves, did not stop. Sometime around the 1840s—no one knows exactly when—the northerners' aggressive raiding resulted in a once-in-a-lifetime gathering of Puget Sound warriors at Nisqually. They had come together at the request of the Cowichan on Vancouver Island in response to repeated attacks from the Laich-Kwil-Tach, who lived at the north end of the Strait of Georgia.[22]

As the warriors gathered, each told of the depredations against their people—Suquamish, Squaxin, Snohomish, Skokomish, Nisqually, Klallam, Duwamish, and Cowlitz—and vowed to join together for an unprecedented retaliation against their common enemy from the north. Kitsap, a famous Suquamish warrior, said "I'm going to die or kill Laich-Kwil-Tach!"[23] He then urged everyone to meet on Whidbey Island for the seventy-mile paddle north across the Strait of Juan de Fuca to Maple Bay, between Salt Spring Island and Vancouver Island. Here they would join up with dozens of other Coast Salish groups who had been terrorized by the Laich-Kwil-Tach.

Nearly two hundred canoes, each carrying ten or twelve men, paddled to the rendezvous, where as many as five thousand warriors united for battle. After sending scouts north to watch for the approaching Laich-Kwil-Tach, who were reported to be planning a raid on the Klallam on the south side of the strait, the assembled warriors at Maple Bay sharpened spears, applied poison to arrows, and prepared their canoes.[24]

To entice the enemy, the southerners sent out decoy canoes into Maple Bay with men wearing "big hats, such as the women commonly wore."[25] When they first saw the Laich-Kwil-Tach, the decoy men were supposed to hoot like an owl and then make a wolf call when the enemy began their pursuit. Those hidden on shore for the ambush would bark like a dog to let the men know they were ready.

Attracted by the decoys, the Laich-Kwil-Tach powered their war canoes into the bay and failed to see the ambush. Soon arrows were flying: "A Laich-Kwil-Tach man would yell, 'a . . . !,' and go overboard with an arrow in him."[26] As the canoes came into contact, the warriors battled with clubs. The smaller, more maneuverable Coast Salish canoes allowed the paddlers to use their spears, but the northerners were able to shield themselves by throwing "their weight to one side, raising the gunwale toward the enemy and depressing the other almost into the water."[27]

Accounts differ as to how many days the battle lasted and whether the southerners suffered no losses or many dead. There is little dispute, though, about the defeat of the Laich-Kwil-Tach. When they tried to escape by paddling along a bluff, men atop it pelted their canoes with rocks. When other canoes made for the open sea, one of them swamped, three capsized on submerged rocks, and the rest were caught and the men slaughtered by the united warriors. In the end the bay "became red with the blood of the slain."[28] After the battle, the southerners took the Laich-Kwil-Tach canoes, paddled north in disguise, and destroyed villages and rescued their enslaved relatives. Peace finally came after two Laich-Kwil-Tach women married Cowichan warriors.

Anthropologists who study warfare on the Pacific Coast often cite the Battle of Maple Bay as one of the most important in the region. It involved more people with more complex tactics than had been deployed in any previously known battle. It united disparate groups, some of whom had earlier fought each other, against a common foe. It exemplified how social networks, developed through extensive intermarriage, could create political alliances. And it ended the cycle of warfare between the Laich-Kwil-Tach and Coast Salish people.

To Angelbeck and other anthropologists, the most significant aspect of the battle is the demonstration that the people of greater Puget Sound were not merely victims but actively defended themselves. They aggressively protected their home, families, and territory by building fortifications and by resisting attacks. When necessary, they could band together to attack a common enemy. Will Bill Jr. made a similar point to me. "It is super important for people to understand that . . . we had to go to war to protect our lands and our life. . . . We fought and are still fighting for everything that we have. Otherwise we would not exist today."[29]

• • •

The end of warfare among Coast Salish people did not mean, however, that all of Puget Sound's inhabitants could stop worrying about defending their home. The new settlers, who viewed themselves as the rightful owners of the land, now perceived a new threat from the colonists in British Columbia.[30] Although the British citizens to the north were more concerned about American filibusters entering their territory than with any visions of taking back land Britain had ceded, the possibility that the British might want back into Puget Sound still worried the Americans.

Between 1849 and 1855, the US government sent three teams of engineers and military officials to Puget Sound to evaluate the threat from other countries.[31] Their reports mostly agreed that Puget Sound was unequaled for its harbors, ease of navigation, and rich natural resources.[32] But because it was too undeveloped to be a target, it wouldn't merit much more than a small, third-class fort or gun battery. (A battery is a grouping of field artillery, which is defined as large weapons capable of firing ammunition a great distance.) The surveyors wrote that Puget Sound and the Strait of Juan de Fuca, particularly Vancouver Island, could provide the ideal base for a British attack on or blockade of San Francisco, by far the most substantial city on the West Coast. So long as the British retained Vancouver Island, they could control access to the strait and sound and "paralyz[e] our whole western coast," noted a July 1855 report.[33]

Not content with these surveys, the US government decided to send Joseph Gilbert Totten, chief engineer of the Corps of Engineers, to evaluate defenses on the Pacific coast.[34] Totten had entered the West Point military academy at the age of fourteen, became the chief of the Corps in 1838, and was the "dominant figure in American fortification engineering."[35] In his 1860 report, Totten agreed with previous surveyors that Britain's control of Vancouver Island, or what one later official described as a "menacing spear-head," meant that the British could disrupt all commerce in Puget Sound if they so desired.[36] Because of this, and the great potential for the region to become more populous, Totten recognized the "necessity for providing, in due time, security against the effects of this mastery in hostile hands."[37]

Totten, however, misunderstood the British goals on Vancouver Island, or at least overemphasized them to justify building up coastal defenses. From the late 1840s until the end of the century, British officials regularly expressed alarm at the Monroe Doctrine and the US tendency toward continual expansion of its territory, according to a study by the historian Barry Gough of letters and memos by British ministry and military officials. He refers to an editorial in the Victoria, BC, newspaper written in reference to the purchase of Alaska: "[It] places the whole of Her Majesty's possessions on the Pacific in the position of a piece of meat between two slices of bread, where they may be devoured at a single bite."[38] The British didn't want Puget Sound and certainly had no plans to "paralyze" the coast; they simply didn't want to be eaten by the gluttonous Americans.

Totten, who had based his career on fortifications, believed that Puget Sound needed to be defended; therefore the Sound must be blanketed with forts. His 1860 report included proposals for building three forts at the mouth of Admiralty Inlet: one on each shore and one in the middle of the inlet, built somehow in more than 150 feet of water. He acknowledged that the midchannel fort was impracticable but necessary, because otherwise the two land-based forts would be "next to useless."[39] He advocated a second line of four forts across Puget Sound at the south end of Whidbey Island, as well as batteries at the Tacoma Narrows. He also proposed "harbors of refuge" in the Strait of Juan de Fuca where merchant ships could find safety in wartime.[40] Totten concluded his report by noting that despite his observations, he had practically none of the specific information "that is indispensable to an actual determination of the form, extent, and even precise site of the fortifications." In other words, "everything has yet to be done here."[41]

Not until 1884, and nearly a dozen reports later, did engineers and military officials conclude that Puget Sound had "become a national interest" that merited fortifications.[42] In November, Brigadier General Nelson A. Miles forwarded to the adjutant general of the US Army a report by three of his men, who recommended batteries with artillery of "the largest caliber and greatest penetration" and not less than two companies of troops at Admiralty Head, Point Wilson, and Marrowstone Point, across the bay east of Port Townsend, forming what became known as the Triangle of Fire.[43] Totten's technically infeasible midchannel fort was no longer necessary because of advancements in artillery design. Rifled artillery, in which helical grooves are machined into the internal surface of a gun's barrel, could now shoot projectiles several miles. This meant that gunners at the land-based forts could hit any ship that might try to pass through Admiralty Inlet.

As had happened so many times before, officials in Washington, DC, ignored this suggestion from the far side of the continent, even for the protection of what the territorial legislature described as "the finest body of land-locked tide waters in the world . . . [with] numerous growing and prosperous cities . . . enjoying extensive foreign and coastwise commerce."[44] Nor were they swayed by Watson Squire, Washington State's first US senator, who warned in an 1892 speech to the Senate that the British possessed "another Gibraltar" on Vancouver Island that would allow their fleet to "take absolute possession" of every town in the Sound and "destroy their commerce and property" in a single day.[45] Ironically, during the early 1890s the British were contemplating closing their navy base on Vancouver Island and moving it "farther from the border of the United States where they could be better defended against attack."[46]

Finally, in an 1894 report, the Corps' Board of Engineers deemed Puget Sound to have a population and economy substantial enough to be worth defending. The engineers recommended construction of three forts at the headlands specified in the Miles report and several batteries

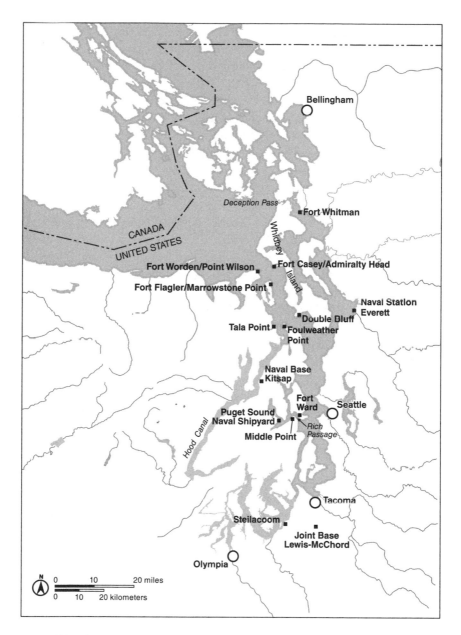

US military facilities and forts described in this book, proposed or built, 1849–present

around Seattle and Tacoma, as well as batteries flanking Rich Passage, to protect entry to the navy shipyard at Bremerton, which had opened in 1891. The total cost would be around $7 million. Two years later the US Congress approved funding for the defense of the Sound.

Puget Sound at the end of the nineteenth century was far different than when the first military engineers had arrived in 1850. Washington was now a state and not merely an outgrowth of Oregon. No longer limited to arriving by a poorly defined trail or occasional ship transport, new residents had been pouring in on the four transcontinental rail lines that reached the Sound, which had increased the waterway's population to almost 260,000, or about 130 times what it was in 1853. In four decades the newcomers had built cities, developed industries, and opened up trade networks. They also had fashioned a relationship with this place based to a large extent on its natural resources, such as salmon, Olympia oysters, and logging. For the settlers, Puget Sound had been transformed from a wilderness into a home.

Fort construction began in 1898. Built atop high, forested bluffs, the sites required extensive clearing and land reshaping, along with creative solutions to transportation challenges. At Marrowstone Point, which would become Fort Flagler, crews cut down twenty-four acres of old-growth forest, excavated 178,400 cubic yards of sediment, and poured 18,800 cubic yards of concrete.[47] To construct Fort Worden at the top of the Point Wilson bluff, engineers designed a railway powered by a steam-powered winch. Across the water at Admiralty Head, workers set up an aerial cableway to transport supplies for building Fort Casey. Wharves had to be built for landing construction materials and armaments at the sites, though they could not always be used because the astoundingly heavy artillery would have crushed the wooden docks. A twelve-inch gun capable of shooting one-thousand-pound shells had a barrel thirty-four feet long and weighed fifty-two tons. Instead the guns were landed directly onshore from barges.[48]

Workers had the guns mounted at Fort Casey by 1898 and continued adding artillery to the forts through 1907. The emplacements included disappearing guns, which could be raised into firing position and then lowered out of enemy view; mortars, which lobbed a round shot high and far; and barbette guns mounted on rotating carriages. By 1910, when the Triangle of Fire was at maximum strength, Fort Worden, with forty-one barbette guns, disappearing guns, mortars, and pedestal guns, had the most firepower, followed by Fort Casey, with thirty-four artillery pieces in ten batteries. They were supplemented by three small forts: Fort Whitman on Goat Island near La Conner, built to stop enemy ships that might try slipping into Puget Sound via Deception Pass; and Fort Ward and Middle Point flanking Rich Passage.

After decades of discussions and planning, Puget Sound now boasted one of the best lines of defense of any harbor in the country. "No more terrible collection of offensive and defensive weapons and no more remarkable mathematical system of rangefinding and plotting exists in the known world than the defenses at Worden, Flagler, and Casey," wrote one *Seattle Times* reporter.[49] Any fleet of ships trying to penetrate the triangle of forts would be met by twenty tons of steel projectiles per minute fired with near-perfect precision, noted another local newspaper writer. With the completion of the forts, residents had an additional reason to feel secure in their relationships to Puget Sound.

Well before this gushing tribute from the *Seattle Times* reporter, however, the Triangle of Fire was heading toward obsolescence. These coast defenses had been designed for fleets that no longer existed. Because the artillery on early-twentieth-century ships had a greater range than land-based weapons, enemy ships could start attacking the forts before the

A twelve-inch mortar like this one from Fort Casey, ca. 1910–16, could accurately shoot a seven-hundred-pound shell and hit a moving target seven miles distant. A single battery could include four mortars, which made them challenging to load. (Courtesy of the Coast Defenses Study Group Inc.)

ships came in range of their guns. Newer ships also incorporated armor far more resistant to shelling than previously. In 1912, Captain John Gulick of the Coast Artillery Corps wrote that "it may be frankly stated that the sinking of such a ship by long range fire of coast guns is entirely out of the question."[50]

Other defense problems were specific to Puget Sound. Admiralty Inlet was too deep for conventional underwater mines, an essential supplement to onshore artillery. Most of the guns at Fort Worden faced east, in the opposite direction from any likely enemy attack. Nor had the forts' designers considered the possibility of a land-based assault from Discovery Bay six miles west of Fort Worden. (Perhaps they should have read their history: in 1792, Vancouver named the island at the mouth of Discovery Bay Protection Island. "Had this insular production of nature been designed by the most able engineer, it could not have been placed more happily for the protection of the port.")[51] Engineers were able to make partial fixes for both of these problems.

When the United States entered World War I, military officials finally found a legitimate use for Puget Sound's artillery. They moved about half the guns to strategically more important sites in the United States, as well as to Europe. None of the artillery made it back to Puget Sound, and by the end of the war, technology had advanced so far, especially with developments in airplane design, that the forts were completely obsolete. During World War II, the forts served as training grounds but were mostly inconsequential. By 1943, no guns remained. All three forts were deactivated in 1953 and are now state parks.

•   •   •

Wandering through the remains of the forts is a surreal experience, evoking a mixture of wonder at what went on here, trepidation at the dark passageways, and fascination at the stark structures, all overlaid with a sense of mystery and discovery. Fort Worden is the hardest to comprehend, particularly on a foggy February day. As I follow the old roads and trails through a second-growth Pacific Northwest forest, I suddenly come across a ruin of concrete. It is massive, with walls several feet thick and substantial steel doors, many of which appear to be permanently sealed. I walk along gloomy corridors encrusted with yellow lichen and green moss and venture into dank rooms, which lead to darker and danker ones. In several, pencil-sized stalactites hang from the ceiling. At the top of a stairway, I find a courtyard and a large ring of metal out of which rise two-inch-long bolts, where I assume one of the great guns sat long ago. After a quick search I locate a ladder that takes me onto the top of the complex, where a slope of concrete angles down toward the water.

In front of me is a stand of Douglas fir. I know the Strait of Juan de Fuca lies beyond it, but I cannot see it through the trees. A hundred years ago, I would have had an unimpeded view of the water and any potential enemy trying to sneak into Puget Sound. Behind me would have been an array of artillery: ten-inch barbette guns that could propel a 617-pound projectile at 1,544 miles per hour; twelve-inch disappearing guns, which could shoot a half-ton shell 9.9 miles, roughly the distance from the Amazon headquarters in downtown Seattle east over Lake Washington to the Microsoft campus, in Redmond; and massive mortar guns, positioned so that four of them could simultaneously lob seven-hundred-pound, basketball-sized shells. Hidden and fortified under the concrete were rooms for storing shells and powder, plotting projectile trajectories, and communications, as well as hoists designed to lift the giant shells.

Across Admiralty Inlet, Fort Casey has a more tangible "Stop or we'll shoot" feel. The fort's historic landscape, a grassy field with no obstructing vegetation, has been preserved. On my visit, the sun emerges for a few minutes and shines on the structures. From most of the gun locations, I have direct views across the shimmery water of Admiralty Inlet west to Fort Worden and southwest to Fort Flagler. Fort Casey's most impressive sights are the two disappearing guns, one of which I can look into and see the grooves inside the barrel that spun the long narrow projectiles and gave them their accuracy. The other is in its lowered position, completely hidden from the view of any ship entering Admiralty Inlet. Nor could the enemy have seen any of the walls of the batteries, which were angled so that anyone looking up from a ship would have seen a flat horizon and a sandy bluff. Of course, if they had been paying attention they would have perceived these as a sure sign of something unusual and perhaps menacing in this normally heavily forested landscape.

Atop the batteries, with my unimpeded views of the gateway to Puget Sound, I can imagine the sense of power and authority that must have developed in the men who worked here. No enemy would dare penetrate the zone of death of the forts. If they tried, more than fifty thousand pounds of armor-piercing shells and exploding mortars could drop out of the skies upon them.[52]

Yet I also find it difficult to imagine why so many people placed so much importance on building these forts. What country realistically would have wanted to attack Puget Sound in the 1890s, much less the 1860s or 1870s, when the waterway was little more than a collection of small towns hoping to become small cities? To understand the reasoning that led to the construction of these forts requires looking into the larger scheme of the American military of the time. Although Puget Sound was a backwater, it was also at the edge of what was envisioned as a single country extending from the Atlantic to the Pacific. Like the adolescent it was, the United States didn't know its boundaries and was constantly testing them. Here at the north end of Puget Sound was one of the fuzziest borders, where not everyone had faith in the treaties signed with Britain. As recently as 1859, the United States and Britain had almost gone to war over a hungry pig at their mutual boundary in the San Juan Islands. Then, eight years later, the United States' purchase of Alaska turned British Columbia into a potential Union Jack sandwich.[53]

In 1886, a recently established military and civilian board under the authority of the secretary of war, William C. Endicott, alerted Congress that the nation's coast fortifications had not kept pace with changes in ship and artillery design. "It is impossible to understand the supineness," they wrote, that had allowed the country's navy and coastal defense system to become "obsolete and effete."[54] Other nations had built powerful armies and were spending lavishly on armored forts, including many around the Pacific Ocean. America had to respond and upgrade as soon as possible.

The Endicott Board calculated that it would cost $126.4 million to protect twenty-seven ports in the continental United States, or $191 billion in today's dollars.[55] With the backing of Congress, the military began a complete modernization, eventually constructing dozens of fortifications at twenty-eight harbors around the country, including Puget Sound.

The fact that Forts Casey, Worden, and Flagler were seen as part of a unified system defending the United States shows that Puget Sound had at last become an integral part of the country. For nearly five decades, the non-Native residents of Puget Sound had strived to be deemed worthy of protection by their fellow US citizens. With the construction of the Triangle of Fire, they had finally achieved that goal, as well as validated a belief that had permeated the lives of the previous generations of Puget Sound residents—that this was a place and home worth protecting.[56]

5

The Maritime Highway

In 2017 I decided to ride all of the ferries in greater Puget Sound, from the San Juan Islands to Olympia. I completed my goal in August 2018 when I boarded the three-minute ferry to Jetty Island, an artificial island adjacent to the Everett waterfront. It was the twenty-second, and shortest, of my trips, which included the ten routes of the Washington State Ferries (WSF) system, as well as ferries operated by the Port of Everett and King, Kitsap, Pierce, Skagit, and Whatcom Counties. For an extra challenge, I also rode ferries owned by several private homeowners' associations.[1]

I was not alone. In 2017 the Puget Sound ferries carried 26,567,061 riders, 92 percent of whom were on the best-known routes, those run by WSF.[2] The next most popular ferry system in the nation, the Staten Island Ferry, carried 24,421,745 people that year on one single route, which operates twenty-four hours a day, 365 days a year. Across the border, BC Ferries manages the system most similar to WSF. In 2017 its boats carried 21,034,746 people on twenty-five routes to forty-seven ports.

Riding ferries is one of the simplest ways to see Puget Sound, the landscape, and some of the people. On the early morning ride to Seattle from Bremerton or Bainbridge Island, you'll encounter the professional rider—the commuter—butt plomped down in a favored (some might think "reserved") seat, eyes focused on some sort of electronic gadget, hand clutched around an insulated mug. Don't make the mistake of getting in the way of these commuters disembarking, when the scrum surges forward and the laid-back island lifestyle rapidly reverts to the ways of the urban jungle. Then there are the tourists, struggling to figure out which way to orient their ticket when passing through the turnstile, bags and kids exploding into a seating booth, smartphones constantly in hand for texting and picture taking, generally having a fine time. In between are people like me who are running errands, going to a social event, or traveling. We are the most common category, and the least fun to observe.

Of the three private ferries that take people to their island homes, only the Homeowners Association of Herron Island both allowed me on their boat and permitted me to set foot on their island. The Decatur Island homeowners' group wouldn't even let me on their boat, and the Hat Island Community Association wouldn't let me off theirs after my ride from the mainland. Hat Island was, though, the only ferry ride I took on which the passengers sang "Happy Birthday" to the captain.[3]

More accessible to those of us who dwell on the mainland are the many publicly run short hops. The two shortest after Jetty Island are in the north, from Anacortes to Guemes Island, and across Hale Passage to Lummi Island. The crossing to Lummi, which is the longer of the two rides, takes about nine minutes. These ferries are so small that a crew member often walks from car to car and passenger to passenger collecting fares; on the Lummi ride this was accomplished en route, as the boat rocked in the waves. (In contrast, WSF passengers generally pay for a ticket at a booth and wait in line before boarding.) Ferry workers are also masters of geometry, adept at packing in the maximum number of vehicles. A friend told me of watching a crew walk up the line of waiting cars on a summer weekend and wave a VW Beetle out and onto a ferry. The crew then bounced the car sideways into a more secure position, to the applause of other riders.

One of the pleasurable aspects of riding the small vessels and short routes is that they harken back to the roots of maritime transportation on Puget Sound. Passengers and crew call each other by name. Pedestrians board via the car ramp and can stay close to the water on the open car decks. If you're lucky, you also might see strange items come aboard, as I did when I watched passengers drive four John Deere ride-on mowers onto a ferry. Long ago, when Puget Sound was not a destination for tourists or techies and few roads cut into the forests, hundreds upon hundreds of vessels of what was known as the "mosquito fleet" sailed into every cove and cranny of the Sound carrying all manner of goods and people. Critical to the region's economic and social development, these predecessors of the ferry system helped knit people together as surely as any state-controlled, planned network.

The Sound today remains accessible to anyone with a watercraft. No one owns the water: there are no tolls and no legal barriers to travel. The small boats may be more faithful to the old ways, but the larger vessels do their part in defining Puget Sound. Each boat that ferries people and goods is essential to the Sound's long history as a maritime highway.

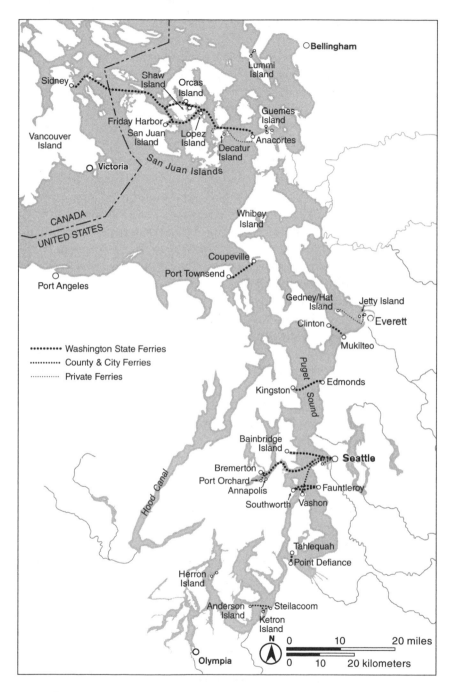

Ferry routes in Puget Sound (state, county, city, and private) as of 2019.

Riding them is as much a signature of the waterway as salmon, rain, and orcas.

Few saltwater expanses around the continental United States are as favorable as Puget Sound proper for year-round boat travel. In the Gulf of Mexico you get hurricanes, mosquitoes "beyond description," and mangroves that create what one early surveyor described as the "most formidable difficulties" in navigation.[4] The eastern seaboard features long stretches of shoals and banks that are, in the words of one maritime historian, "constantly in motion, governing the course of navigation and often claiming those who ignore or are ignorant of their ephemeral and deadly characteristics."[5] On the West Coast, maritime visitors to San Francisco Bay encounter a long, crescent-shaped bar, cloaking fog, and swift currents that create "one of the most hazardous port entries in the world."[6] South of Puget Sound, coastal mariners have to contend with the mouth of the Columbia River, dubbed the "graveyard of the Pacific," where, since 1800, more than two thousand ships have wrecked, claiming an estimated seven hundred lives.

In contrast, consider the words written in 1855 by Isaac Stevens about Puget Sound: "Nothing can exceed the beauty and safety of these waters for navigation. Not a shoal exists within them; not a hidden rock; no sudden overfalls of the water or the air; no such strong flaws of the wind as in other narrow waters."[7] The governor may have exaggerated, but compared to many sections of the continent's coasts, Puget Sound offers a comparative serenity. This does not mean that navigators don't need a thorough knowledge of the waterway or that Puget Sound lacks challenges such as boat-thrashing currents, perpetual days of rain, and salmon chowder fog. At least boaters aren't generally going to be consumed by bugs, cooked by the sun, frozen by snow, or cudgeled by 100-mph winds.

For as long as people have inhabited the Sound, they have taken advantage of its relatively benign nature to journey across the water by boat. Traveling by water would have been far easier than traveling overland. There is a dearth, however, of supporting archaeological evidence for navigation of the Sound by the earliest inhabitants: boats would have decomposed long ago. All evidence for early watercraft is circumstantial. It includes artifacts found on islands, which would have required a boat to reach, as well as bones from animals, such as porpoise and halibut, which would have required a boat to catch.

In the absence of evidence, archaeologists can only speculate about the earliest modes of water transportation in Puget Sound. Early residents might have used three types of boats: hide boats, bark boats, or canoes. These watercraft would have faced a range of different conditions—out in the wind and currents in the Strait of Juan de Fuca, on the rivers that flowed into the Sound, and on its relatively quiet waters—and served different needs, such as ferrying large groups of people and their goods, hunting and fishing for prey ranging in size from herring to whales, and navigating swift river currents. Canoes became the defining mode of transport in the Sound, though canoe carvers would not have had access to western red cedar, the best tree for making canoes, until five thousand years ago. The Bear Creek people could have made canoes from other trees, but archaeologists have not found any evidence to prove or disprove this possibility.

The early residents eventually created canoes that "reached [their] highest development in the world," according to the marine historian Bill Durham.[8] When the first European explorers sailed into this region, they noted the sophistication of canoe culture. In June 1788, a British fur trader reported that "a great number of canoes . . . in which there could not be less than four hundred men" paddled out to meet his boat near the entrance to the Strait of Juan de Fuca.[9] One of Vancouver's officers wrote that canoes made of a single log could hold thirty people and were "very sharp at the stem and stern, and well adapted to going fast," and Wilkes wrote in his report: "The canoes of this region differ from any thing we have seen on the voyage. They are made from a single trunk, and have a shape that may be considered elegant. . . . [T]hey are preserved with great care, being never suffered to lie exposed to the sun."[10]

A few of the early European explorers included black-and-white drawings of the canoes they encountered, but my two favorite images of canoes come from two mid nineteenth-century painters. The two paintings have essentially the same view—a canoe crossing Puget Sound with Mount Rainier in the background—as if the stunning landscape were incomplete without a canoe. Sanford Robinson Gifford's 1875 *Mount Rainier, Bay of Tacoma—Puget Sound* features the northern-style canoe, which was about forty feet long in real life.[11] In contrast, Albert Bierstadt's *Sunrise on Mt. Tacoma* depicts a Nootkan canoe, an ocean-going craft that could be up to eighty feet long and hold several dozen people. T. T. Waterman and Geraldine Coffin, who published a thorough study of the local canoes in 1920, wrote that the animal-head shape of the Nootkan bow gave the canoe "an air of alertness, as though it were moving of its own accord."[12]

The painters' choices to depict these styles of canoe is curious; both were more common elsewhere. Within Puget Sound proper, the everyday canoe was the Coast Salish style. It came in two varieties: a heavier canoe for hauling freight and a more mobile troller, used for fishing,

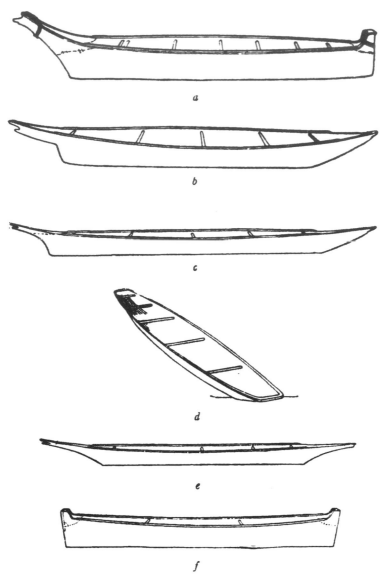

DIAGRAM REPRESENTING THE SIX TYPES OF CANOES ON PUGET SOUND

(*a*, the "war canoe"; *b*, the "freight canoe;" *c*, the "trolling canoe"; *d*, the "shovel-nose canoe"; *e*, the "one-man canoe"; *f*, the "children's canoe," used by children and as a knockabout.)

Common types of canoes used in Puget Sound. The drawings are based on research conducted by ethnographers Geraldine Coffin and Thomas T. Waterman around Seattle in the 1910s. (From Waterman and Coffin, *Types of Canoes on Puget Sound*) duck hunting, and harpooning porpoise and sea otter. Both types had a bow and stern that angled gracefully: the bow ended in a notch like "an open mouth," and the stern "curved up like a duck's tail."[13] For faster travel, the freight canoe could be equipped with a sail made from cedar bark or cattails. This style was called a women's canoe, because it "was used on the Sound proper almost exclusively by women," according to the ethnologist Marian Smith.[14]

A fourth type was designed for navigating rivers; far upriver it was the only type of canoe in use. Typically ten to forty feet long, it had a squared bow and stern, which scooped upward like a shovel, and could be either paddled or propelled by a pole pushed against the river bottom. Although not so elegant or stable as saltwater canoes, these river craft allowed a person standing in the bow, balanced by a paddler in the stern, to be ideally positioned to spear salmon directly underneath the canoe.

The canoe was essential to life on Puget Sound. In the words of the archaeologist Ken Ames, "It . . . seems clear that literally everyone, at least on the Northwest Coast, had one."[15] This included the young. Waterman and Coffin described a more roughly hewn canoe that they called a children's canoe, which despite being used for the "commonest purposes" was still "more manageable than a white-man's boat."[16] It had to be. Although the protected waters of Puget Sound are not washed by the great waves of the outer coast and the Strait of Juan de Fuca, the Sound's tidal currents are not the realm for novices. During the flood tide—what the University of Washington oceanographer Parker MacCready calls Puget Sound's biggest river—saltwater from the ocean squeezes through Admiralty Inlet. One to two hours later, the incoming water, which is about equal in volume to the water that flows over Niagara Falls in twenty-five days, reaches Olympia.[17] Because of the way water piles up against an obstacle, in this case the Sound's southern terminus, tidal variation is much greater in the south than in the north. The range between high and low tides averages 8.3 feet at Port Townsend, compared with 14.4 feet at Olympia.

One of the easiest places to see the action of the tide is on the bluff at Fort Casey Historical State Park. On one memorable visit, I watched the white-capped river of ebb water ripping noisily out of the Sound. In the smooth water of an eddy along the current floated pigeon guillemots, loons, logs, and great rafts of kelp. What made it more notable is that I knew that the flow would soon reverse itself, and I would see a very different pattern of water formed by the flood tide.

The motion of this great volume of water is complicated by the irregular underwater topography and scalloped shoreline. People who traveled the Sound's waters needed to have a comprehensive knowledge of the currents and tides, particularly if they were moving canoes laden with people and goods. Such a journey could take hours longer if the paddlers had to battle against the tides. In bottlenecks such as Tacoma Narrows and Deception Pass, where the current can reach speeds of 5.5 and 10 knots respectively, or two to three times faster than a typical canoeist can paddle, the mass of water could be dangerous and as impassable a barrier to travel as any terrestrial feature.

In 1977, the University of Washington oceanographers John Lincoln and Noel McGary published *Tide Prints*, a guide to the surface currents of Puget Sound.[18] They created maps for each of the Sound's four basins, with arrows and lines depicting current direction and speed. The maps look like fingerprints: each is unique, with loops, curls, and swirls showing currents heading in all directions, shooting through channels, and warping around headlands. Then you flip the page to the next map—showing the same location, with the tide now ebbing instead of flooding—and the pattern has completely changed. As complex as these maps are, they only begin to show the navigational challenges, because they don't take account of the effects of wind or how water moves near shorelines, in restricted bays and inlets, or across tidal flats.

"In their youth, Indians of the Skagit Region acquired a complete familiarity with canoe navigation, the tides and currents, and the winds of their home village areas," wrote Natalie Roberts in her dissertation on the Swinomish Tribe, who live in the north end of the Sound proper.[19] This familiarity would have been acquired firsthand, by travel on the water both alone and with an elder who could have shared his or her knowledge of the waterway. Over time, and aided in part by the numerous descriptive names given to features of the landscape, paddlers would have developed a finely tuned mental map of the Sound. They would have supplemented their spatial knowledge with an awareness of the relationship between the moon and the tides—recognizing, for example, that the greatest tidal range occurred at the new and full moons. How few among us now even notice the moon and its phases, much less any effect upon our primary method of transportation? To navigate Puget Sound required an intimacy with the landscape, the waterways, and the natural processes and rhythms of the days and seasons.

• • •

European settlers took a different approach to navigating the Sound, relying on engines instead of people for propulsion. The first steam-powered vessel reached Puget Sound only three years after the Hudson's

A Snohomish man and woman sit near a canoe on the Tulalip Indian Reservation in 1907. She is sitting next to a cattail mat. Photograph by Norman Edson. (Courtesy of UW Special Collections, Image NA729)

Bay Company established Fort Nisqually. Built on the Thames River as a paddle wheeler, but then outfitted for ocean travel as a sailing ship, the 101-foot *Beaver* left London in August 1835 and sailed across the Atlantic and around Cape Horn, reaching Hawaii in February 1836. Two months later the *Beaver* arrived at HBC's Fort Vancouver on the Columbia River, where crews converted her back to a wood-burning steamship by reassembling the engine, boilers, and paddle wheel. With this conversion the *Beaver* became one of the earliest steamers in the Pacific Ocean.[20]

On June 18, 1836, the Fort Vancouver manager, John McLoughlin, sent the *Beaver* to visit HBC outposts farther north. The paddle-wheeler ultimately made it to Fort Tongass, near Ketchikan, Alaska, before returning south. On November 12 it reached Fort Nisqually, where it overwintered. Although the trip was deemed a success and the *Beaver* went on to serve as a floating HBC trading post in Puget Sound for several decades, it had a major limitation: it lived up to its name, eating through wood for its boilers at a rapid clip. It took six men two days to cut enough wood to fuel twelve to fourteen hours of travel, or a journey of about 230 miles. Because the *Beaver* could store only forty cords, "she is at least as much at anchor as she is under way," wrote the HBC governor, George Simpson.[21] Later in its life, after a conversion to coal, the "little black steamer" could travel for several days without stopping to refuel.

Like many later Puget Sound–based steamships, the *Beaver* was a multipurpose vessel, serving at different times as a towboat, anchored gunpowder magazine, and survey ship. Its end—one shared by many local

HBC steamship *Beaver* anchored near Victoria, British Columbia, ca. 1880. At this point, the ship was privately owned and used for general freight. Photograph by Asahel Curtis and Walter Miller. (Courtesy of Seattle Public Library, spl_shp_5093)

CHAPTER 5

ships—came when it crashed into the shore at Calamity Point in Burrard Inlet (now Prospect Point in Vancouver's Stanley Park) on July 25, 1888. Stuck on the rocks, it became a popular attraction and site for souvenir seekers, even after the wake from a large steamer further damaged the wreck in 1892.

After the *Beaver's* arrival, seventeen years passed before another steamship reached Puget Sound. A September 1852 editorial in the *Columbian* noted that "the business men on the Sound, as well as the traveling public, have heretofore experienced the most serious inconvenience" because of a lack of steam navigation. The Sound's American residents could move only as fast as the wind on the fleet of small sloops, schooners, and scows that ran on an irregular basis between the settlements from Olympia to Port Townsend. If the settlers wanted to travel or send their goods to more distant destinations, such as San Francisco, they could do so only on sailing vessels. Even worse, in the eyes of many settlers, they often had to resort to Native-powered canoes for transportation within Puget Sound, a mode of travel that typically made the news only because of drownings or editorial complaints about the paddlers.

Puget Sound's second steamer was the British-made, 122-foot, propeller-driven *Otter*. It was not, however, brought in for the use of the settlers. The vessel was intended to supplement the *Beaver* on runs for the HBC. Finally, on October 31, 1853, amid a celebratory firing of cannons and a mass gathering of the populace, an American ship arrived, the side-wheeler *Fairy*, though not under its own power. It rode from San Francisco to Olympia on the deck of the bark *Sarah Warren*.

Within weeks of the little *Fairy's* arrival, advertisements appeared in the *Columbian* touting the *Fairy's* regular run to Steilacoom, Seattle, and Alki.[22] One-way travel from Olympia to Steilacoom cost five dollars and a journey to the northern destinations ten dollars—a significant expense when an ordinary laborer made two to three dollars per day.[23] Described as "undersized as well as cranky," the *Fairy* had a short life: it blew up and sank in October 1857.[24] But it had demonstrated that steamships could carry freight and passengers, as well as the mail, whose delivery had been erratic. Finding a bigger, more reliable vessel would "add more towards the growth and prosperity of our territory, than any other project," wrote the editor of the Olympia-based *Pioneer and Democrat*.[25]

Over the next few decades, steamship after steamship chugged into the Sound, eventually forming the waterway's mosquito fleet. Typically owned and operated by one person, the vessels operated on the principle of "Where there's a will, there's a way"—to land, to transport goods of every size, and to travel anywhere with enough water to float them. Even

Typical scene on the Seattle waterfront ca. 1885, showing a mix of sailing ships and early steamships of what would later be called the mosquito fleet. (Courtesy of Seattle Public Library, spl_shp_13474)

that was not always a requirement: one legendary boat "walked" across a mudflat on its side wheel.[26] The fleet quickly became the main mode of transport for Puget Sound's growing settler population.

Although it is often associated with Puget Sound, the term *mosquito fleet* was first applied to military vessels. The earliest reference I could find in the United States was in a letter written by New York governor George Clinton on October 12, 1777. He referred to a "Musquito Fleet" commanded by Sir James Wallace on the Hudson River. References to mosquito fleet vessels also appear in accounts of the War of 1812, battles against pirates in the Caribbean around 1823, and the Civil War. In Puget Sound, the term began to show up regularly in newspapers around 1890, appearing first in papers from towns to the south. An article in the *Tacoma Daily Ledger* on February 21, 1889, noted that "'The Mosquito Fleet' is the name very aptly applied by L. F. Cook to the swarms of small steamers that skim over the green waters of the Sound." We will never know if Cook was the first to use the term in the Sound, but we do know that it is retroactively used to describe Puget Sound's pre-1889 steamers.[27]

By the time the term was in common parlance, the mosquito fleet was entering its peak era. Hundreds of vessels crisscrossed the Sound annually, carrying hundreds of thousands of passengers and hundreds of thousands of tons of goods. The maritime historian Joe Baar estimated

Built in San Francisco in 1862, the *Yosemite* was one of the more elegant mosquito fleet vessels. The ship started to operate in Puget Sound in 1906, often carrying up to one thousand passengers between Seattle and Bremerton. The *Yosemite* ran aground on July 9, 1909, at Port Orchard and was a total loss. (Courtesy of Cherie Christensen)

the minimum size of the fleet to be 700 vessels; some sources state that it totaled 2,500.[28]

There is no agreed, precise definition of the boats and ships that made up the mosquito fleet, but, to paraphrase Justice Potter Stewart's definition of pornography, people knew a mosquito fleet vessel when they saw it. The archetypical "pointy-ender" was made of wood, steam powered, wood fueled, propeller driven, and about ninety feet long. It had a narrow hull and long, tapered bow with a flat bottom and very shallow draft to facilitate access to the shore. Nothing, though, was uniform about mosquito fleet vessels. They ranged in size from the 19-foot *Polky* to the 283-foot *Yosemite*. A handful were made of steel or iron. Many were paddle wheelers (or "paddle-wagons"), with the wheel at either the stern or the side. Some were elegant, some crotchety, some scary. No two looked alike.

Part of what might be considered the charm of the mosquito fleet is that few of the boats corresponded to any formal design. Most smaller vessels were simply built to the specifications of the owner, who often united equal parts of nautical knowledge and gumption. In an account of his Puget Sound childhood in the early 1900s, the historian and novelist Archie Binns described one such boat, which ran between Shelton and

Olympia. The *Old Settler* was "a bastard creation: a common scow with a donkey engine which had been induced on board under false pretense and then persuaded to turn a pair of homemade paddlewheels." And, yet she regularly ran her route, providing a generally safe, if not altogether efficient, method of travel.[29]

Failure, though, was common in the mosquito fleet. Bad financial choices, bad equipment, bad captains, bad routes—all played a role. In his *Ships of the Inland Sea*, Gordon Newell calculated that almost 40 percent of the mosquito fleet was abandoned, burned, stranded, sunk, or wrecked. Some boats even suffered twice, sinking and being refloated, only to run aground later.

What united the mosquito fleet vessels was location; their skippers conducted their business primarily in Puget Sound, though ships also ventured north to Canada, up the larger rivers, and into Lake Washington and Lake Sammamish. Most of the early routes ran north-south, such as the course long traveled by the *Eliza Anderson*, one of the most famous ships of the mosquito fleet, which steamed from Olympia to Victoria, BC, for most of the second half of the nineteenth century. The orientation of the routes started to change when the populations of Seattle and Tacoma began to skyrocket. The fleet eventually became more of a cross-Sound system, transporting people and supplies between urban centers and small rural outposts on the islands, the Kitsap and Olympic peninsulas, and in Hood Canal. Service to the hinterlands became a stronger focus for the fleet when railroads spread along the eastern shore of Puget Sound—beginning slowly in the late 1870s and advancing rapidly after the transcontinental railroad reached Seattle in 1893—and overland travel between north and south became easier.

In a time when no roads existed, as well as for several decades into the era of automobiles and trains, the mosquito fleet provided transportation for every far-flung settler and community. Stops were known as dock stops where a dock existed, and rowboat stops where people made do by rowing out to meet a steamer. No one knows how many official stops there were. Information from newspaper articles from the early 1900s suggests that the number exceeded 350. Named stops, such as Aquarium, Bee, Detroit, Gettysburg, Joe Elliott's Bay, Nibbeville, Pleasant Beach, Pleasant Harbor, Sunnybay, Venice, Whiskey Spit, and Zenith, persist today only as abandoned docks, silent testimonials to the dreams of former settlers.

For many nineteenth- and early twentieth-century Puget Sound residents, the mosquito fleet was their lifeline, a combination of post office, transit system, UPS truck, and general store, plus a good source of neighborhood gossip. Residents knew their vessels' crews by name and trusted and relied on them. They had to, as captains navigated without the benefit of accurate nautical charts, sophisticated navigational equipment, buoys, or lighthouses, a task that was particularly challenging during the many months of winter fog. One trick that fog-bound captains employed along Puget Sound's bluffs was to blow a whistle and listen for the echo off the land to determine how close they were to shore. Some captains heeded barking dogs as another sign of proximity to land.

The mosquito fleet also created jobs, particularly in the days when steam engines were powered by wood. Hazel Heckman, in *Island in the Sound*, wrote that residents of Anderson Island provided at least eighty thousand cords of wood, and probably much more, for the steamers. "Those woodyards were beans and bacon, in one way or the other, for most settlers. . . . The chances are the Island would have been a long time settling without them."[30]

Historians have often overlooked the importance of Puget Sound's natural resources to the success and longevity of the mosquito fleet. Anderson Islanders would not have been alone in providing wood: Joe Baar suspected that "almost every tree less than a foot and a half in diameter and within a half-mile distance to salt water, across the region, would have been cut and split for fuel by 1910."[31] In addition, Puget Sound coalfields began supplying the steamboats in 1868, selling coal for eight dollars a ton. By the late 1890s, the price had dropped to less than two dollars a ton, and King and Pierce Counties were producing more than a million tons annually. This was more than enough to fuel vessels in the fleet, one-third of which used coal—though not for long. By 1911, 75 to 85 percent of the steamers ran on oil.

Unregulated, fly-by-night, money-losing, and erratic, the mosquito fleet nevertheless survived because it was functional, practical, and adaptive. It filled a need, enabling settlements to grow and thrive. People could put down roots in isolated locations and still be connected to a larger world. Farmers living in the middle of nowhere could still have access to a market for their products and obtain needed goods. They could be part of a community.

In a world where water, forests, and hills divided the landscape into separate locations, often hard to reach, the vessels of the mosquito fleet were the flexible sinews that held together the people and communities of the region. "There were smiles, tears, laughter and heart break connected with the coming and going of the steamer that linked us with the outside world. . . . When the little steamer made twice a week trips, we felt we were really getting somewhere. When we had a daily boat we felt we were really on the map," wrote Lillie Christiansen, who grew up in the little town of Brinnon, on Hood Canal, in the 1890s.[32] The ships of the mosquito fleet—the steamers with their churning paddlewheels, towering smokestacks, and graceful bows, and also the little launches buzzing in every direction—gave Puget Sound a maritime pulse we no longer feel today.

• • •

In 2019, only two mosquito fleet vessels were still running in Puget Sound. The younger and better-known is the *Virginia V*, which began operating on June 11, 1922, running from Seattle to Tacoma. Now docked at Lake Union and owned by a nonprofit foundation, it weathered storms, owners, and route changes until 1968, when the ship was purchased and protected by a group of steamship aficionados. Five years later, the *Virginia V* was listed on the National Register of Historic Places, which ultimately helped lead to a multiyear restoration to its former beauty.

Much less well publicized is the *Carlisle II*. Built in 1917 and originally serving Lummi Island, the sixty-five-foot, diesel-powered, passenger-only ferry is remarkable for having made the same run, between Port Orchard and Bremerton, from 1936 to the present. For two bucks each way, you can ride the *Carlisle II* for the morning and afternoon weekday commutes.[33] One afternoon I waited in a long line of commuters at the Bremerton dock for the *Carlisle II* to arrive. It pulled in smoothly, on time, its long, narrow bow gliding along the dock. A Kitsap Transit crew member leaped off, tied down the lines, opened a small gate, and let out the few passengers directly onto the dock. He then let passengers board for the return journey, scanning our ORCA transit cards or taking fares. Most of the riders appeared to know the crew by name.

Space on the double-decker ferry was standing room only. The ceilings were not much more than six feet high. Inside, the *Carlisle II* was all wood, its floor unpainted and well worn, the rest painted white from the ceiling down to the top of the dark green benches running around the outer edges of both decks. Covering the walls were photos and articles about historic vessels from the era of the mosquito fleet, and near the entrance were several ancient-looking coin boxes.

Ten minutes later we had crossed Sinclair Inlet to Port Orchard. There was nothing fancy about the ride: it was quick, cheap, and efficient. Most people stood in small groups, either inside or on the exposed outer decks, chatting with their companions. The ride may or may not have saved anyone any time; I suspect people found it less stressful than driving and the journey time more predictable, with no worries about traffic. In the spirit of the mosquito fleet, the short ride on the *Carlisle II* was a community builder, allowing people to live in the neighborhood of their choice and to connect to the larger world beyond.

• • •

Although the practical and adaptable nature of the mosquito fleet vessels had made it possible to carry automobiles—generally one or two cars shoehorned onto a deck—the first vessel officially adapted to transport cars was the *Bailey Gatzert*. The 194-foot stern wheeler underwent surgery in March 1920 to add a ten-ton steam elevator, which allowed cars to be placed on the car deck at any level of the tide. The vessel was an immediate success and led to the subsequent conversion of numerous other passenger-only steamers. Riders of today's roll-on, roll-off ferries might have found them odd, as cars entered and exited from the same point.

What maritime historians describe as the first ferry built to hold vehicles on Puget Sound was the *City of Seattle*, a side-wheeler built in Portland, Oregon. She began operating between downtown and West Seattle across the south end of Elliott Bay on December 31, 1888.

Built in Ballard in 1890, the *Bailey Gatzert* had a 22-foot-diameter sternwheel, had a top speed of over 20 miles an hour, and was one of the fastest ships in Puget Sound. Named for Seattle's first Jewish mayor, the *Bailey Gatzert* operated in the Sound until the 1920s. (Courtesy of Cherie Christensen)

Double-ended, with a wide bow and stern like modern ferries, the *City of Seattle* was designed to carry horses and wagons. The initial fare of fifteen cents per ride soon dropped to a nickel and then to forty rides for a dollar during a price war, which the *City of Seattle* won because a mysterious fire destroyed the competition, the steamer *Lady of the Lake*.[34] The *City of Seattle* continued the run until 1913.

Realizing that cars were the future, shipbuilders began to fashion ferries in the 1920s that enabled cars to drive on at one end and off at the other. Ships were eventually built that could carry hundreds of passengers and dozens of cars and often included the elegant dining and sitting rooms that had glorified the largest vessels of the mosquito fleet.

By the end of the 1920s, as roads spread around Puget Sound, particularly on the east side, the days of passenger-only service were numbered. Expensive conversions, along with route consolidation, ultimately led to the elimination of small, private operators and the rise of corporate ownership, according to the historians Carolyn Neal and Thomas Kilday Janus in *Puget Sound Ferries: From Canoes to Catamaran*.[35] The most successful was Alexander Peabody and Joshua Green's Puget Sound Navigation Company (PSNC), best known for its Black Ball Line ferries. Through mergers, acquisition, and ruthless competition, PSNC soon monopolized the local ferry system. "Suddenly, in the mid-1930's, the people of Puget Sound found that their Mosquito Fleet was gone. It surprised them and made them a little sad. . . . They had been part of the peculiar charm and magic of their lovely inland sea. . . . Only when they were gone did they begin to look out over the quiet reaches of the Sound and feel that something fine and exciting was suddenly missing," wrote Gordon Newell. A system that had been quirky, independent, and adapted to the unique conditions of the Sound had been replaced by "big, efficient, ugly" ships with "little personality" that were slaves to the automobile.[36] By the early 1940s, the Black Ball had fifteen routes and 452 daily sailings, with the capacity to carry 22,500 cars and 315,000 passengers every day.[37] During World War II, Black Ball ran ferries every hour on the hour around the clock between Seattle and Bremerton, home of the US Navy shipyard.

But with the end of the war, PSNC could not maintain the regular service and low fares it had offered when thousands of people needed to be at their war-related jobs. Not only did the company reduce the number of runs, but they also sought a fare increase of 30 percent, which would raise the price on the Seattle-Bremerton run from 52 to 68 cents for passengers and from $1.19 to $1.55 for a car and driver.

Despite their reliance on Black Ball, riders began to sour on the company's monopoly and perceived price gouging, prompting Governor

The *Kalakala*, pictured on this brochure, was built in 1935 for the Puget Sound Navigation Company and was the largest and fastest ferry in the Sound. The *Kalakala* operated in the Sound until 1967, then was used in Alaska, and ultimately ended up in Tacoma, where the ship was parted out in a 2017 auction. (Courtesy of Paul Dorpat)

Mon C. Wallgren to issue a proposal for the state government to take over Black Ball. On August 30, 1948, over Peabody's objections, Black Ball's shareholders agreed to accept the state's offer of $5,975,000 cash for twenty-one ferries and associated facilities. Passengers did not necessarily support public ownership—some opponents of the proposal described it as "creeping socialism"—but most people had decided that Peabody's ownership was even worse. With a ninety-day option for the state to pay, it appeared that Puget Sound ferry riders' long-ambivalent relationship with the Black Ball Line would soon end.

But 1948 was an election year pitting Wallgren, a classic New Deal Democrat, against the Republican Arthur Langlie, who called Wallgren's plan to buy the ferry system a fiasco. Instead, he favored acquisition by condemnation, saying that the state shouldn't have to purchase a system that it had been "goaded" into buying by Peabody's selfish maneuvering.[38] This conflict between the candidates resulted in the state's failing to follow through on the buyout.[39]

After winning the election, with the support of Seattle Republicans, Langlie changed his position and submitted legislation for buying out the ferry service. He also revived a radical idea for ending the ferry problem. "Within seven years there will be very few ferry boats on Puget Sound," said Langlie in March 1950.[40] In his vision, they would be replaced by bridges, which would have the advantage of being available twenty-four hours a day, and once the bridge bonds were paid off, crossing Puget Sound would be free.

The backbone of the proposal was a four-lane floating bridge from Brace Point (south of the Fauntleroy ferry terminal) to Vashon Island. The 14,250-foot-long bridge would be more than twice as long as the Lacey V. Murrow Memorial Bridge across Lake Washington (on present Interstate 90), which had opened in 1940. The total cost for the floating bridge and more than a dozen others would be $60 million, or as much as $3.4 billion in 2019 dollars, which would be paid for by tolls of 75 cents per car and 15 cents per passenger.[41]

The Vashon project was merely the beginning, wrote Charles Andrew, the principal engineer on the design team for the Lake Washington floating bridge. He proposed a pair of submerged concrete tubes, each carrying two lanes of traffic, between Alki Point and Restoration Point on Bainbridge. With walls three feet thick, the tubes would float fifty feet below the surface, anchored by cables to the bottom of Puget Sound. Andrew favored this plan in part because the tubes would not interfere with shipping traffic. His proposal also called for a second pair of submerged tubes to connect Skiff Point on Bainbridge with West Point (Discovery Park), and most ambitious of all, a combination of floating bridge and submerged tubes linking Richmond Beach with Point Jefferson on the Kitsap Peninsula. The total length of this crossing would be approximately twenty-one thousand feet, or about four miles, and it would take advantage of a "submerged island" offshore from Point Jefferson. Another floating bridge would cross to Port Orchard, on the west side of Bainbridge Island.[42]

As plans moved forward for the cross-Sound bridge system, Langlie continued to promote the purchase of the ferry system. On December 30, 1950, the state of Washington finally acquired the Black Ball Line. Now that the state owned the ferry system, it would better be able to "integrate our highway program with the ferry routes best located to convenience the traveling public and redevelop the travel habits that have dwindled during the past several years," said Langlie.[43] State management of the ferry system began on June 1, 1951.[44]

Langlie's goal of bridging Puget Sound in some ways envisioned the return of an aspect of travel in the waterway that had prevailed for thousands of years. Using canoes, travelers were free to get in and go when and where they pleased (subject to weather and tide conditions). With the rise of the mosquito fleet, individuals had lost that independence. The vessels could and would go almost anywhere around Puget Sound, but travelers had to organize their journeys around someone else's schedule. Nor was the traveler in the driver's seat, literally or figuratively: that position had been ceded to the vessel's captain. Crossing Puget Sound by bridge would give back that independence, providing travelers "free, 24-hour-a-day transportation between the Seattle area and the growing sections to the west across Puget Sound," noted the governor, with a typically myopic view of the centrality of Seattle to all things concerning Puget Sound.[45]

Langlie's secondary, and arguably more realistic, vision of integrating the ferry and freeway system sought to make a fundamental change in Puget Sound transportation, one that we still feel today. Throughout the history of human habitation of the Sound until the era of the car and ferry, boats had been the area's sole transportation system. They were the easiest, the most direct, and often the only means of getting from point A to point B, particularly for those who lived in isolated localities along the 1,332-mile shoreline. Langlie proposed that boats would now become part of an integrated transportation system—in essence, an extension of the car-oriented highway system.

Modern maps and modern experience reflect this thinking. Ferry routes are imprinted on the water like roads on the land. Traveling from Seattle to Port Angeles, on the Olympic Peninsula, you drive north to Edmonds, wait in the ferry line (which you might consider a regularly scheduled traffic jam), get on the ferry, get off in Kingston, and continue driving for another ninety minutes or so. The ferry ride is integrated into the car-based road network. No doubt the current system is faster, more efficient, and easier than depending on the mosquito fleet, but it is less in harmony with the long-term history of Puget Sound.

The modern ferries have not, however, severed our connections with the past. In December 2017, I spent part of a day with WSF Captain Marsha Morse. Few people have as deep a relationship to the maritime highway of Puget Sound as Marsha, who began working for WSF in 1975 and has worked most officer and crew jobs and every route in Puget Sound proper. On the day we chatted, she was working as chief mate on the Southworth to Fauntleroy run. "Oftentimes the mate navigates eastbound and the captain navigates westbound," she commented. "As one person said, 'The captain has the responsibility, the mate does lots of the footwork.'"[46]

In her four decades of service, Marsha has seen it all. She has been involved in births and deaths, been threatened by a man with a gun, and saved people's lives. She has watched the passenger demographics change as techies have supplemented and replaced the blue-collar workers on runs like the one between Seattle and Bremerton. "In the old days it was rough on that run." She lamented another change: today, fewer people look out the window or go outside. Instead, they are on their cell phones and tablets. "To me that's very sad," said Marsha.

One thing the cell-phone-absorbed passengers miss is seeing wildlife, in particular orca. Earlier in the day Marsha had seen a dozen splashing between Vashon and Fauntleroy. "Where else do you work [that is] like that?" she says. Because ferries regularly encounter orca, researchers have recommended a transition to quieter, more fuel-efficient vessels, to reduce the interference of vessel noise with orca echolocation. The Washington State Department of Transportation has also initiated use of a whale-alert smartphone app, which enables the public to report whale sightings in real time, to try to prevent collisions between ferries and orca.

Marsha places part of the blame for passengers' indifference on modern boat design. The old boats were smaller, slower, gentler, and closer to the water, she says. "These [newer] boats have encapsulated people more and made them more separated from nature. You can see out, but you can't get out as easily." (During this part of the conversation she used my favorite ferry term, *pickle fork*, to refer to the two sections of the upper deck where you can stand above the car deck.) Ferry designers, she says "are not conscious of how important that connection is, for people to be able to get out and look out."

Marsha believes, however, that some riders still appreciate the opportunity that comes with riding a ferry in Puget Sound. She spent her childhood in the desert of eastern Washington. "When I am on the water, it's kind of like the desert. It's flat. It's open. And I do think there's

Captain Marsha Morse on the M/V *Kitsap*, 2018. Her more than four decades of experience with Washington State Ferries has given her deep insights into the spiritual as well as the practical impacts of ferries in Puget Sound. Photograph by Terry Donnelly. (Courtesy of Terry Donnelly)

more of a spiritual connection being on the water. Or openness that can happen. Now, you're on a ferry, which is public transportation, it's a bit different, but you're still on the water. I imagine that people who ride the ferries, they take a minute, I know I do, and they look out, and they connect with nature and can reflect on their lives because they have an expanse. I cannot speak for everybody, but I would not be surprised if people felt that."

Marsha's insight into the relationship between people, Puget Sound, and ferries provides an additional way to consider the threads that connect the modern ferry system back through the decades to the mosquito fleet and through the centuries to canoe culture. I suspect that many boat travelers on Puget Sound have felt, as she does, that there is a spiritual aspect to being on the water, with its great views, connections to nature, and time to think. In the twenty-first century, perhaps most travelers are focused on the practical concern of getting from A to B, but we cannot forget the importance of the spiritual: both play a part in the 12,500-year-long story of traveling by boat on Puget Sound.

• • •

Six months after my conversation with Marsha Morse, I traveled to Alki Point for a celebration of the origins of Puget Sound's maritime highway. I had come to see the Tribal Canoe Journey, an annual event bringing together Native peoples from the Salish Sea and beyond to honor the heritage of the canoe. The first such journey was held in Seattle in July 1989, in conjunction with the centennial of Washington State. The Native Canoe Project, coordinated by the Quinault elder Emmett Oliver, sought to revive carving and paddling traditions. Tribes would craft traditional-style canoes from old-growth cedar trees provided by the US Forest Service and use the new canoes on a monumental journey, the Paddle to Seattle.

On July 20, members of twenty-five tribes and nations from the United States and Canada gathered at Suquamish. People from Puget Sound were joined by members of the Quileute and Hoh tribes, who had journeyed 170 miles from the Pacific Ocean side of the Olympic Peninsula, and the Heiltsuk First Nation, who paddled five hundred miles from Bella Bella, north of Vancouver Island. The next day more than thirty canoes traveled across the Sound to Golden Gardens, a small park on the water in north Seattle, for celebrations, canoe races, and ceremonies.

Reading through the accounts of those who participated in the event, I am struck by the stream of related words: *community, healing, rebirth, sacred, spiritual, teamwork, traditional.* For many tribes in Puget Sound, the project was a turning point. "The Canoe Journeys have given me a whole new perspective on where I grew up," said Will Bill Jr. of the Muckleshoot Indian Tribe. "I have deeper understanding of my ancestors and the depth of knowledge they must have had, how to know tides and currents, and when to harvest. The journeys have helped us relearn traditional protocols and how to engage with each other. Canoe society is helping to restore connections to home."[47]

When I arrived at Alki around noon for the 2018 Tribal Canoe Journey, a half dozen canoes had already landed. They had been carried up the beach and placed in a row above the tide line. Painted in elaborate and detailed designs of black, red, white, and blue, the canoes were elegant and beautiful. The biggest could comfortably hold more than a dozen people.

Over the next couple of hours, I watched more than one hundred canoes arrive from dozens of tribes and nations within Puget Sound, the Salish Sea, and along the Pacific Coast from Oregon to Alaska. As each canoe approached, a representative of the Puyallup tribe, which hosted the final days of the journey, formally welcomed the paddlers: "We give thanks to everyone for being here. We will sing. We will dance. And we will feast together. Come to shore now, and we will enjoy visiting each other."

As I watched the canoes arrive, listened to the evocative words of the hosts, and observed the participants and bystanders, I felt the paddlers' sense of joy, companionship, and pride. It was thrilling, too, seeing Puget Sound dominated by canoes, each one gliding smoothly and efficiently, reminding all of us at Alki of how, for thousands of years, these vessels have made life possible for people on this waterway, and how the water continues to shape the values and actions of those who perceive the connective threads between people and place.

6

Forests in the Sound

In March 2017, while eating a garlic and sun-dried tomato pizza for lunch, I became a kelpophile. The person who showed me the light was Tom Mumford, an expert on kelp in Puget Sound. Before our meal, I thought of kelp as the spinachy-looking, often slimy, sometimes stinky, usually dead seaweed I tried to avoid on beaches. By the time Tom and I had finished eating, he had taught me that the great kelp forests under the surface of the Sound are the equivalent of the temperate rainforests above it, and equally critical to the ecosystem. When Tom offered to take me out in the field and look at kelp once the weather improved, I took him up on his generosity. That is how, in June 2017, I ended up on a small beach on the west side of Whidbey Island.

Now retired from the Washington Department of Natural Resources (WDNR), Tom has been studying and rhapsodizing about kelp for decades. He had chosen this rock-strewn beach because it faces directly toward the Strait of Juan de Fuca, with nothing blocking the waves and weather. It isn't ideal habitat for kelp—most kelps grow in deeper water, typically attached to a rocky substrate—but the Whidbey Island field of cobbles provides a good place to sample the diversity of kelp and other seaweeds in the Sound.

Scientists such as Tom who study marine algae, called phycologists, refer to kelp as brown algae. For most of scientific history, kelps were classified as plants, certainly a logical idea considering that kelps share many of the attributes of plants, such as photosynthesis, a sedentary life, and a three-part morphology of root, stem, and leaf. In the past few years, however, taxonomists have decided that brown algae have more in common with single-celled organisms known as diatoms than they do with roses or tulips, and they have removed kelp from the plant kingdom. Kelp has now been placed in the Chromista kingdom, along with the colorfully named water molds, downy mildews, and blister rusts. To further confuse things, the term *seaweed* is suspect, as it is not a specific scientific term and generally refers to marine macroalgae, or algae visible without magnification. These include one of the better-known seaweeds, nori, which actually is a plant. Even so, I continue to refer to kelp as a plant or seaweed because experts, even phycologists, still do.[1]

At the beach, Tom and I headed across the sand to the cobbles, most of which were about the size of a basketball and covered in a seaweed with the common name of sea lettuce (*Ulva* spp.). Since it's a plant, not a kelp, we ignored it, except to avoid stepping on its slimy surface. More agile in his rubber boots than I, Tom reached a pile of two-foot-long brown leaves while I was still navigating the slippery green hazards. "*Pterygophora californica*," he said, pulling a knife out of the pocket of his field vest. Over the next hour or so the vest continued to supply items—a phone, pencils, and magnifying lenses salvaged from old flatbed scanners—necessary for the Kelp 101 class that Tom was giving me.[2]

Lifting up the mass of leaves, or blades, he sliced through the one-inch-wide stem, or stipe, to reveal its tannish internal structure of rings. Kelp 101: Anatomy had begun. *Pterygophora* is unusual among kelps because its age, as with trees, can be determined by counting the annual growth rings. Our specimen appeared to be about three years old. "*Pterygophora* is what I'd call an old-growth kelp," said Tom. In contrast to an annual species such as bull kelp (*Nereocystis luetkeana*) or even the perennial giant kelp (*Macrocystis pyrifera*), which lives three to five years, *Pterygophora* has the potential to achieve a grand old age: a specimen growing in Barkley Sound on the west side of Vancouver Island was twenty-eight years old when biologists cut it down in 2018 and age-dated it.[3]

At the base of the stipe, Tom pointed out the holdfast, the root-like structure common to all species of kelp that anchors the organism to a substrate on the sea bottom, in this case a granite cobble. Holdfasts consist of fingers, called haptera, that are negatively phototrophic, meaning that they grow away from light rather than toward it. As the holdfast gets bigger and anchors itself more firmly to the substrate, the fingers split and resplit to fill every microscopic crevice so precisely that when researchers removed holdfasts in experiments, they discovered that the haptera had formed an exact reverse impression of the substrate. To further strengthen their bonds, haptera exude a mucilaginous substance that glues them to the rock.

The *Pterygophora* holdfast is light brown, speckled with white, and dotted with tan tubeworm casings. About the size of a grapefruit, it looks very much like a root. But unlike the roots of a plant, kelp holdfasts do not transport nutrients or water to the structure above. Instead, their primary function is to keep the kelp in place.

Holdfasts are an important microhabitat for other organisms, especially in species such as sea tangle (*Laminaria* spp.) and giant kelp, which can have holdfasts up to six feet tall and nine feet wide. One study found almost ten thousand individuals living in a single holdfast. Thronging with invertebrates and vertebrates, the holdfast ecosystem is a safe haven for crawlers, creepers, slitherers, and swimmers. Less mobile critters find it suitable, too; they simply sit and wait for the rain of nutrients that sloughs off surrounding kelps and seaweeds.

Leaving the shore of cobbles, Tom headed into the water, and I followed for the second part of his class, Kelp Diversity. Our goal was a forest of brown stipes and blades, all folded over as if the kelp were doing a downward dog yoga pose. Each stipe rose no higher than the top of Tom's boots and ended in a blade with the consistency and sheen of fruit leather. It was split almost to its base into numerous narrower sections, giving the kelp the look of droopy fans imagined by Salvador Dali. "*Laminaria setchellii*," said Tom.[4] It's one of the more common kelp species in the intertidal zone of the Sound.

Laminaria setchellii, sometimes called sea tangle (a term of Norwegian origin), grows in the lower intertidal and upper tidal zones, in areas impacted by waves. Species of *Laminaria* are found from Alaska to Mexico. Photograph by the author.

CHAPTER 6

As we continued to explore, every step seemed to produce another name. *Alaria marginata*: "Take it, wrap it around a piece of bacon, it's excellent," said Tom. *Egregia menziesii*—"known as feather-boa kelp."[5] *Saccharina latissima*, or sugar kelp—"often found on docks around Puget Sound, where it tends to have thinner, more ruffled blades than ones that get hit more often by waves. This species is also grown for biofuel." *Cymathaere triplicata*—"Note the three ribs of the stipe. It also has a really cool holdfast, which looks like a suction cup." Tom even stopped to point out a couple of nonkelp species, *Stephanocystis* and *Mazzaella*, and several red coralline algae, which crusted over many boulders.

When Tom and I had met earlier in the year, he had told me that Washington State has twenty-two species of kelp, eighteen of which occur in Puget Sound. Few places in the United States approach this level of kelp diversity. "We are in a good place where we have many species that don't occur south of us and many that don't grow to the north," says Tom. We further benefit from Puget Sound's cold water, rocky substrate, and topography, the latter two of which developed because of its glacial origin.

All of the kelps we have seen so far are understory species, which grow beneath other kelp whose blades float on the surface. As in a terrestrial forest, the marine understory provides habitat, refuge from predators, and temporary homes for migrating animals. In particular, studies in the San Juan Island kelp forests have shown enhanced growth rates and survival for several invertebrates, such as mussels, barnacles, and tubeworms, that live beneath the understory canopy. With their networks of stipe and holdfast, lower-growing kelps also provide a safe harbor for schools of fish, including Pacific herring, Pacific sand lance, and surf smelt.

The most recognizable floating kelp in Puget Sound, and arguably the most critical to the ecosystem, is bull kelp. To Tom, it's simply *Nereocystis*.[6] The species grows on the Pacific Coast from southern California to about halfway out to the Aleutian Islands archipelago. Shaped like a flexible turkey baster on steroids and adorned with streamers, bull kelp produces a long stipe, solid at the bottom but changing to hollow, topped by a turnip-shaped bulb, the gas-filled structure that keeps the plant on the surface. Out of this float grow several dozen blades, where photosynthesis occurs. In one of the first scientific reports about the species, the German botanist Karl Mertens, who reported that the Russians called it "sea otter's cabbage," wrote that the people of the Aleutians employed the stipes, which were said to be up to 45 fathoms (270 feet) long, for fishing lines, and that the blades were 27 feet long. In Puget Sound, single stipes top out at about 80 feet and blades at about 30 feet.

Tom and I found a handful of *Nereocystis* on the beach, rooted to small boulders by their wonderful, burnt-lemon-colored, multifingered holdfasts. None of the stipes were longer than about ten feet. Far more bull kelp grew in the deeper water just offshore, where we saw bobbing brown floats and blades, as well as a harbor seal patrolling through.

No one has ever reported single stipes of the length described by Mertens. He may have been mistaken in thinking that the Aleutian fishing lines consisted of a single stipe. James Swan, who lived on the Olympic Peninsula from 1852 until 1900, wrote that the Makah at Cape Flattery tied together the lower parts of stipes to make fishing lines up to six hundred feet long, or about the height of the Space Needle. They used these lines for fishing for be-shó-we or black cod, also called sablefish.

A more common use of the lines, wrote Swan, was for halibut fishing, which required attaching specially made hooks to a kelp line and sinking them to the ocean bottom. The hooks were U-shaped, with a sharpened barb attached to one side and pointing back toward the bend in the hook. The Makah made the hooks, called *čibu·d*, by taking the hard knots of hemlock trees, cutting them into narrow lengths, and inserting them into kelp bulbs, which were placed in a bed of hot ashes to steam the wood and make it pliable. The softened wood was then bent, tied into the desired shape, and allowed to cool until hardened and inflexible.[7]

To obtain the stipes and bulbs, Makah fishers formed two sticks and a knife into an A shape, which they slipped over the bulb at the surface and slid down the stipe with a weight. When the cutting tool reached the bottom, a simple pull severed the stipe. When they had gathered a sufficient quantity of stipes, they placed them in a stream for five or six days until they had been bleached white. "They are then partially dried in the smoke, knotted together at the ends, and further dried in the sun, after being stretched to their full length, and to their utmost tension," wrote Swan in 1869.[8] A study in the 1980s showed that each step in washing, drying, and stretching the strands was essential in taking advantage of bull kelp's physical qualities to create the strongest and most elastic rope possible.

Nancy Turner, an ethnobotanist at the University of Victoria, reports that properly treated and stored bull kelp ropes could last several years. People who had used the ropes told her that they were "much easier on the hands than modern hemp or nylon line."[9] She has also described how the Koskimo of Quatsino, on Vancouver Island, bound their babies' heads with bull kelp stipes to create an elongated, "sugar-loaf" skull shape, "which was said to be a sign of importance."

The anthropologist Franz Boas further reported on another ingenious and creative use of kelp stipes. In the days preceding their Ghost Dance,

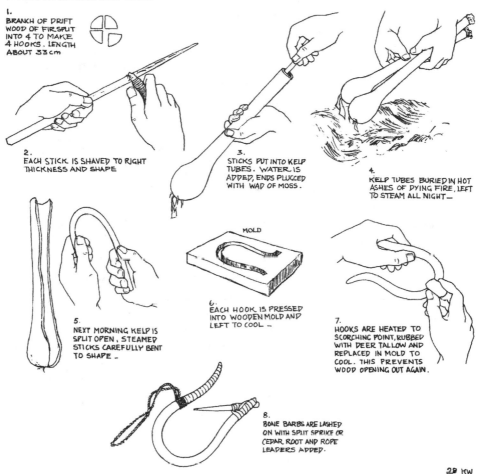

MAKING LARGE BENTWOOD HOOKS

1.
BRANCH OF DRIFT
WOOD OF FIR SPLIT
INTO 4 TO MAKE
4 HOOKS. LENGTH
ABOUT 33 cm

2.
EACH STICK IS SHAVED TO RIGHT
THICKNESS AND SHAPE

3.
STICKS PUT INTO KELP
TUBES. WATER IS
ADDED, ENDS PLUGGED
WITH WAD OF MOSS.

4.
KELP TUBES BURIED IN HOT
ASHES OF DYING FIRE, LEFT
TO STEAM ALL NIGHT—

5.
NEXT MORNING KELP IS
SPLIT OPEN, STEAMED
STICKS CAREFULLY BENT
TO SHAPE —

MOLD

6.
EACH HOOK IS PRESSED
INTO WOODEN MOLD AND
LEFT TO COOL —

7.
HOOKS ARE HEATED TO
SCORCHING POINT, RUBBED
WITH DEER TALLOW AND
REPLACED IN MOLD TO
COOL. THIS PREVENTS
WOOD OPENING OUT AGAIN.

8.
BONE BARBS ARE LASHED
ON WITH SPLIT SPRUCE OR
CEDAR ROOT AND ROPE
LEADERS ADDED.

29 KW

The traditional method of making a čibu·d led to a hook that selectively caught halibut, specifically smaller males, which meant that larger females were left uncaught and alive, so they could continue to reproduce. (From Stewart, *Indian Fishing*)

Kwakwa̱ka̱'wakw dancers would surreptitiously run kelp tubes from outside the dancing house and under the floor boards "so as to terminate in the fire." At the height of the ceremony, the dancer would sink into a ditch behind the fire, followed by hidden assistants who spoke through the stipe tubes, giving the impression of ghostly voices emanating from the fire. The ghosts told how they had taken away the dancer, who would eventually return. Other groups used hollow stipes for "calling" underwater to attract seals.[10]

The kelp bulbs had multiple uses, too. Describing a practice probably common to most of the Indigenous people along the northern Pacific
Coast, Boas wrote that Kwakwaka'wakw women on Vancouver Island
collected bull kelp following berry season in the fall. The women submerged a cutting tool to slice the stipe, which they pulled ashore with
the bulb always facing inland. Using a precisely broken cockle shell, the
women scraped the stipe, always with their right hands. Meanwhile,
the men built elaborate frames of hemlock in order to fire dry the kelp.
They then blew into the dried kelp until the bulbs were as full of air as
possible, tied them off, and tested for leakage. Bulbs that held air would
be further dried and worked to produce bottles.

The bottles were used to hold water and oil from eulachon—small
smelt, also known as candlefish because of their high oil content. For
thousands of years, the fish oil was an important economic commodity
for coastal people, who traded it to inland dwellers. The trade led to an
extensive network of "grease trails" from Oregon to Alaska.[11] Some historians even argue that the name *Oregon* comes from the Chinook Jargon
for the fish, *ooligan*.

These relatively recent Indigenous uses of kelp may reflect the longest continuous relationship between a plant and people in the Western
Hemisphere. In 2002, a team of international researchers, including the
Oregon State University archaeologist Jon Erlandson, argued that kelp
was essential to the movement of people to the New World around fifteen
thousand years ago. Moving from kelp forest to kelp forest, interconti-
nental boaters could have voyaged out of Asia to the Americas, never far
away from food, never having to cross high mountains, and never having
to experience the bitter cold of the middle of the continent. "Puget Sound
certainly would have been one of the sweet spots," or off-ramps, of what
Erlandson and his colleagues dubbed the "kelp highway."[12]

One challenge the long-distance travelers would have faced was
knowing what to eat in an environment they had never visited. It's a
problem that still persists: why, after all, do so many tourists eat at the
McDonald's on the Champs-Elysées in Paris? For those migrating around
the Pacific Rim, the kelp forests were the McDonald's of the day, ubiquitous and filled with familiar food, but with a menu offering more than
two hundred choices, from moon snails to salmon to the now-extinct
Steller's sea cow—a ten-ton kelp eater.[13] "Relatively rich in calories,
fiber, protein, iodine, calcium, fatty acids, and other nutrients essential
to human health and nutrition," wrote Erlandson, algae and seaweeds
would have been an ideal supplement to the diet.[14]

Although the kelp-highway hypothesis has only recently become widely accepted, the connection between people and Pacific Rim coastal marine ecosystems may illustrate a far deeper and more persistent history than Western science can imagine. In her work with Indigenous people throughout the Salish Sea and surrounding areas, Nancy Turner has noted the widespread incorporation of kelp into communal knowledge, from place names to ecological awareness to mythology. "It is possible that the antiquity of these narratives extends to peoples' earliest experience with the North American coastline," she writes.[15] If Turner is correct, the human-kelp relationship in Puget Sound may be as old as any story about the region.

•   •   •

Back on Whidbey Island, Tom picked up a bull kelp blade and we began the sex-ed section of Kelp 101. The blade is eight feet long, smooth, four to five inches wide, and light olive-drab in color, except for an elongated patch that is slightly darker and surrounded by a thin, whiter rim. Known as a sorus, the patch is the reproductive region of the kelp blade. Like all kelp and seaweeds, bull kelp have two alternating life phases. Out of a single kelp's sori will come billions of spores that drift and flimmer with the current.[16] After landing on the sea bottom, spores develop into the kelp's microscopic life phase, sperm-producing male and egg-producing female gametophytes. The fertilized eggs then mature into the kelp's visible life phase, the sporophyte. It is not a plan that meets with regular success; a Canadian study found that a forest of kelp producing nine billion spores per square meter resulted in nine million gametophytes and one sporophyte.

Despite the abysmal odds, this two-phase lifestyle has been successful. Tom and I spent the day looking at kelp sporophytes—the holdfast, stipe, and blade that make up a single kelp organism. He referred to this dual form of life as an evolutionary "trick" that allows kelp to "move." He observes: "We tend not to think of kelp as moving like an animal, but they do in a way. It's just on different scales of time and place." Gametophytes are thought to be perennial, long-lived, and inconspicuous. Sporophytes tend to be annual and very conspicuous. They live for a only a few months when conditions are good, unless they are one of the perennial species. The two phases occupy different ecological niches and are cued by different seasonal changes: the long days and low temperatures of spring and the short days and warm temperatures of autumn. In this sense, kelp live a life neither static nor immobile.

Kelp expert Tom Mumford holds a bull kelp blade, which features a dark sorus patch, the kelp's reproductive region. Photograph by the author.

Kelp live an incredibly productive life, too, taking in carbon via photosynthesis on a scale that rivals any ecosystem on Earth, including the nearby temperate rainforests. Blades grow at anywhere from 1.5 to 20 inches a day, depending on conditions and species (giant kelp is the fastest growing, followed by bull kelp). The nature of kelp growth varies with the wavelength of light at different water depths. Studies conducted in the late 1970s discovered that blue light, which penetrates the deeper water, stimulates stipe elongation. Closer to the surface, where more red light penetrates the water, the growth of stipes slows and eventually stops. The opposite occurs with blades; red light stimulates blade growth, which is held in check by underwater blue light. By the time you have read this chapter, a blade of giant kelp will be another half inch longer.

The huge blades were endlessly useful to Coast Salish coastal communities. Canoers placed kelp blades on their boats' thwarts to reduce the sound of a striking paddle and wrapped fish with the blades to keep them cool and wet during transport. On the San Juan Islands, the blades were laid out in the sun to create a salt efflorescence that could be harvested, and in many places, people used chopped kelp to make food more fla-vorful. Probably the most widespread use was to line pits with the blades when steaming foods such as camas, deer, seal, and porpoise. Not only did the blades add moisture, but they imparted flavor, too.

• • •

Although some ecologists prefer the term *kelp beds, kelp forests* is a better way to visualize the multitiered kelp ecosystem. On a clear day, light ripples down through the waving kelp blades, painting the underwater world in hues of bronze, ocher, and honeydew. Not all of the plants extend to the surface. Slow-growing and late-starting *Nereocystis* reach to all levels of the water column. Underneath is the complex understory of smaller kelps and seaweeds, their blades gently fluttering in the current.

Looked at anthropomorphically, kelp engineers its environment to its own advantage, as well as to the benefit of uncountable other marine species. At every level, from the sea bottom to the surface, the plants help limit the effects of wave action, influence sedimentation rates, and slow the movement of water, reducing coastal erosion, protecting the understory algae and seaweeds, and allowing fish and invertebrate larvae to remain in the highly productive forest instead of being carried into less favorable habitat. Kelp forests also offer shelter to boaters, as well as safe spots for fishing. James Swan observed that the Makah could find temporary refuge or spend the night with their boats tied to the kelp.

Within the kelp forest, life abounds. Red and green sea urchins itch along the substrate in search of bits of kelp; bacteria by the multimillions eat and excrete; cinnamon-roll-sized abalones rasp at detritus with barbed tongues; olive-green pillbug lookalikes nibble on holdfasts; tightly packed mussels suck debris through their feeding filters; Pacific blood stars gnaw on sponge-covered boulders; kelp crabs shaped like a sheriff's badge sidle on long, pointed legs up stipes and over blades; shrimp-like amphipods the size of pinto beans graze like Lilliputian cows; perfectly balanced, ptero-dactylesque great blue herons hunt from atop buoyant bulbs; immense schools of Pacific sand lance and juvenile herring twist and turn in a mesmerizing ballet of motion; five- to six-inch-long tubesnouts missile in and out of the kelp blades; and orca ply the forest in search of salmon, which, as recent studies show, use the forests as juveniles. (Orca are known to drape themselves in kelp; no one knows why.) These are a few of the hundreds of species that live in and regularly visit these forests, which researchers such as Tom have come to recognize as one of the most dynamic, diverse, and essential underwater communities in Puget Sound.

One ecologist I know described a scuba dive into the kelp as similar to parachuting into a terrestrial forest, "except the fall is slow and controlled. Gravity is not such a concern." The marine ecologist Anne Shaffer described a kelp forest at its peak of beauty on a clear day: "It's very calm. The colors are muted and tranquil. It's as close to feeling in a cathedral as I have felt in the wild."[17]

• • •

Living kelp is only half the story. Dead and degraded kelp is like that old advertising trope, the gift that keeps on giving. A typical kelp blade resembles a flag worn by the wind, intact near the stipe or bulb and tattered at its outer edge, where it constantly sheds senescent bits. Once in the water column, this mostly microscopic detritus provides food for other organisms, working its way through the food web and transferring carbon and nitrogen to progressively larger creatures.

If, as has been argued, trees are made of salmon, many animals are made of kelp. After eating salmon, bears and eagles deposit their meal or leave the leftovers in the woods, where the nutrients feed the rainforest community. The same argument can be made in the marine ecosystem. For example, 50 percent of the carbon in Beaufort Sea snails comes from kelp, the same percentage as in pelagic cormorants, a common Puget Sound seabird. Ninety percent of the carbon in kelp greenling and black rockfish along the West Coast, cormorants in Norway, and Alaskan amphipods and sea stars is estimated to come from kelp. About 10 percent of detrital kelp sinks to the ocean bottom and is buried by sediment, which removes it from the ecosystem. A recent study concluded that kelp has been overlooked and may play as essential a role as terrestrial forests in carbon sequestration and slowing global warming.[18]

Bull kelp and giant kelp play an additional ecological role. Floating or washed-up dead kelp, called wrack, harbors its own community of invertebrates and fish. Anyone who has walked on a beach of wrack, with its acrid aroma of decomposition and salt, has probably noticed that each footstep sends a host of organisms hopping around. No species depends solely on kelp wrack for its home, but the ability to provide a home on land as well as in the sea is another often overlooked ecosystem service provided by kelp. At sea, the buoyancy of kelp may also have contributed to the migration of other species. One recent study hypothesized that two small crustaceans colonized Antarctica after floating five thousand miles on a raft of southern bull kelp. More than fifteen thousand years later, their descendants still live there.[19]

As we are starting to better understand the ways in which kelp-derived carbon is woven into the marine ecosystem, we are developing a fuller understanding of the ecological complexity of Puget Sound, according to Tom. We have been justifiably concerned with the top of the food web, with animals such as salmon and orca, and we have started to recognize the important role of midlevel species, such as herring, surf smelt, and sand lance. The next step, he says, is to look closely at the bottom-level producers such as kelp and, to a lesser extent, eelgrass.

· · ·

The final part of my Kelp 101 class focused on the environmental challenges faced by local kelp, and particularly the continuous, long-term effects of climate change. Imagine a kelp forest as a balanced teeter-totter, which an environmental change can force out of equilibrium. One such perturbation is a rise in water temperature. This has already changed the balance in places. On the central California coast, the discharging of heated water from the Diablo Canyon nuclear power plant starting in May 1985 raised the seawater temperature in a small cove by 3.5 degrees Celsius. The bull kelp couldn't tolerate the heat, and within a decade of the plant reaching full power, none remained. In the Salish Sea, researchers determined that a water temperature above 17°C, such as occurs in the summer in the Strait of Georgia, significantly reduces bull-kelp spore germination. The kelp has not yet disappeared, but without strong recruitment of the next generation, forests in the strait are more susceptible to external stress.

Researchers identified another temperature-related tipping point in 2011 when a change in the flow of ocean currents warmed the sea surrounding Tasmania. The warmer water allowed long-spine sea urchins, which feed on kelp holdfasts, to extend their range south into kelp forests around the island. Like a horde of Dickensian urchins, the sea urchins spread across this unsuspecting community and laid waste to the residents, leaving behind what scientists call "urchin barrens," extensive tracts of sea bottom devoid of life, including giant kelp. The study's lead scientist, Craig Johnson, described it as "a bit like an animal coming in and bulldozing a rainforest back to bare earth."[20] A similar process is occurring in other places around the globe as warming temperatures are forcing plants and animals to relocate up and down in elevation as well as latitude, creating new marine communities with unforeseen effects.

Closer to Puget Sound, scientists have seen similar clearcutting by sea urchins. Wherever red sea urchins (*Mesocentrotus franciscanus*) flourished on the west side of Vancouver Island, kelp forests disappeared, and wherever kelp forests thrived, the red urchins didn't. Temperature did not tip this balance: sea otters did. The otters' appetite for the urchins keeps populations in check, but pelt hunters extirpated many sea otter populations, including those of the Salish Sea, by the mid-1800s. In the past few decades, as sea otters have been reintroduced around Vancouver Island, they have laid waste to the urchin population, and the kelp forests have returned.

The relationship between sea otters, sea urchins, and kelp exemplifies the conclusions drawn from one of the most important scientific studies conducted in Washington. In the 1960s, the University of Washington biologist Robert Paine began studying ochre sea stars (*Pisaster ochraceus*) and the animals they ate—limpets, barnacles, chitons, snails, and mussels. On an isolated outcrop of rock near Cape Flattery, Paine began to pry up sea stars, often with the aid of a crowbar, and fling them into the ocean, to see what would happen if he removed the top predator. Would the sea stars' prey become more or less diverse, more or less abundant?

Scientific theory at the time held that the number of prey regulated the number of predators and the abundance of species higher on the food chain. The role of predators, people thought, was relatively small in this bottom-up ecosystem model. Paine proved that this paradigm was incorrect, and in doing so rewrote the basic understanding of ecology. His removal of the sea stars led to an immediate loss of diversity, from fifteen species to eight and eventually to one surviving species, the mussel *Mytilus californianus*. Realizing that sea stars were critical to the equilibrium of the entire community, Paine coined the term *keystone species* to describe this top-down model. Like the keystone of an arch, predators were of paramount importance in maintaining a balance of producers, consumers, and predators in the ecosystem.

Within Puget Sound, sea stars have long been recognized as a keystone species. Unfortunately, their numbers began to decline in 2013 because of sea star wasting disease, which affected more than twenty species, including two of the more ecologically important: sunflower stars and ochre sea stars. Sunflowers are the biggest and most fearsome sea stars around, growing up to three feet wide and sporting twenty arms or more. Bob Paine's chosen species, the classic five-armed orange- to purple-colored ochre sea star, is perhaps the best known because it occurs intertidally throughout the Sound.

Both species dispense any idea one might have about the benign nature of sea stars. Speeding along at up to eighteen feet per minute, sunflowers outsprint sea urchins, capture them, and swallow the urchins whole, allowing the spines to puncture their stomachs, which heal quickly. Taking a more leisurely approach, the ochres seek out less mobile critters, wrench them off their home substrate, and pry them open. Everting its stomach, which resembles a plastic bag, the ochre then secretes digestive juices and devours its meal, leaving behind the empty shell.

Between 2013 and 2015, sea star wasting disease caused sea stars from Mexico to Alaska to disintegrate into piles of limbs and skeletal bits. Puget Sound suffered wholesale losses that left some areas completely devoid of sea stars. The disease is caused by a member of a group of viruses known as densoviruses. Researchers have found that warming ocean temperatures significantly worsened the prevalence and severity of the wasting disease in shallow, nearshore environments.

The decline of the sea star population concerns ecologists because removal of these keystone species can domino through the ecosystem. For example, north of Vancouver, BC, in Howe Sound, researchers observed a marked increase in the abundance of green urchins, with a corresponding reduction (of around 80 percent) in kelp cover. "What's scary is that we are going to have more ocean warming and more ocean outbreaks, and we are not paying attention," says Joe Gaydos, coauthor of a recent paper on the disease and science director for the SeaDoc Society. "We are already seeing changes in the ocean that are seemingly small, but have had cascading effects that are large. Nobody thought that sea star wasting disease outbreak could be connected to ocean warming, but it was. And nobody thought that the massive decline in sunflower stars could result in urchin increases that exacerbated loss of kelp forests, but it did. Climate change and ocean acidification are not looming, they are here."[21]

Rising water temperature and sea otters are not the only factors affecting the health of kelp forests. Cutting down trees and replacing them with miles of impervious concrete has increased sediment runoff to the Sound, where clay, silt, and sand inhibit kelp spore settlement and smother the microscopic gametophytes and incipient sporophytes. A significant accumulation of sediment can also convert the rocky bottom into a soft sediment substrate ill-suited to kelp. Too much sediment floating in the water further limits photosynthesis, as do solid objects such as docks, piers, ferry terminals, and moored boats, which have become more prevalent in the Sound over recent decades. Increased nutrients and toxic substances originating from agriculture, roads, sewage, and industry also negatively affect kelp, as do invasive species, such as sargassum, which can outcompete kelp.

So what does all of this mean for Puget Sound and its kelp forests? Anecdotal evidence points to a general decline; the reduced acreage of kelp is simply one more manifestation of how humans have mistreated and befouled the waterway, making life more challenging for species such as salmon and rockfish. Although they may agree with the locals about kelp loss, scientists prefer to have empirical evidence rather than simply anecdotal recollections to determine how the Sound's kelp forests are faring.

Fortunately, researchers have a unique historical record of the local distribution of kelp. Mariners have long noted its importance as an aid to avoiding submerged rocks. Charles Darwin wrote in *The Voyage of the Beagle*, "I believe, during the voyages of the *Adventure* and *Beagle*, not one rock near the surface was discovered which was not buoyed by this floating weed [kelp]. The good service it thus affords to vessels navigating near this stormy land is evident; and it certainly has saved many a one from being wrecked."[22] The same could have been written about Puget Sound—and was. Fifteen years after Darwin's book appeared, George Davidson, a surveyor for the US Coast and Geodetic Survey, surveyed the Sound and the Strait of Juan de Fuca. On September 18, 1854, he wrote his supervisor, Alexander Bache: "The experience of this season has confirmed what I have hitherto found on this coast with regard to sunken rocks—*that where such exist there is sure to be kelp upon and about them.*"[23]

One manifestation of Davidson's concern shows up on the survey's topographic sheets. These T-sheets, as most mariners knew them, were mappings of nearshore features in unprecedented detail, including kelp. On the 1877 T-sheet of Puget Sound from Point Defiance to Ketron Island, numerous snake-like squiggles, the symbol for kelp, run along miles of shoreline.[24] Because of the prevalence of the kelp—or the rocks it was anchored to—and other obstacles, Davidson wrote, "It would be almost useless to attempt to describe the route between Olympia and Steilacoom because a pilot or a chart is absolutely necessary in making the passage." Ultimately, Davidson concluded in his letter to his boss: "The deduction is short—*always avoid the kelp.*"[25]

A second set of maps depicting Puget Sound's kelp forests owes its origin to world politics. In December 1911, the US secretary of agriculture, James Wilson, submitted a report to Congress on the fertilizer resources of the United States, in particular potash. Historically produced by soaking wood ash in water, then boiling the ashes in a large iron pot to concentrate the solids—hence the name—potash was essential to the production of fertilizer, as well as black gunpowder, acetone, soap, glass,

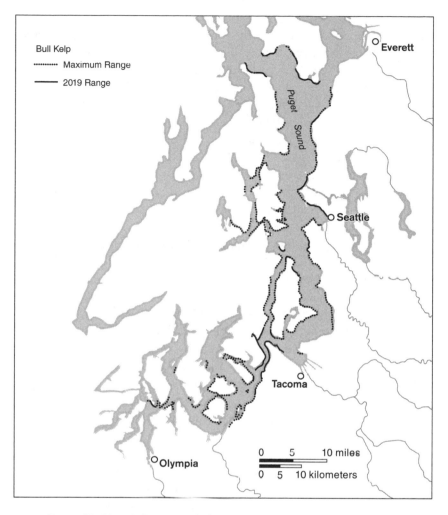

Range of bull kelp in Puget Sound, showing the historical maximum and 2019 extents. (Based on data from Washington Department of Natural Resources, Nearshore Habitat Program)

and alum. (Curiously, the term *kelp* may have first been used in reference to the ash rather than the seaweed.) Wilson was concerned that the country depended solely on Germany for potash, and if the Germans decided to stop shipping it, American farmers would suffer.

Wilson's scientists scoured the country looking for potash sources. The only high-quality, cost-effective source, according to Wilson's team, was kelp. Wilson valued the kelp resources on the Pacific Coast alone at more than $240 million. As part of the project, George Burton Rigg, a professor of botany at the University of Washington, surveyed for bull and giant kelp in Puget Sound and the Strait of Juan de Fuca. He produced more than a dozen maps showing the kelp forests, ranked from very thin to very heavy. The richest areas occurred in the San Juan Islands; other good stands occurred around Squaxin and Anderson Islands.

Soon after Rigg had started to announce some of his findings, newspaper stories began describing plans to build plants to convert the local kelp to potash. "There is every prospect that the enterprise in which they are to engage will constitute a big local industry," wrote a *Seattle Times* reporter.[26] Eventually plants opened at Port Townsend and Port Stanley on Lopez Island, though neither yielded much except a handful of jobs. When World War I ended and Germany began exporting potash again, the Puget Sound plants closed.

Aided by these historic documents, Tom Mumford, Helen Berry at WDNR, and Cathy Pfister of the University of Chicago have begun to assemble a story of change in Puget Sound's kelp forests. On the outer coast of Washington and the Strait of Juan de Fuca, kelp forests have remained relatively stable except close to Puget Sound. East of Dungeness Spit the forests have declined. In the South Sound, kelp forests in the Tacoma Narrows are sustainable, whereas south to Olympia and west into the fingered inlets, most of the kelp forests have decreased dramatically. The one relatively healthy location is the forest at Squaxin Island, though it too has shrunk recently. Between the south and north, the Main Basin kelp forests have mostly declined, particularly around Bainbridge Island, Mukilteo, and Edmonds.

An interesting counterpoint to the general reduction of kelp in Puget Sound is Elliott Bay. On early charts, bull kelp was conspicuously absent from the Elliott Bay shoreline. In recent years, however, it has become a common sight along the shoreline from the Elliott Bay Marina to the Seattle Aquarium. Some parts of this shoreline, such as the Elliott Bay Marina jetty and Myrtle Edwards Park, have been sites of habitat restoration projects. Other new beds are likely the result of development: seawalls and other structures have increased the available hard substrate for kelp to attach to.

The historical data do not tell a complete story, warns Helen. For instance, the early kelp observers probably excluded smaller beds, or beds not important to navigation, and may have missed beds if they surveyed when high tides or fast currents hid the bull kelp. Moreover, because the early navigation charts and many other sources denoted bull kelp with generalized symbols on small-scale maps, they are probably not highly accurate. Helen further notes that there are huge annual variations in floating kelp, such as bull kelp and giant kelp. She has shown that between 1989 and 2016, the area covered by these canopy species in Puget Sound varied as much as fourfold from one year to the next. In addition, past surveyors took no notice of understory species. Nor are they easily detected by aerial surveys, though citizen volunteers have started to survey the Sound by canoe, kayak, and paddleboard to seek out kelp below the surface.

Despite the limitations of the data, Helen and Tom have concluded that the extent of bull kelp beds in Puget Sound has changed significantly since people like George Davidson first began to notice them. In areas such as south Puget Sound and Bainbridge Island, the losses are so pronounced that they overwhelm all of the data uncertainties. For example, when researchers compare presence versus absence over miles of shoreline south of the Tacoma Narrows, the results show a transition from kelp beds being generally present before 1980 to persistently absent after 1980. In contrast, bull kelp beds in the Tacoma Narrows showed high persistence in both time periods.

Taking the long view, the early data offer more than simply a historical record. The maps and reports illuminate the long-term connection between kelp and people. Rarely does a plant merit so much focus for such diverse reasons. By showing where kelp forests can grow, the data help illustrate the ecological differences between the Strait of Juan de Fuca and Puget Sound proper. In particular, ecologists such as Helen and Tom have used the historical record to better understand how human-created stressors, such as rising water temperatures and increased nutrient load and sedimentation, affect the health of kelp and the numerous species that rely on kelp forests.

• • •

Equipped with information about the historical distribution of Puget Sound kelp and guided by their understanding of kelp's multiple roles in the marine environment, private citizens, nonprofit groups, tribes, and government agencies across the Sound have started to focus on restoration and recovery. "Many of the things we eat and think about when it comes to Puget Sound, including iconic species like salmon, crab, and rockfish, are made in part of kelp. From providing habitat to supporting food webs to potentially mitigating local effects of ocean acidification, kelp is essential to this ecosystem," says Betsy Peabody, the founder and executive director of Puget Sound Restoration Fund (PSRF), one of the principal groups working on kelp restoration.[27]

In April 2018 I visited one of PSRF's projects, at Hood Head on Hood Canal. Three months earlier, Brian Allen, PSRF's director of Olympia oyster and kelp programs, along with others, had unfurled 8,500 feet of twine wrapped around seventeen lines of heavier rope. The twine had been inoculated with sugar kelp spores, which made the strands brown and fuzzy. Small white buoys and larger round black floats, some speckled with bird poop, marked the boundaries of this underwater plant trellis.

"This is top-shelf product. Look at all this gold," said Brian, as he and a PSRF staffer, Stephen Schreck, collected samples.[28] Growth had been spectacular; after a slow start, the sugar kelp blades were now several feet long, golden brown, and wavy like lasagna noodles. For the next three hours or so we motored between the rows, pulled the kelp-laden lines on board, and snipped, photographed, and hole-punched blades to create markers of how fast they grow. Because of the strong tides and dense kelp, we occasionally had to stop and untangle lines that had wrapped around each other. The main challenge was lifting the heavy lines, which were hard to see because of the dense growth. We had to stop work when a Trident nuclear submarine and its half dozen or so escorts passed by us on their way out to sea from their home base in Hood Canal. A minute before the sub reached our location, a heavily armed boat with a heavily armed guard zoomed across to us to let us know in no uncertain terms that we should stay where we were.

The PSRF and its many partners, including the University of Washington and the National Oceanic and Atmospheric Administration (NOAA), had several goals with the Hood Head experiment. At the north and south ends of the kelp "farm," sensors on large yellow buoys collected data on the water chemistry so that researchers could see how kelp affected pH, carbon, and nitrogen levels. Other researchers tracked net production of kelp and its biomass, and NOAA divers surveyed the site for marine life.

"Growing kelp is easy. We have that part figured out," said Brian. The hard part is restoration and recovery, because so many other species interact with kelp in so many different ways—when it's growing or decomposing, as habitat and as food, from the sea bottom up to the surface. "Kelp restoration cannot be done in a vacuum. We need to embrace it as part of a multipronged strategy to building resilience in Puget Sound," says Betsy.

The decline of kelp forests may be connected to global climate-change issues, adds Tom Mumford. "Is the problem temperature, ocean acidification, pollutants, or something we have overlooked? Until we figure out what made kelp disappear, we cannot fix the problem," he says. Tom worries that without that understanding, we will be wasting money, but he is hopeful that if we can address the larger issues, kelp can return to the Sound.

When I first asked Betsy about the importance of kelp to the future of Puget Sound and why she and her group work to restore it, she described our species' long relationship with kelp. Ever since humans followed the kelp highway to reach these shores, our lives have been interwoven with kelp. We have navigated by it, found safe harbor in it, eaten it, used it in cultural practices, and harvested animals great and small that live in it. Now, says Betsy, we should look to it for our future. "We have unleashed anthropogenic carbon into the world, both the atmosphere and the oceans, and we need all the natural allies we can find to help soak it up. Perhaps kelp can help chart a path forward, as a natural mechanism for transforming carbon into life-building biomass."

All of the recent research in Puget Sound on kelp and kelp forests reveals their vital importance to the health of the waterway and, as with so many other plants and animals, their vulnerability to global temperature rise. Dead or alive, no other plant can rival kelp as a marine nursery, safe harbor, home, and carbon source. "If people can understand the goods and services that kelp provides, they will be more aware of the need for concern of such a fundamental species," says Tom.

7

The Silver Wave

"Surf scoters," said my friend Lyanda Lynn Haupt, and I knew that, like Brigham Young, we had found the right place. Standing on the south side of Alki Point, we were the odd people out in our chosen spot. We had come not because it was one of the first sunny weekend days in Seattle in months. Instead we had come in search of Pacific herring, or more specifically their eggs, which local blogs had reported were washing ashore in unprecedented numbers.[1] I wasn't sure what we were going to find. The blogs showed photographs of egg masses and gulls feeding on the adult fish, but I knew we had missed the main spawning event. I hoped that we still might encounter some evidence of the ecological role of a fish that has been called the "critical gatekeeper of energy flow" in the Puget Sound ecosystem.[2]

Herring merit this label because they are one of the Sound's major first-level consumers, vacuuming up detritus and microscopic life forms called plankton at the base of the food web and in turn getting eaten by secondary consumers, such as salmon.[3] As one biologist described the role of herring, "They are really good at eating tiny, crunchy things and converting them into delicious fatty meals" for dozens of other species, from western grebes to lingcod to Dall's porpoises.[4] In this intermediate role in the food web, the herring, nine to eighteen inches long, connect everything in Puget Sound, says Ole Shelton, a NOAA fisheries biologist. "They connect the open ocean to the coast. They link predator and prey. They transmit nutrients between ecosystems. They are very much the hub in the wheel of the Sound."[5]

Not only do many animals eat adult herring, but an equal number eat their eggs, larvae, and young, which was why I was at the beach. I knew that I wouldn't see wolves, humpback whales, or bears, which eat the nutrient-rich eggs farther north in the Salish Sea, but if I was lucky,

I might see harbor seals and bald eagles. If not, I would still be satisfied by one of the Sound's most visible herring eaters, surf scoters.

I had a second reason for coming to Alki to see herring. In the past century, human behavior has altered the Puget Sound ecosystem to the point that people have petitioned to have local herring populations placed on the endangered species list. We have eliminated their habitat, poisoned their waters, and harvested too many of them. Not all of the news is bad, though. In 2012, for the first time ever, biologists observed herring spawning in Elliott Bay. Scientists are still debating why the fish arrived, where they came from, and why they keep returning, but I take their presence as a positive sign, as hope for the future, as proof that even in the heart of Puget Sound's most industrialized region, the fish have found a way to survive.

Lyanda, who lives nearby in West Seattle, is a writer, a naturalist, and a much better birder than I will ever be. We had just walked south past the Alki Lighthouse when she raised her binoculars to her eyes and said, "Wow, look at the birds." Looking up, where I normally think birds are to be found, I couldn't see anything. Lyanda kindly suggested that I might want to lower my perspective to the water, where I finally located the gathering of black birds that she called scoters.

They were floating in small rafts about a hundred yards offshore. Lyanda told me to look for the surf scoter's classic white head patches on the forehead and nape, which I later discovered gave the species one of its other common names, skunkhead. Another less common name is snuff-taker, apparently a reference to the "variegated colors of the beak [that] suggest a careless snuff-taker's nose."[6] In contrast to dabbling ducks, such as mallards, with their characteristic tail-to-the-sky feeding stance in water, surf scoters vanish below the surface in search of food. Other members of the aptly named diving duck clan include harlequins, eiders, and buffleheads. Scoters tend to dive less than thirty feet deep, seeking penny-sized mussels on the bottom, at least in autumn. A study in Penn Cove and Padilla Bay in northern Puget Sound found that scoters shift to eating crabs and marine isopods (related to pillbugs) in summer and segmented worms in winter. Come late winter and spring, when the herring spawn, a scoter's thoughts turn to fish eggs.

The scoters' feeding frenzy occurs here because herring tend to return to roughly the same nearshore spawning site at about the same time each year. At least in the Sound, the fish are seeking beds of eelgrass and other underwater vegetation where they can deposit their eggs, each about a millimeter in diameter. During spawning, male herring broadcast milt in such great quantities that it can turn the water a creamy turquoise.

Females release between ten thousand to forty-five thousand unfertilized eggs apiece. These settle and stick on the vegetation, where they come into contact with the milt, and fertilization occurs. Spawning events may involve more than three hundred million fish. Several weeks later, after they have satisfied their procreational imperative, the fish migrate back to their normal feeding grounds, either someplace else in the Sound or out in the open ocean.[7]

The lives of herring and scoters are so intertwined that a team of Canadian and US biologists coined the phrase *silver wave* to describe how the birds' migration corresponds with the location and spawning of the silver fish.[8] As they migrate from as far south as Baja California to their breeding areas in the boreal forests of western British Columbia and southeast Alaska, Puget Sound is one of their stopover points. The researchers found that 60 percent of the tracked surf scoters stop at a herring spawning event during their migration. The eggs offer what the researchers described as "easily accessible, high-energy, lipid-rich food," on which the ducks can fatten up for their migration.[9]

Lyanda estimated that as many as three hundred scoters, and a dozen or so harlequin ducks, were feeding off Alki Point. Dispersed in clusters of fifteen to twenty birds, the scoter packs periodically disappeared, one bird seeming to be the instigator of an round of diving in which each bird lunged up before heading under. Ten to fifteen seconds later, each scoter popped to the surface, some wriggling their wings and most seeming to be resting or perhaps eating. A few minutes later, another bird would decide that down under was better, and the raft of scoters would vanish again, leaving behind a slightly rippled water surface.

Intermingling with the ducks were immature glaucous-winged gulls, who looked a bit like bemused uncles overseeing rambunctious young-sters. The gulls simply floated along. If they were eating the eggs or even adult herring, as some blog photos had shown, we missed it.

We saw only one adult herring during our afternoon at Alki, dangling from the talons of an osprey flying past us onshore. Then the herring and the osprey reappeared, headed toward the water, which puzzled us until we saw an adult bald eagle in pursuit. The osprey continued to fly away from shore, juking here and there, until he made an abrupt turn and dropped the herring. Intent on the fish, the eagle broke off her pursuit and descended toward the water, but then she appeared to realize the futility of trying to catch the fish and veered away. The osprey continued to put distance between himself and the eagle, and both were soon out of sight.

Lyanda and I didn't see any herring eggs on the beach that day, but at a subsequent herring spawning event, my wife and I saw uncountable numbers. We were on Hood Canal at Right Smart Cove, about six miles south and two coves west from a location known to the Skokomish people of Hood Canal as "landing for herring," attesting to its importance as a spawning ground. On the water were several hundred ducks: scaups, surf scoters, buffleheads, American widgeons, and goldeneyes. Another raft a quarter mile south was less diverse, consisting almost entirely of surf scoters, but bigger, with what looked to be more than a thousand birds. (Flocks in Alaska can number seventy-five thousand.) I hoped that the presence of this many birds signaled a correspondingly huge number of herring and even more eggs.

On the cove's rocky shoreline, I had tried to find eggs, though I didn't know what I was looking for. I had given up and started walking the pebbly and sandy beach when Marjorie called over that she had found some. As I walked toward her, she pointed down to the tan wrack lines I had bypassed, where the receding tide had left debris ashore. Most of the wrack, which stretched the length of the quarter-mile-long beach, consisted of eelgrass covered with pinhead-sized eggs.

One of the key plants on which herring deposit their eggs, eelgrass (*Zostera marina*) is not a true grass, but it does have narrow, grass-shaped blades that can reach six feet in length. Growing on a sandy substrate, it is the shallow-water equivalent of kelp, slowing currents, dampening waves, offering protection from predators, providing essential habitat for dozens of species, and fixing carbon via photosynthesis. The audio engineer Jeff Rice told me about a recording he made in eelgrass beds, which he described as the "sound of photosynthesis" as plants released bubbles of oxygen. "Eelgrass beds must be pretty noisy places underwater, on warm sunny days," says Rice.[10] Like kelp, eelgrass has suffered from human impacts that have reduced its distribution in the Sound.

Farther down the beach, eggs had accumulated in a depression where a stream washed into the cove. The eggs formed islands four to five inches deep, up to fifteen feet long, and several feet wide. In a small nearshore eddy, they were so thick that the water had the consistency and color of watery Malt-O-Meal. These eggs had either been washed free of the eelgrass or had been detached as surf scoters fed.[11]

Reaching my hands into one of the piles on shore, I scooped up a football-sized mass of eggs. About one in five encased a thin whitish body bearing two black dots—surprisingly cute eyes—indicating they had been deposited about ten days ago. Other eggs had barely visible eyes, which meant they were about six days old. Younger still were eggs that looked to be empty, although each one contained a see-through embryo a couple of days old.

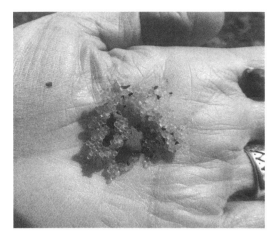

Herring eggs can wash ashore in uncountable numbers, providing food for all manner of animals from bald eagles to wolves. Photograph by Marjorie Kittle. (Courtesy of Marjorie Kittle)

Eggs that accumulate onshore will die in the heat, suffocate under their sisters and brothers, or get eaten by basically "everyone," one biologist told me. Those that remain attached to underwater eelgrass and are not eaten by scoters and others, which may total less than 10 percent of the original brood, hatch in about fourteen days into rice-grain-sized larvae, each bearing a yolk sac that provides nutrients and ballast. They spend the next two to three months feeding and drifting with the currents; at this life stage, herring larvae have little control over where they travel, though they can migrate vertically in the water. If they are fortunate, they end up in a sheltered cove or bay. But they are far more likely to meet their end in the mouth of one of a long list of consumers, including cannibalistic adult herring. Larvae that survive to reach a length of about an inch—perhaps as few as 1 percent of larvae make it to this stage— metamorphose from a big-eyed, transparent noodle into a pigmented miniature adult herring.

During this juvenile phase, herring adapt two new behaviors that guide the rest of their lives. First, they begin to gather in schools, which can comprise millions of individuals. (The name *herring* appears to come from a Teutonic word, *heer*, or army.) Toward the end of their first summer, juvenile herring start to migrate from their nearshore habitat into deeper water.[12] As fingerlings, they stay separate from adults. After another year or so, they reach adult status and begin their yearly return to the same nearshore spawning location. Tagging studies have shown that adult fish remain in the same school for years, unless they fall prey to the birds, mammals, and other fish who have attuned their lives to this prodigious resource.

Herring are an important food for people as well as animals. John Lord, one of the earliest naturalists to visit Puget Sound, wrote: "Garnering the herring-crop is the Coast Indian's best 'sea-harvest'; lodges spring up like mushrooms along the edges of bays and harbours; large fleets of canoes dot the water in every direction, their . . . crews continually loading them with glittering fish."[13] Herring were particularly valuable to people throughout the Salish Sea for their abundance and timing. Adult fish began to arrive in early winter and late spring and provided meat and oil at a time when other foods might not be available. In addition, the fish attracted birds and mammals that represented additional food resources.

Most animals, salmon being one notable exception, tend to reproduce in ways and places that humans rarely encounter and benefit little from. By contrast, the reproductive cycle of herring made them an easily obtainable and reliable food. Consequently humans developed unusual biological and cultural connections with the fish. Until the last decade or so, however, archaeologists and ethnographers tended to downplay the cultural significance of herring and other marine food resources in favor of salmon. So ingrained was this tendency that the Canadian archaeologist Gregory Monks coined the term *salmonopia* to describe it.[14]

Monks went beyond a simple criticism of salmonopia and showed how people relied on other fish as well. Central to his thesis was the idea that people found it advantageous to gather in a single location to harvest a wide variety of resources. As an example, Monks referenced an archaeological site in Deep Bay on the central east side of Vancouver Island. For approximately 2,500 years, humans occupied the site and at some point built a rock wall on a tide flat that enabled them to trap herring. Herring were the most abundant fish remains found at the site across the entire time span. Other remains included the bones of seals, dolphins, gulls, eagles, and diving ducks, all known to consume herring or their eggs, as well as those of other animals, such as deer and clams, that could be harvested when herring spawned. To Monks, the evidence from Deep Bay suggested that people came there specifically to take advantage of a food web centered on herring.

Since Monks's paper appeared in 1987, archaeological studies from Washington to Alaska have provided compelling evidence to back up his assertion about the importance of herring. In 2014, Canadian researchers published a comprehensive study based on fish-bone data from 171 Canadian and American archaeological sites dating back to 10,700 years before the present (BP). Herring were the most numerous fish in ninety-five of the sites, as well as the most ubiquitous fish, occurring in all but two of the sites and representing 56 percent of the 435,777 analyzed bones. The Canadians concluded that herring were "both widespread across the coast and a mainstay of ecological and socio-ecological systems over the Holocene."[15]

Studies based on more recent history have drawn similar conclusions. One of the most thorough focused on southeast Alaska, where archaeologists and anthropologists interviewed Alaskan Natives and non-Natives and synthesized hundreds of reports and studies. They concluded that "Southeast Alaska Native space and time were to a significant extent coordinated by herring."[16] Residents established settlements, marked the seasons, and planned when and where to seek food according to the presence of herring. Although no similar all-encompassing study has yet been conducted in Puget Sound proper, a similar picture has begun to emerge here.

One of the first local studies to show reliance on herring focused on Vashon Island, at an archaeological site known as Burton Acres. Excavated in 1996, the site consisted of a shell midden with cultural artifacts, including more than 1,700 mammal and bird bones and about 9,000 fish bones. The material dates back to about one thousand years BP through European contact. The Bear Creek archaeologist Bob Kopperl, who also worked at Burton Acres, catalogued 5,326 bones that he could identify by species, including dogfish, rockfish, and ratfish; skate, sculpin, and, salmon; and herring, which were by far the most prevalent, totaling 4,281 specimens, compared with fewer than 570 salmon bones.[17]

Bob does not discount the significance of salmon, particularly at river sites such as those found along the Duwamish and Black Rivers, where fish remains consist almost exclusively of salmon, but he recognizes the equally enduring cultural importance of herring. Even though the herring remains found in Puget Sound so far don't predate the appearance of middens around five thousand years ago, it's logical to assume that people have been eating them for as long as humans have lived here, he says. Bob bases his observations on his Burton Acres work as well as other sites in the Sound, including a unique artifact from Old Man House in Suquamish, consisting of a herring nested in a littleneck clam nested in a butter clam—a Pacific Northwest precursor of a turducken. Archaeologists dated these remains to between 800 and 960 years BP.

Locally, place names are another signifier of the importance of herring. During his work on Hood Canal, William Elmendorf recorded three place names that refer to herring, including the spot near Right Smart Cove where I saw so many eggs. The other two places were known only as *herring*, one about a mile south of Hood Point and the other a village at what is now Potlatch State Park.[18] Probably the best-known Native name is one still used: Herring's House, or Tohl-ahl-too, was a village site adjacent to the Duwamish River tide flats, near the present-day Duwamish Longhouse and Cultural Center.[19]

Bob further points to the historic reliance on the fish as described in early ethnographic studies. The reports refer to four means of obtaining herring. During the spring run to spawn, fishers headed out in canoes equipped with a herring rake—a wooden pole eight to twelve feet long, flattened on one side for about half its length. Jutting out from the flattened part were teeth an inch long, made of hemlock, fir, or bone (or later of nails), spaced about one inch apart. To catch herring, the fisher swept the rake through the water, impaled fish on the teeth, and dropped them into the canoe or a basket.

Even greater quantities could be caught using brush weirs, which consisted of brush woven between pilings to create two walls that funneled fish into a large circular trap. Built in tidal flats, weirs could trap two to three tons of fish in a single tide, wrote the naturalist John Lord.[20] Adult herring were eaten fresh or dried and used as bait for larger fish and gulls. Other informants of Elmendorf told of catching seals that followed the herring into the traps.[21]

People also harvested herring eggs during the spawn by submerging cedar or hemlock branches in eelgrass beds. The practice still occurs today, mostly in the northern part of the Salish Sea. Floating a few feet above the bottom, the branches provide a perfect spot for adult herring to deposit their eggs. Egg harvesters place additional branches on beaches, weighted with rocks. After the spawning run, they collect the branches on which eggs have collected after washing ashore. The eggs are dried or eaten raw. "Fresh herring eggs were considered a treat, especially when they popped deliciously between the back teeth," writes the historian David Buerge about the Duwamish people. They also stuffed salmon skin and deer intestines with herring roe and cured them like sausage.[22] In the north, Franz Boas reported, the Kwakwaka'wakw baited duck traps with herring roe.[23]

Another long-practiced method of catching herring, which was popular with Puget Sound anglers seeking bait for salmon, was to find herring baitballs. These tight aggregations form when predators, such as rhinoceros auklets, common murres, harbor seals, and spiny dogfish, hunt herring and force them together in dense swirls of thousands of fish.

Biologists still exploit this phenomenon, as I learned when I spent a day in Admiralty Inlet with the US Geological Survey biologist

Jake Gregg in a fourteen-foot Zodiac rubber boat. We had a simple plan; look for accumulations of gulls. They would be swarming around the herring baitballs. We had a simple goal: catch the herring, which Jake was studying to see if they had diseases. When the gulls found the fish, the birds' repetitious diving underwater and quickly popping up made them appear to be attached to some sort of cosmic yo-yo. When we couldn't find a frenzy of gulls, we would look for birds flying "resolutely"—looking like they were late for a meeting, flying hard and straight, as opposed to soaring or milling about. When we saw such birds, Jake would tail them in the boat, once following one across the four-mile-wide inlet. This made me feel like the harpooner Tashtego, who famously followed a line of seabirds to locate Moby Dick. The bird eventually led us to a gull swarm.[24]

On our first successful attempt to catch a baitball, Jake sped the few hundred yards to the swarm of squawking birds. After he brought the boat to a stop, I plunged a net on a ten-foot pole into the frenetic ball and pulled it up with what Jake estimated to be three to four thousand fish. A subsequent catch was two or three times larger.

Unfortunately for Jake's study, the fish were Pacific sand lance, which along with surf smelt and herring, rank among the three most

The great accumulations of forage fish such as these herring are essential to a healthy Puget Sound ecosystem. Photograph by Margaret Siple. (Courtesy of Margaret Siple)

numerous forage fish in the Sound. Basically high-fat fast foods for other animals, and arguably some of the waterway's most critical food resources, the three forage fish share a similar lifestyle of spawning on or near the shore, aggregating in schools, and having wildly fluctuating populations.[25] Although they failed to aid Jake's study, the sand lance I caught still revealed the enviable bounty of the Sound and how easy it was to harvest forage fish; if my little net caught five thousand or so fish, imagine the numbers that must be swimming throughout the Sound. (As with all the field studies where I tagged along, the researchers released whatever they caught, unless they needed specimens for a specific purpose.)

As we left one of the throngs of gulls, Jake said, "When I used to watch birds gathering or flying in a specific direction, I didn't think anything of it, but now I realize that they often have a purpose, which I hadn't noticed before." This observation is probably obvious to people who spend much time boating, fishing, or diving in Puget Sound. But most of us don't have the opportunity to encounter such patterns of behavior, so we miss the complex connections among the wild lives around us.

This realization was brought home most keenly for me on the F/V *Chasina*, a fifty-seven-foot trawler. I was with a Washington Department of Fish and Wildlife crew of biologists who were on their annual survey of bottom-dwelling wildlife in the Sound, investigating five locations ranging in depth from about 100 to 360 feet. At each spot, the crew unloaded a net they had dragged along the sea floor into a wooden box about the size of a ping-pong table and one foot deep. Wearing heavy-duty rain pants and jacket, thick rubber gloves, and protective goggles and helmets, the biologists and I took out every specimen to identify it and add it to the count. WDFW uses the population data for fishery- and ecosystem-based management.

Never before had I seen such an array of creatures in Puget Sound. Most obvious were *Metridium*, a common sea anemone that can often be seen on pilings or rocks close to the surface. Out of the water, they had withdrawn their feathery white tentacles and looked like glistening orange fishing floats, ranging from grapefruit to volleyball size. Most numerous were the flatfish, such as starry flounder, Pacific sand dab, and English sole, with their curious, flattened bodies bearing both eyes on one side. Most to be avoided were the Dungeness crabs. The first time I stuck my hand into the box to pull out a specimen and place it with others outside the box, I grabbed a paperback-book-sized crab from behind, between its rear legs, a trick I had learned in my youth to avoid the crab's pincers. Unfortunately, this crab had learned to reach around and grab its attacker. My glove failed to protect me against a pinch that broke the skin of my index finger.

I was also warned to watch out for spotted ratfish, which may be the most abundant fish in Puget Sound, though biologists don't fully understand why: other members of the ratfish family typically live in far deeper water. Related to sharks and rays, ratfish have golden brown bodies with white spots; iridescent, milky green eyes; and nostrils that resemble a rabbit's. Their genus name, *Hydrolagus colliei*, means "water rabbit." The male ratfish sports a white, club-like structure on the forehead called a tenaculum, which is used to grasp the female during mating. In front of the dorsal fin of both sexes is a single sleek, venomous spine. I figured that since the biologists would be out on the boat for more than two weeks and needed the experience, I would allow them to handle the more worrisome species.

Other totally cool-looking fish included plainfin midshipmen, whose rows of narrow white dots on the head, flank, and belly reminded me of Australian Aboriginal art; buffalo sculpin, which are green, white, pink, and brown with bright blue "horns," or spines; longnose skates, with a face that made me think of stereotypical space aliens, with wide-set eyes, an undefined nose, and pursed mouth set on an elongate head; and giant pink sea stars, which I have more to say about later in the book. In a total of ten thousand specimens we identified fifty-eight species.

· · ·

One of the reasons that modern biologists have to be concerned with species diversity and populations is the long-term effects of natural resource consumption in Puget Sound. The early practices were so bad that even some commercial fishers complained. One of these was John P. Hammond. Around 1870, about seven years after San Francisco newspapers first reported that the Sound could soon have an unsurpassed herring fishery, Hammond started to produce herring oil in Port Madison, at the north end of Bainbridge Island. His earliest nightly hauls totaled two to three hundred barrels (each holding two hundred pounds) of fish, yielding three hundred gallons of oil a day. The unguent was used in tanneries for greasing skins and in logging camps as a skid grease. A gallon of oil sold for thirty-five to forty-five cents. Hammond had hopes, too, of selling what he called fish guano, or scraps, to markets on the East Coast for twenty dollars per ton, but he worried that herring stocks were crashing. In 1886, he wrote to the eminent fisheries biologist Spencer

Commercial herring drying and processing business, ca. 1900. Within a few years after this photograph was taken, a local fishing magazine reported that the rapid extermination of herring had reduced the fishery to two locations, Port Discovery Bay and Nanaimo, British Columbia. (Courtesy of the Washington State Historical Society, Image 2012.0.360)

Baird that after 1877, his typical harvest at Port Madison had dropped to twenty barrels a night. Hammond blamed a lack of laws protecting the fish, as well as Chinese fishermen and mill owners, who threw "gurry, sawdust, and every description of filth and rubbish" into the Sound.[26] He would not be the last to worry about declining fish harvests or about what people tossed into the waterway.

By the 1890s, commercial herring fisheries operated throughout Puget Sound, using brush weirs, purse seines, and drag seines to catch spawning herring. The brush weirs were based on the original Coast Salish model, except that chicken wire substituted for brush. Seines are nets. Drag, or beach, seines worked best in shallow water, where fishers set out long, narrow nets (more than one hundred feet long and less than ten feet wide), forming an arc facing the shore, the one long edge floating and the other weighted so that it sank to the sea bottom. The two ends of the net were then pulled together and the entire net dragged ashore, capturing all the fish and most other species inside it. Purse seines were set from a boat in deeper water: a net was suspended from a line of floats, and it could be closed, or pursed, by another line at the bottom. A 1941 Washington State Department of Fisheries report concluded that both types of seines "caused considerable damage on the spawning grounds."[27]

Researchers still use beach seines. In August 2018, near Olympia, I helped a crew from the Washington Department of Fish and Wildlife (WDFW, the successor to the Department of Fisheries) to set a 125-foot-long net in which we caught more than a dozen species, including juvenile Chinook salmon, pencil-thin bay pipefish, thousands of transparent, grape-sized blobs called ctenophores, and beautiful, quarter-sized jellyfish. In the past few decades, researchers have observed a significant increase in jellyfish abundance in Puget Sound, particularly near urban areas. Probably the best known are the large, opaque, umbrella-shaped moon jellies, which can accumulate by the millions in what is known as a smack, or bloom. Although scientists don't know exactly why jellyfish populations have risen, they have observed that jellies benefit from warmer water, which likely means that huge smacks will become more frequent with climate change. What makes this problematic is that jellyfish compete with forage fish for food, eat their larvae and those of salmon, and provide limited calories to other marine organisms.

Despite the large harvests in the twentieth century, little of the commercially harvested herring was eaten by people around the Sound. Instead, most of it became bait, either fresh or frozen into cakes, for catching halibut, cod, soupfin shark, and dogfish shark. (No one ate either type of shark; shark processors simply cut out the livers, which were used as sources for vitamins A and D, and tossed the bodies back into the Sound.)[28] Holmes Harbor, on the east side of Whidbey Island, consistently generated the largest herring harvests, all via brush weirs.

Around the turn of the century, commercial harvesters, like Hammond earlier, began to note a decline in the populations of herring. The reasons, according to newspaper articles, included whales, Italian fishermen, sawdust dumping, and poor harvesting practices, such as using the wrong size of mesh, dynamiting, and fishing the spawning grounds. The more likely reason was an unregulated fishery, which meant that commercial interests harvested the fish with little regard to the animals' biology. In 1915, the state passed laws to protect the fish, such as making it unlawful to fish for herring on weekends and creating herring reserves at the most important spawning grounds: Port Hadlock (near Port Townsend), Holmes Harbor, Deception Pass, Jackson Cove (Hood

Canal, next to Right Smart Cove), Hale Passage (Lummi Island), and Birch Bay Point. Within the reserves, catching fish during spawning season was illegal.

Halibut fishermen immediately complained about the three-inch minimum mesh size on purse and drag seines, which had been mandated in order to protect young salmon. (The measure didn't work, and salmon harvests continued to shrink.) The three-inch-mesh made it impossible to catch the relatively small herring used as halibut bait. As a result of the new regulations, the amount of herring caught dropped from more than two million pounds in 1915 to less than 165,000 pounds in 1921. The smaller harvests allowed the fish to multiply quickly, which ironically led to increased fishing, followed by another population crash.

By the 1950s, another recovery had pushed the herring population high enough to start another round of harvesting. Seeking to exploit all possible markets, harvesters took herring at every life stage. They caught adult herring, extracted the females' egg sacs, and sold the roe, primarily to Japanese markets. They also captured juvenile herring to sell as bait for recreational fishing and netted adult herring for fish meal and oil. The

Hauling in a drag seine of herring along Vashon Island, south of Burton Dock, ca. 1920. Nets such as this, which indiscriminately captured all fish, were detrimental to herring and other fish such as salmon. (Courtesy of the Washington State Historical Society, Image 2001.141.2.8)

harvesters reached annual peak consumption at more than 7,100 tons. By 1983, the fisheries had to be closed because herring populations had crashed yet again.[29] As of 2019, only the bait herring fishery exists in Puget Sound, taking less than 6 percent of the total estimated spawning biomass (that is, the estimated weight of all fish capable of reproducing). There are no tribal herring fisheries within Puget Sound.

Local herring numbers in Puget Sound today send a mixed message. Every year since 1970, WDFW biologists have assessed the cumulative spawning biomass by examining populations of fish at different spawning grounds, called fish stocks—a useful management unit because of the way herring populations return annually to spawn at the same time of year in the same location. In practical terms, this allows fisheries managers to direct their efforts at individual stocks of genetically related fish based on recent abundance, compared with a twenty-five-year mean abundance.

The good news is that state biologists consider the total herring population to be "moderately healthy," the second-best category. Less positive is the story for most of the individual stocks. Except for the Quilcene Bay stock, which is by far the healthiest and which skews the total numbers, herring stocks have experienced a steady population decline, particularly at historically the largest and arguably the best-known stock, at Cherry Point, north of Bellingham. Between 1973 and 2004, the Cherry Point spawning biomass plummeted by 90 percent, which led several organizations to file a petition to have the herring listed as "threatened" or "endangered" under the Endangered Species Act. In the petitioners' view, the herring faced "a very high risk of extinction in the near future." As of 2018, and with no formal federal listing, the numbers have continued to drop, with only 3 percent of the 1973 Cherry Point population remaining.

This difference between the overall assessment and that of individual stocks creates challenges in Puget Sound's herring management. Because of Cherry Point's precipitous reduction in biomass, more energy and publicity have been focused there than on the overall picture. The University of Washington ecologist Tessa Francis observes, though, that the story of Puget Sound herring is not simply about Cherry Point. "If we focus too much on Cherry Point, we may reach the target there, but what about the rest of the Sound? The Cherry Point population is so local." Instead, she says, we need to take a holistic approach to applying science and management throughout Puget Sound. She backs up her statement with recent studies that offer new ways to look at the challenges herring face, in particular genetic studies. "I am hopeful that as we learn about the differences, we can see how they add up to create sustainability for the whole population," says Tessa.

As an example, she cites the work of Eleni Petrou, whose PhD dissertation from the University of Washington focused on herring genetics, using DNA from Puget Sound herring and herring remains from two archaeological sites. Normally, geographically close herring stocks spawn within a three-week window. In contrast, Puget Sound herring spawn between January and mid-April. The Cherry Point stock is an outlier that doesn't spawn until mid-May. Biologists and fisheries managers have long wondered if the variation, particularly at Cherry Point, is due to genetics, geography, or some combination of these factors, and whether stocks spawning at different times interbreed.

Eleni's research found limited reproduction between stocks with disparate spawning times, which means that if Puget Sound's early- or late-spawning stocks disappear, they might be irreplaceable. "This is a unique type of diversity that we should protect, a diversity of life history."[30] She adds that because small, isolated stocks are more vulnerable to extirpation and genetic harm, fisheries managers need to be more aware of how fishing activities are distributed around the Sound. In particular, targeting a single area for fishing, and depleting an individual stock, could remove a unique subset of genetic attributes, thus weakening the overall diversity of herring populations and making them more susceptible to changing environmental conditions.

Hoping to understand whether this diversity of spawning times also supported Puget Sound Native peoples in the past, Eleni worked with Suquamish and Puyallup tribal biologists to obtain permission to sequence DNA from herring bones from archeological sites at Burton Acres and Port Orchard. She was able to identify early and late spawners. Bob Kopperl, who assisted Eleni, told me that Coast Salish people probably adapted to fishing herring (and other species, including salmon) in different places at different times soon after they first arrived here and noticed the diversity of herring spawning behavior. They continued to refine the practice over time, as human populations grew and new limitations arose, such as population fluctuations among different fish stocks or people encroaching on others' territories. Bob sees these adjustments as yet another manner in which the long-term residents of Puget Sound adapted to place and the rhythms of life.

Several other studies underscore the importance of management plans that take into account life-history diversity in Puget Sound herring populations. Two of the studies, published in 2018, looked at herring migration. The researchers were inspired by observations from Native fishers, one of whom said, "Herring have lost their big chiefs and no longer know where to spawn." Both teams of researchers independently developed models that showed that young herring learn from older fish how to migrate to the open ocean to forage and then back again to spawn.[31]

Illustrating what is known as the adopted migrant, or "go with the older fish" (GWOF) hypothesis, these models highlight the importance of older fish to the distinct populations in Puget Sound, says Margaret Siple, a University of Washington postdoctoral research associate involved with one of the GWOF studies. A loss of older fish could mean that the younger fish in individual stocks might not be able to complete their migratory journey and help repopulate the stock.[32] "If this is the model for herring behavior, then it could explain local extinctions under the present fisheries model," says Margaret.[33] Like Eleni, Margaret says her research points to the importance of managing herring with attention to individual stocks.

Margaret and her colleagues, including Tessa Francis, cite data showing that Puget Sound's herring population became younger between 1973 and 2012.[34] By 2008, the total number of three-year-old herring outnumbered all older fish. In addition, no fish more than eight years old was found in spawning-site surveys after 2007. The loss of older herring in Puget Sound compounds researchers' concerns for several reasons. Older fish not only know where they are going, they know what to do once they arrive at the spawning grounds. Older fish are markedly more fecund than younger ones. "Fewer older fish will mean that the dynamics of the population as a whole are more driven by things that affect younger fish, such as environmental variation and rearing habitat quality, which are already highly variable in space and time and likely to grow more so in the future," says Margaret. In essence, the wisdom and productivity of the older fish provide a buffer for the vagaries and mistakes of youth.

A second, persistent problem is the way herring accumulate toxic chemicals in their tissues, such as polychlorinated biphenyls (PCBs), dichlorodiphenyltricloroethane (DDT), and flame-retardant polybrominated diphenyl ethers (PBDEs). Despite more than twenty years of cleanup, researchers have found that PCB concentrations in herring in south and central Puget Sound have not dropped. "They rival [the levels in] herring found in some of the most industrial waters in places such as Poland and Germany," says Jim West, a WDFW toxicologist.[35] Jim and his colleagues do not know what amounts of these chemicals herring can tolerate, or how these toxic substances interact with other human-generated chemicals found in Puget Sound fish, such as Prozac, nicotine, Lipitor, cocaine, and caffeine. If he found similar levels in salmon, he told me, he would expect the fish to have compromised immune systems, slower growth, or both.

CHAPTER 7

Part of the problem, says Jim, is the Sound's great depth. The pollutants glom onto sediment, dead organic material, and tiny organisms floating in the water. In shallow estuaries, such as Chesapeake Bay and San Francisco Bay, the polluted particles sink to the bottom, where they cause problems for bottom-dwelling fish such as flounder and sole. In the deep Sound, they tend to be consumed at intermediate depths by plankton, and they are lipophilic, meaning that they attach to fats in the plankton. As the herring continually eat these poisoned microinvertebrates—particularly krill and copepods, two key items in a herring's diet—the toxins concentrate, or bioaccumulate, in the fish. The Sound's toxic load is further exacerbated by the waterway's circulation pattern, which I describe above as its long-term memory: reflux tends to return about two-thirds of total pollutants during each tide, which results in a more contaminated open-water food web.

Although concentrations in herring of DDT and PBDEs throughout the Sound and PCBs around Cherry Point dropped between 1999 and 2014, their levels still trouble biologists. Puget Sound's southern resident orcas have high levels of all three toxic chemicals, primarily because they eat salmon that eat herring. A 2016 report concluded that orca calves exposed to these poisons could have "impeded growth and development, delayed or premature physical or sexual maturity, reduced future fecundity, or reduced perinatal survival," as well as reduced learning ability. Because orcas are extremely social animals whose lives revolve around an extended family, or pod, biologists worry that these changes could result in unsuccessful foraging or poor interaction within Puget Sound's three pods.[36]

Margaret's research with Tessa also helps address the conundrum posed by the state's "moderately healthy" assessment population and the status of the Cherry Point stock. Their work focuses on what ecologists call the portfolio effect. Just as a diverse financial portfolio results in less volatility during economic upheavals, a diversity of genetic makeup, habitat, and life history within a species enhances its stability. If one stock is down, others may be up, and the population's overall status is not as dire as it would be in a species without the complexity exhibited by Puget Sound herring. In the Sound, Tessa's and Margaret's work has shown that multiple spawning locations stabilize the overall population of herring, making it a more reliable food source for higher-level predators, especially mobile predators who can move among spawning populations. These findings complement Eleni's work showing the benefits to overall herring survival of spreading out the timing of spawning among isolated populations. They also indicate, says Margaret, that thinking

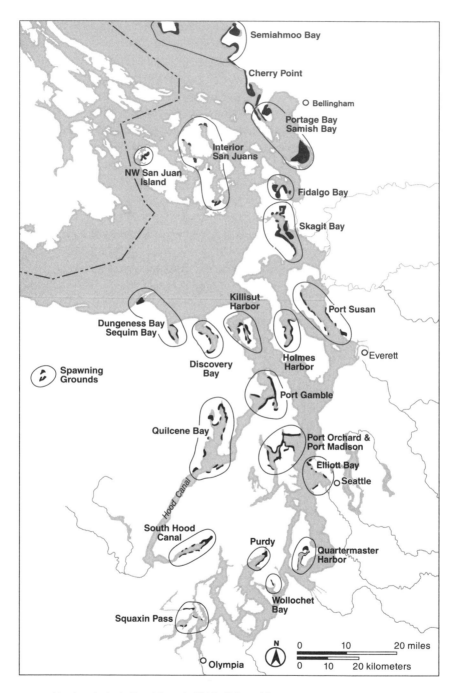

Herring stocks in Puget Sound, 2019. (Adapted from a map by Adam Lindquist, Washington Department of Fish and Wildlife)

about herring on a smaller scale (e.g., by monitoring and managing individual spawning beaches) is a good idea for the health of the Puget Sound stock as a whole.

Although levels of some notorious pollutants are declining, the effects of other toxic substances are now coming to light. Among these are polycyclic aromatic hydrocarbons (PAHs), strong-smelling toxic chemicals that occur naturally in coal, crude oil, and gasoline. They also form during the burning of oil, gas, coal, garbage, tobacco, and meat. If you smoke, you inhale PAHs. If you grill meat, you eat PAHs. If you drive, you generate PAHs.[37]

Prior to the 1990s, scientists did not understand the damage that PAHs caused in fish. In the years following the 1989 *Exxon Valdez* oil spill, researchers began to observe problems with herring and pink salmon in Prince William Sound that could be traced to these toxic chemicals. The NOAA toxicologist John Incardona found that PAHs led to disruption of cardiac function in embryos in these two species. The embryo hearts were malformed, pumped more slowly, and exhibited arrhythmia. If the fish survived to adulthood, which is less likely in less fit individuals, they appeared superficially normal, but they were living on borrowed time. When John gave PAH-exposed adult herring the equivalent of a stress test, he found that the fish swam more slowly and had reduced aerobic capacity. "This was not a problem in the lab, where there were no predators. In the real world, though, they would suffer," says John.[38]

Although the lasting image from the *Exxon Valdez* spill is of oil-covered beaches, birds, and mammals, the insidious problem with PAHs is that invisible concentrations can still damage fish embryos. As one of John's collaborators said, herring embryos, which have no liver to metabolize toxins and no protective covering such as a hard shell, are "perfect little sponges" that soak up contaminants. John found that as few as 110 parts per trillion of PAHs (one part per trillion is equivalent to a single grain of sand in an Olympic-sized swimming pool) resulted in heart disease as well as smaller eyes and deformed jaws. The threshold for damage may be even lower, as he and his colleagues observed similar problems in fish with PAH concentrations below what could be detected. (A biomarker gene within the herring embryo that was sensitive to PAHs confirmed their effects.)

The problem in Puget Sound, says John, is that "in urban streams, we have continuous small oil spills happening all the time."[39] Runoff with high concentrations of PAHs generated by fuel-burning automobiles (and from tire dust) washes into the Sound, creating the same cardiac issues in herring as those found after a crude oil spill. A related study showed that creosote-treated pilings—of which there are probably hundreds of thousands in the Sound—are a significant source of PAHs. It's not simply an urban problem: one cannot travel the shoreline for more than a mile or two without encountering a stream or old piling that could be a source of PAHs.

PAHs are not the only toxin that flows from urban streams into the Sound. Along the Duwamish River, for example, approximately two hundred public and private drains, ditches, streams, and combined sewer overflows discharge oils, grease, heavy metals, and fecal coliform bacteria into the lower five miles of the river. Other studies of stormwater runoff show that the Duwamish exemplifies what happens throughout Puget Sound. During a typical day, more than 52,000 pounds of pollutants and 1.1 million pounds of suspended sediment enter the Sound from surface sources. In 2018, a report by the King County Water and Land Division estimated total untreated stormwater runoff in the county at 118 billion gallons annually.[40] To remediate this discharge of untreated water, the county expects to spend almost $2 billion over the next decade.

The challenge of stormwater runoff is that it cannot be traced to a single source, as would eventually happen with industrial waste flowing directly into waterways. But it also offers an opportunity, because we can identify one of the major sources of pollution, and it is us, the human residents of the Sound. Each of us contributes to the problem. We pee unmetabolized caffeine. We dump prescription drugs down our toilets. We drive. We wash our vehicles in our driveways. We buy goods that others deliver to our homes by truck. We pave natural habitat. We use fertilizers, pesticides, and herbicides in our yards. We let our pets poop outside. These actions and many others contribute contaminants that end up in our stormwater or sewage system and ultimately in Puget Sound.

"Is this why herring populations have stayed down in Puget Sound?" asks John. He cannot definitively answer yes, but his research provides an insight into how the current human residents around the Sound contribute to the problem. PAHs are not simply a story of previous poor fishing practices or external issues or industry-generated problems. "It's all of us and everything we do," says John. Measures such as controlling storm runoff, removing creosote-treated pilings, driving less, and making the hulls of tanker ships more resistant to damage can mitigate the problem, but he is not optimistic that we have the will to pay for or to implement them.

Other biologists I spoke with also wondered whether we have the political will to act for the benefit of herring. For them, it's about the fish and their role as the "gatekeeper of energy flow" in the Sound, as the US Geological Survey biologist Paul Hershberger described herring. "We need to realize the value of these fish, which drive and maintain the health of Puget Sound," he says.

Herring stand out among the fish of the Sound because of their critical ecological roles throughout the habitat, from shoreline to deep water, and at all life stages. They are the conduit through which nutrients from lower-level organisms, such as krill and copepods, pass through the food web to salmon, scoters, seals, and hundreds of other fish, mammals, and birds. Without herring, and sand lance and surf smelt, the top-level consumers would die; in the words of Tessa Francis, "Seals wouldn't deign to filter feed at the bottom of the web."[41]

Because of the critical ecological roles of herring, every action we take for their protection has effects throughout the food web. Cleaning up PAHs, PCBs, PDBEs, and DDT means this toxic stew won't accumulate in the bodies of salmon, seals, and orca. Protecting and restoring eelgrass habitat translates to more food for surf scoters and the dozens of species that feed on herring eggs. Focusing on good management of individual herring stocks helps increase ecosystem stability throughout the Sound. Ensuring that we better understand and safeguard microscopic plankton not only provides food for herring but also benefits their larger, better-known predators.

Nowhere is the importance of herring better illustrated than in the current status of orca and salmon. After what happened to the orca Tahlequah and her calf, in March 2018 Washington governor Jay Inslee established the Southern Resident Orca Task Force, consisting of tribal, federal, and state officials and representatives from the private sector, nonprofit organizations, and the government of Canada. Their goal was to "identify, prioritize and support the implementation of a long-term action plan for the recovery" of the orcas. Eight months later the task force published its initial report. It identified three issues threatening orca: lack of prey, an ever-increasing mixture of pollutants, and noise disturbance from boat traffic. Linking the first two were herring. One recommendation to increase sustainable populations of Chinook salmon, which are the primary food source for orca, was to increase herring populations. But the task force acknowledged a problem: the way in which herring consume contaminated zooplankton and pass toxins up the food chain through salmon to orca. Despite this, Todd Sandell, one of the senior WDFW biologists working on herring, put the problem succinctly: "No herring, no orca."

Most of the biologists I spoke with were cautiously optimistic about herring prospects, despite the long-term population decline. Many based their views on the astonishing ability of herring to reproduce. In a handful of good years herring can produce astronomical numbers of young, and their populations have the capability to bounce back from steep decline if the conditions are right. "At this point, I don't think we can say that we are beyond the point of no return," says Correigh Green, a NOAA research biologist.[42] The big question that he and other biologists ask is whether we can create an environment that will allow herring to procreate as they evolved to do.

Phil Levin, lead scientist with the Nature Conservancy of Washington, thinks we can. "I think the problems are solvable because they are focused on what we do in Puget Sound," he says.[43] Unlike species such as orca and salmon, which spend much of their lives outside the Sound, herring are attached to Puget Sound, and the waterway's future lies with the agencies and people who are based here. "The solution to helping herring is not going to be one thing. It has to be all of them," says Phil. Despite that, he is still optimistic. "If we can get our shit together and do the right things, we will give herring the chance. We need to set the table and wait for them to show up."

8

Old Fish and New Laws

If salmon are the most iconic fish of Puget Sound and herring the most central to the ecosystem, rockfish are the most quintessential resident, with more species, more habitats, and a more direct connection to the Sound's geology than any other fish. Of the 253 fish species in greater Puget Sound, slightly more than 10 percent are rockfish. The genus—the aptly named *Sebastes*, meaning magnificent—includes twenty-seven species.[1] The next largest genus, *Oncorhynchus* (salmon), includes a mere seven species. Rockfish win on style points, too. One rockfish species bears a yellow swoosh on a yellow-freckled, blue-black body; another has dark vertical stripes set against a pinkish background; and a third sports fluorescent orange blotches that seem to glow from within. As Shawn Larson, curator of Conservation Research at the Seattle Aquarium, told me: "We have salmon, but rockfish are more interesting. They are what make the Sound colorful underwater."[2]

With their rich diversity in size, food preference, and life history, rockfish have been able to spread across and take advantage of the full range of Puget Sound's glacially influenced topography. From the light-filled surface down to the darkest depths, from sandy eelgrass flats to rocky reef kelp forests, above old wrecks and under fishing docks, these multihued fish have filled nearly every niche, natural or artificial, in the waterway.

The great taxonomic variety of *Sebastes* stems primarily from their means of reproduction. Unlike most marine fishes, in which males and females broadcast their sperm and eggs and simply hope for the best—a process marine biologists sometimes refer to as "spray and pray"—rockfish have sex. Their mating, a sort of dance, shudder, and penetration, results in fertilized eggs that develop into embryos within the female fish, which are released, or extruded, as larvae about half the length of a grain of rice. The number of larvae depends on the species: the bigger the better. A female of the checkbook-sized, Puget Sound rockfish species extrudes about 3,330 larvae, compared with up to 3,000,000 for the three-foot-long, twenty-five-pound yelloweyes. The biggest and longest-lived species can keep procreating for decades, annually cranking out millions of live young, which eat anything they can fit into their tiny mouths. As happens with most fish, a vanishingly small number reach adulthood, but it's hard not to admire rockfish productivity. When it fails, though there can be dire consequences.

From an evolutionary perspective, reproducing through copulation instead of group spawning means that when a physical or physiological variation arises, a female may choose to mate only with a male that possesses that trait, which facilitates passing it along to the next generation, who now have the potential to evolve into a new species.[3] Combine sex with high fecundity and diverse and dynamic habitats, such as those found all along the West Coast and in Puget Sound, and you have a perfect recipe for evolving a range of magnificent species.

Another factor influencing rockfish evolution is the series of underwater sills in Puget Sound. Researchers hypothesize, for example, that soon after glacial retreat, some unknown number of brown rockfish colonized Puget Sound. Over time, the sill at Admiralty Inlet limited the subsequent interchange of larvae and adults between the inland waters and the outer coast, which led the founding brown rockfish to evolve and become genetically isolated from their coastal relatives.

A copper rockfish (*Sebastes caurinus*) caught as part of a Washington Department of Fish and Wildlife study, 2017. The distended eyes resulted from a pressure change as the fish was pulled up from a depth of 250 feet. Photograph by the author.

The lifestyle of several species, particularly yelloweye and copper, has compounded the effects of this topographically influenced genetic bottleneck. In contrast to salmon and their wandering ways, rockfish find a rock, hunker down, live by it for the rest of their lives, and have little chance to exchange genes with fish from outside their homewaters. In Hood Canal, limited adult movement and reduced water movement caused by the sill at the canal's mouth have isolated a population of yelloweye rockfish that is genetically different from yelloweye in Puget Sound proper and from those on the outer coast.

Despite their adaptability, all is not well with Puget Sound rockfish. Because the sills limit water flow, shrinking Puget Sound populations have not been augmented by fish from the outer coast. This might not have been a problem if humans hadn't started catching rockfish in unprecedented numbers. Overfishing has led to two rockfish species, bocaccio and yelloweye, making it onto the federal list of endangered and threatened species, along with several of the Sound's salmon and the southern resident orca. Unfortunately, the dire predicament of rockfish is yet another defining example of their quintessence in Puget Sound.

• • •

Much as understanding how George Vancouver ended up in Puget Sound required a side trip to Venice, the story of rockfish requires its own side trip. This one is shorter, going only as far as the coast, but it features a foray into Cold War politics.

In the predawn hours of September 20, 1966, a strange engine noise woke Bob Hitz while he slept on the R/V *John N. Cobb*, a US Fish and Wildlife Service vessel. Instead of the sonorous hum of a cruising boat, the sound was quieter, indicating that the pilot had placed the *Cobb* in neutral and stopped the ninety-three-foot boat. Bob got out of bed, dressed, and headed up to the pilot house, where the skipper, Pete Larson, told him, "We have some company."[4]

More than fifty ships, nearly all bearing the Soviet Union's red hammer-and-sickle flag, surrounded the *Cobb* as it floated about three miles off Cape Elizabeth on the Washington coast. "It was like what I imagine a person must have felt when they saw the arrival of ships at D-Day," says Bob, who was the chief scientist on the ship. Although the encounter occurred during the middle of the Cold War, the Soviets had come not to invade the United States but to fish for schools of hake and Pacific ocean perch.

The Soviets had first begun to catch these species in the Bering Sea in 1959, operating in a manner that could be compared to forest clear-cutting: harvest as much as you can until the resource is exhausted, then find a new source. After ransacking the Bering Sea fishery, the Soviets moved to the Gulf of Alaska in 1962, then a year later to the Aleutian Islands. The fleet ventured below the Forty-Ninth Parallel in 1966. With factory ships the length of a football field, side trawlers, oil tankers, water tankers, personnel transports, rescue tugs, and freezer ships, the Soviet fleet employed hundreds of people and could stay at sea for months at a time, freezing millions of pounds of fish. (One of the appeals of Pacific ocean perch is that they retain their freshness after being frozen.) And the ships stayed in Washington, fishing the coast until the first week of December 1966. By the end of the year, Soviet crews had harvested thirty-four million pounds of Pacific ocean perch from Oregon, Washington, and the east side of Vancouver Island. The following year, the total regional catch, which included a small amount of Japanese-harvested fish, was under twenty-seven million pounds. By 1969 the harvest had plummeted to about a million pounds.[5] In only three years, the Soviets had nearly eradicated Washington's Pacific ocean perch.

Despite the name, the Pacific ocean perch is not actually a perch; it is a rockfish (*Sebastes alutus*), known colloquially as a redfish or rosie because of the color of its flesh. The common name originated as a marketing ploy to take advantage of the reputation of the ocean perch of the East Coast, another species of rockfish (*S. marinus*). The Atlantic fish had in turn acquired its name because of the popularity of the yellow perch of the Great Lakes, which actually is a perch (*Perca flavescens*).[6] Known as rosies when first commercially fished in 1946, these fish were rebranded as Pacific ocean perch in 1951. Only then did diners respond and propel a dramatic rise in the harvest.[7]

Continued Soviet harvests, as well as those of other nations, so close to the coastline of United States eventually led Senators Warren Magnuson of Washington and Ted Stevens of Alaska to propose a two-hundred-mile fishing limit. The Fishery Conservation and Management Act of 1976 (generally known as the Magnuson-Stevens Act, or MSA) passed with the goals of eliminating foreign fishing within two hundred miles of the US coast, preventing overfishing, and allowing depleted fish stocks to recover. (The MSA applies only to federal waters and not to state-controlled waters such as Puget Sound.) To facilitate the recovery process, the MSA called for the development of fisheries management plans (FMPs), with which regional councils would establish harvest guidelines and sustainability goals for fisheries.[8]

In response to the Soviet-induced decline of Pacific ocean perch, the Pacific Fishery Management Council adopted an FMP in 1981 with the goal of rebuilding the population by 2001. The main requirement of the plan was limiting the harvest by American fishers (since the MSA excluded foreign vessels) to 1.3 million pounds per year in Washington and Oregon and 2 million pounds around Vancouver Island. Despite meeting those goals, the population did not recover, and in 1999 the fishery council declared that Pacific ocean perch needed more help.

One of the challenges of rebuilding the stock was a long-held misunderstanding of the life span of Pacific ocean perch and other rockfish species. In 1976, the NOAA biologist Percy Washington told a *Seattle Times* reporter that he believed that some rockfish might live as long as seventeen or eighteen years, which would be exciting; at the time most biologists thought that rockfish lived only about seven or eight years. To test his hypothesis, Washington was collecting different species of rockfish in Puget Sound and extracting an ear bone, or otolith, and counting the microscopic rings on its surface. Like trees adding rings to their trunks, fish add yearly rings, called annuli, to their bones, rays, scales, and otoliths. The otoliths of most rockfish are about as thick as a dime, as long as a nickel, and shaped like an oval or an arrowhead. Two years later, Washington published a study showing that he had underestimated the life span of rockfish. Among his Puget Sound data were otoliths from four yelloweye rockfish that had lived to be twenty-six years old and a copper rockfish that had made it to nineteen years old.[9]

Biologists now know that even these new findings grossly underrepresented how long rockfish actually live. In November 1977, Dick Beamish was working for Canada's Pacific Biological Station on Vancouver Island when a well-known fisherman contacted him about what he thought was an unfished population of Pacific ocean perch.[10] If the location had never been fished (which would have been surprising because the Soviet fleet had also plundered Canadian waters), the fisherman argued, he should be allowed larger catches than had been allotted for heavily exploited rockfish sites. The determining factor would be age. If Beamish found an abundance of older fish, then he would know that the foreign fleet had not fished this location.

Unlike most previous sclerochronologists—or age readers, as they call themselves—who had counted the annual rings only on the surface of otoliths, Beamish sliced them open. He then charred them, painted them with cedarwood oil, and polished them, which highlighted the light and dark pattern of the annuli. Beamish's method eliminated inaccuracies caused by the tendency of the rings to be crowded on the edges and reabsorbed over time. It did not, however, eliminate the challenges of counting them. The retired sclerochronologist Kristin Munk told me that

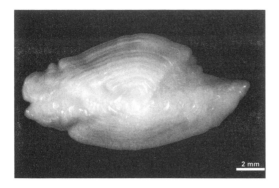

An otolith, or ear bone, from a rougheye rockfish (*Sebastes aleutianus*) that was 43 centimeters long and weighed 1,200 grams. Note the annular rings, which indicate that the fish was around fourteen years old when it died. Photograph by Kevin McNeel. (Courtesy of the Alaska Department of Fish and Game)

2 mm

you quickly learn not to blink when counting, or else you will miscount the microscopic dark and light rings. "I always ended up buying eye drops for new people in the lab," she says.[11]

What Beamish found astonished him. In addition to counting seventy-six annuli on the otolith of one of his Pacific ocean perches, he found seven other species of rockfish that had lived into their fifties. Studying thousands of otoliths from a wide variety of species, subsequent age readers have learned that a seventy-six-year-old rockfish is a youngster among *Sebastes*. The yelloweye rockfish species that Percy Washington had aged to 26 years can live up to 121 years, and quillback, which in Washington's observation topped out at age 15, can make it to 95 years old. Pacific ocean perch are now known to break the century mark. The record holder, at 205 years, is a rougheye rockfish caught in 2000 in Clarence Strait, south of Wrangell, Alaska. Normally resident in deep water, rougheyes have been harvested a handful of times in Puget Sound proper and the Salish Sea. As they age, these fish don't simply grow longer: like people, they have a tendency instead to get stouter.[12]

Biologists have yet to catch a double centenarian rougheye in Puget Sound, but they are nevertheless the longest-lived animal in the Sound. To be precise, rougheyes are the oldest according to a specific method of recording yearly growth, such as annuli, as opposed to animals whose ages are estimated on the basis of chemistry. For example, researchers have estimated that a deep-sea sponge in the East China Sea is more than seventeen thousand years old based on "silicon isotopes and germanium-to-silicon ratios."[13] No one has investigated Puget Sound sponges to determine their longevity, but authors of a recent paper on aging described sponges and other simple animals, particularly sea anemones, as "potentially immortal" because of their ability to "grow, regress, regrow, and regenerate their bodies as needed."[14] Although we may never know, I like to believe that there are individual animals, perhaps many of them, who have lived in Puget Sound for thousands of years.

It is not surprising that it took so long to recognize the longevity of these ocean animals. We see the world in terms of human life spans. If we do consider other long-lived animals, we tend to think about larger mammals, such as giant tortoises or orca, some of which have lived more than one hundred years. We certainly don't think of small creatures such as geoducks, the oldest known of which lived to be 173 years old, or sea urchins, which could compete with rougheye rockfish for longevity.[15] Nor is it common knowledge that fish can outlive us, in part because our best-known example—salmon—don't live longer than ten years. Sadly, this lack of knowledge has led to poor fisheries management in Puget Sound.

The problems originated with the National Standard Guidelines for fisheries managers. Written into the original Magnuson-Stevens Act and subsequently modified to reflect updated science, the guidelines are based on a management concept known as maximum sustainable yield (MSY), which one skeptic summarized this way: "Any species each year produces a harvestable surplus, and if you take that much, and no more, you can go on getting it forever and ever (Amen)."[16] MSY assumes that fish annually produce excess young and that managers can accurately determine the maximum number of fish that can be taken while still maintaining a sufficient number of fish to reproduce and sustain the population.[17]

The problem with this assumption is that not all fish reproduce on the same schedule. For short-lived species, such as forage fish, the number of reproductive fish that survive to enter a fishery, collectively known as recruitment, may fluctuate greatly from year to year, but they have a higher likelihood of quickly increasing their population after a poor recruitment year, or couple of years. Long-lived rockfish, on the other hand, tend to have very sporadic and highly productive recruitment years. Even when the fish hit the jackpot, the survivors from those years won't reach sexual maturity for another decade or two.

Known as bet hedging, this strategy of sporadic recruitment is an evolutionary adaptation that allows rockfish to wait for favorable environmental conditions to reproduce. As with herring, studies have found that older rockfish are essential to the success of their local populations. Elderly rockfish improve the odds of the bet-hedging reproductive strategy by producing more eggs and more fit larvae than younger fish and by doing so earlier in the year. Unfortunately, according to biologists such as Dick Beamish, fisheries managers have often overlooked the importance of older fish and their significance to the resilience of a population. Commercial fishing tends to remove the oldest and biggest fish, which can result in a fish stock made up mainly of younger fish without the ability to produce recruitment classes that can keep a population viable. Beamish calls this problem *longevity overfishing*. Removal of older, more fecund fish *can* lead to younger fish becoming more productive, but they produce less-fit eggs and larvae. Ultimately, the loss of older, bigger fish can result in an evolutionary change in which subsequent generations of older fish produce less-fit eggs.

Declining numbers of rockfish lead to a secondary problem. Because of their prolific lifestyle, "we probably should consider rockfish as a forage fish," says the NOAA biologist Dan Tonnes, recovery coordinator for the Yelloweye Rockfish and Bocaccio Recovery Plan. Like herring, the highly nutritious rockfish larvae may provide essential food for juvenile Chinook and coho salmon. Researchers have begun to collect data on the importance of rockfish larvae to salmon, because any fish that can pump out three million live larvae at one shot must be providing a valuable nutrient source, says Tonnes.[18]

Longevity overfishing appears to have affected Pacific ocean perch. After the Soviets' devastation of the fish stocks in the 1960s and the subsequent loss of bigger, older fish, recruitment dried up, and the population didn't have a chance to rebound until the management plan of 1981 restricted the harvest. Those limits may not have been enough: when managers reevaluated the species in 1999, they decided to sharply curtail the annual allowable catch, which dropped from an average of 2.5 million pounds from 1981 to 1999 to about 203,000 pounds from 2000 to 2016.[19] Finally, in December 2017, managers declared that the Pacific ocean perch stock had been rebuilt, due in part to several jackpot recruitment years since 1999.[20] Biologists cannot say definitively why recruitment was high—whether because older fish were becoming more plentiful or because of an influx of young females—but they note that the successful rebuilding of the Pacific ocean perch population points to the importance of understanding the life history of a species.

• • •

A similar story, though one that has not yet had a happy ending, has also been playing out in the Puget Sound rockfish population over the past five decades. The triggering event was one of the most important court decisions in Washington history. In September 1970, Stan Pitkin, the US attorney for western Washington, filed suit against the State of Washington on behalf of several Puget Sound and coastal tribes.[21] Pitkin and his clients claimed that the state had not upheld the tribes' rights, which had been defined in act 3 of the treaties of 1854 and 1855: "The right of taking fish, at all usual and accustomed grounds and stations, is further secured to said Indians, in common with all citizens of the United States." Presided over by the federal judge George H. Boldt, the case included forty-nine witnesses and three years of pretrial examinations of history, biology, and anthropology. In his February 12, 1974, decision on *United States vs. State of Washington*, Boldt ruled that the state had violated the treaties and systematically discriminated against the tribes.[22] He furthermore declared that the tribes had the rights to one-half of the annual catch of harvestable salmon and steelhead in the state. In determining the allotments of fish, Boldt based his reaffirmation of the tribes' rights on the definition of "in common with," which meant sharing equally the opportunity to take fish at "usual and accustomed" locations.

The Boldt decision did not sit well with most of the commercial and recreational fishing community, or with many state officials: James Johnson, assistant attorney general for the Department of Fisheries, called the ruling "morally reprehensible and unconstitutional."[23] In 1979, by a 6–3 vote, the US Supreme Court determined that it was neither, and upheld Boldt's decision.

In the wake of this landmark case, tribes have developed extensive fisheries of their own, worked with state agencies to comanage fishing resources, and created numerous fisheries departments focused on biology and ecology and on protecting and restoring habitat. Most recently, two key environmental decisions affecting Puget Sound were based in part on *United States v. State of Washington*. In 2016, the US Army Corps of Engineers denied permits to build what would have been the largest coal port ever proposed in North America, at Cherry Point, because it would have violated the Lummi Nation's usual and accustomed fishing rights.[24] Two years later, the US Supreme Court upheld a decision calling for the State of Washington to pay for the removal of hundreds of culverts that restricted access to salmon habitat and infringed on treaty-guaranteed rights.

Although state officials did not always support the Boldt decision, and some actively tried to circumvent or overturn it, fisheries managers recognized that they needed to respond to the new reality of fishing in Puget Sound. With the tribes now entitled to catch 50 percent of the harvestable salmon, commercial and recreational fishers would have to share the remainder. Making the situation more challenging, both tribal and nontribal groups would be fishing for a dwindling number of fish.

Commercial fish harvesting had begun in Puget Sound in the 1850s, when entrepreneurs caught, salted, and packed fish into barrels for shipping to San Francisco. This relatively small-scale industry was supplanted in July 1877, when a salmon cannery opened at Mukilteo. That industry dominated the salmon industry throughout the twentieth century, mostly taking sockeye and pink salmon with purse seines and gillnets. By the time of the Boldt decision, the industry was on a path to self-destruction, with profits falling and fish populations declining.

Following the Boldt decision, fisheries managers tried to encourage nontribal fishers to pursue other fish besides salmon. This was not easy, as most Puget Sound fishers tended to dismiss any other fish as a consolation prize or worse. Bottomfish, such as rockfish, were thought to be puny, prickly, ugly, unlikely to fight like a salmon, and unworthy of the effort. To combat these perceptions, WDFW began promoting a broader range of recreational fishing in Puget Sound.[25]

The least expensive tactic involved state and federal biologists reaching out to the public via fishing and hunting magazines with articles such as "Bottomfish: Overlooked Gems in Puget Sound," "Often-Ignored Black Rockfish: Feisty Scrapper, Fine Eating!," and "The Key to Rockfish Heaven: Kelp." Each article followed a similar pattern of offering suggestions on how to catch the fish, tips on where to catch them (such as along the piers in downtown Seattle), and how to cook them. "The quillback is in flavor the equal of any Northwest game fish and finer than most," wrote one enthusiast.[26]

One additional challenge that many of these articles attempted to address was what to call these fish, particularly rockfish. Within Puget Sound, orange to reddish rockfish were generally known as red snapper, even though true red snappers are found only in the Atlantic Ocean. If a rockfish was darker, it could be called a black bass or sea bass, whereas the mottled copper and quillback went by the name rock cod.[27] The numerous articles invariably noted that all of these rockfish had unique names.

The second part of this effort led to WDFW's building artificial reefs around the Sound, says Ray Buckley, who worked for WDFW from 1963 to 2008.[28] The objective was to give recreational fishers better access to fish such as rockfish and lingcod. Constructed from quarry rock boulders, tires, and scrap concrete, the reefs were typically within five hundred yards of shore, in water less than one hundred feet deep, and covered more than an acre.[29] They had high relief and many cracks and caves, two features favored by rockfish. By the mid-1990s, WDFW had constructed more than a dozen of what Ray described as "boat angler reefs," designed for the benefit of both "yachting anglers" and "avid small-boat anglers."[30]

Ray and his colleagues also began to construct public fishing piers. "We wanted a way to reintroduce the social aspect of fishing, where people could gather, and when one person caught a fish everyone was happy," he says. The first piers opened in Edmonds (south of the ferry terminal) and Elliott Bay (near the grain terminal) in March 1979 and January 1981, respectively. Each provided access to water fifty to sixty feet deep. More than simply platforms to fish from, the piers incorporated large underwater boulder structures designed to attract fish and provide safe habitat away from the anglers.

The idea of the piers grew out of the loss of the boathouse culture once found in Puget Sound, says Ray. Often little more than a shack or two on a dock, boathouses were important hubs for recreational fishing, where anyone could rent a boat and gear, seek advice, get inspired by the photographs of legendary fish on the walls, and swap stories about the day's adventures. During their peak in the 1950s, more than 140 boathouses and resorts served greater Puget Sound.[31] Boathouse culture began to die out when property prices rose and more people began to own boats. Ray hoped to fill the void with piers and reefs.

When I talked to Ray in 2018 about his past work with rockfish and fishing, he was clearly proud of what he had done, in particular providing better access for families. Fishers of all ages flocked to the piers and boated out to the reefs, where they discovered that rockfish were easy to catch and tasted great. "Unfortunately, we probably did too well," he says. "The structures helped bring fish in that had been dispersed, and they got hammered. We probably promoted rockfish at the wrong time, because they weren't doing well."

In the years following the Boldt decision, rockfish harvests soared, rising from about two hundred thousand pounds to almost nine hundred thousand pounds by 1980. Initially, commercial fishers ruled the harvest. After the mid-1970s, most rockfish were caught by people fishing around the reefs and piers. The change had an unexpected effect. In 2010, two biologists examined more than three thousand recipes from Pacific Northwest seafood cookbooks and found that more than 80 percent of the recipes for rockfish were published after 1980. Prior to 1970, such recipes were exceptionally rare. In the 1990s, when regulations began to reflect the population drop, the number of rockfish recipes declined.[32]

With the rise of the recreational fishers, the rockfish population plunged, and the average harvest dropped to forty-two thousand pounds between 2004 and 2007. "Back then, we didn't have the concept that recreational fisheries could harm the fish populations," says Ray. The problem with rockfish was the same one the coastal fish managers had: "We didn't have an appreciation for how infrequently they reproduced." The huge harvests in Puget Sound had most likely removed the old and big rockfish, and without them, the populations could not recover. It wasn't until 1984 that state biologists responded by lowering the daily rockfish bag limit for recreational fishers from fifteen to ten. They eventually dropped it to five, then to one, and finally to zero in 2010. (I repeatedly heard of people who had filled garbage cans with their daily haul in the years before these limits; they weren't throwing the fish out, they just needed a good, large container to store them.) Over the same period, the state also extended the geographic bans on commercial fishing, ultimately banning it completely in 1999. At present, it is illegal to harvest any species of rockfish in Puget Sound.

• • •

Despite the restrictions, I have gone out fishing for rockfish twice on Puget Sound. In June 2017, I was on Steve Kesling's thirty-one-foot fishing boat as part of a NOAA bycatch study of lingcod and rockfish. When fishers accidentally catch a species other than the one they planned to catch, the "wrong" fish is known as bycatch. The goal of the NOAA project is to determine whether there are better ways to catch lingcod without bycatching rockfish. Begun in March 2017, the study compares three types of bait: frozen herring, artificial lures, and live Pacific sand dab, a type of flounder.

Motoring out of the Edmonds dock, we traveled twenty miles south on quiet water past Elliott Bay to a small island, where we idled in water 250 feet deep. Joining Steve were two fishermen who had volunteered for the opportunity to catch rockfish and Kelly Andrews, the NOAA fisheries biologist who was overseeing the study. Watching us were a pair of bald eagles, a few gulls, and a single seal, who periodically raised her head and peered at us from the water.

For this stop, the fishers were using Point Wilson jig darts, a fish-shaped lure about six inches long, green on top, yellow in the middle, and silver on the bottom, with red eyes and etched fins and facial features. Drifting along at about walking speed, we were over a spot where erosion had carried large rocks into the depths, ideal rockfish habitat. The plan was to let the jig down almost to the bottom, then jerk the line a bit, let the jig descend, then jerk again. When they felt a bite, the fishers were supposed to jerk the jig aggressively to set it.

Within a couple minutes, one of Steve's volunteers had caught a copper rockfish, historically the most common rockfish species in the Sound. Kelly helped bring in the fish, pulled out the lure and measured and weighed the fish—identified as a male by his tiny external urogenital papilla, a reproductive unit akin to a penis (though you may not want to use that word around a fish anatomist). At seventeen inches long and weighing about three pounds, the fish was about average size for the species. Overall he was brownish, with a hint of gold on top that mottled down to white, with hints of pink toward his head and brown toward his rear.

Like most rockfish, this one had stout, sharp dorsal spines, which Kelly astutely avoided. He wore thick work gloves for additional protection. Rockfish are members of the scorpionfish family, which has numerous venomous species. The mild venom of rockfish is described in one scientific study as not "particularly dangerous," but the author of an article in the local magazine *Fishing Holes* wrote that the spines "can introduce the incautious angler to a whole new kind of pain."[33]

Most noticeable was the copper's stomach, which protruded from the fish's mouth looking like a huge thumb. Bottom-dwelling coppers, like other rockfish, achieve neutral buoyancy, which allows them to remain in deep water, by regulating the volume of gas in their swim bladders. This is an adaptation for animals that evolved to stick close to home and not move up and down in the water column. Unfortunately for rockfish, humans have a propensity to bring them up from the depths. At the surface, the gases within the bladder expand, leading to what is known as barotrauma: the fish can have a bloated or ruptured swim bladder, distended stomach, and bulging eyes, making them look like Peter Lorre on steroids. Most fish that experience barotrauma cannot swim back down to their home habitat and typically end up floating on the surface and dying, which has also contributed to the decline in rockfish numbers. (Because so many of the deep-dwelling fish are orange, these floaters are known as pumpkins.)

Over the next eighty minutes—the study calls for fishing one location for ninety minutes—the quartet of fishers kept their lines overboard. When all four were going, their metronomic up-down, up-down jigging was a joy to watch, especially when they had to reel in their lines and water droplets sparkled in the morning light. Periodically Steve moved the boat and placed us over a new spot with a good rocky bottom. His array of high-tech navigation devices allowed him to "see" the bottom in

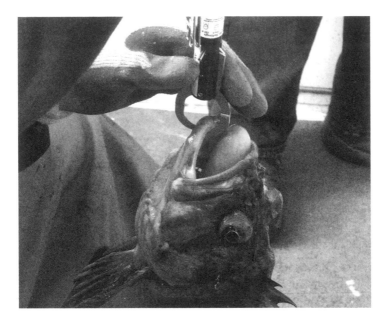

As part of a 2017 Washington Department of Fish and Wildlife study, Kelly Andrews has attached a descender to this copper rockfish (*Sebastes caurinus*), which suffered from barotrauma and exhibited the resultant distended stomach. The descender will help Andrews lower the fish back to its original habitat deep in Puget Sound. Photograph by the author.

great detail. He could even pick out individual fish and schools of fish, including what he called a "knot of herring."

A far simpler tool on the boat was a nifty device known as a descender, a five-inch-long black plastic tube with a pressure-sensitive, spring-loaded clamp on the end. As soon as Kelly finished measuring each rockfish, he clamped the descender to the fish's mouth, attached the descender to a weighted line, dropped it overboard, and returned the fish to its deep-water home, a practice that one person described to me as "just like fishing but in reverse." Prior to the development of descenders, fishers attempted to aid barotraumatized rockfish by using a hook or hypodermic needle to puncture the swim bladder. A study of this practice, known as venting, or fizzing, found that it had little positive benefit, not least because few people, either recreational anglers or knowledgeable biologists, could do it correctly.

Initial studies of rockfish returned to depth with descenders have shown that the recompressed fish typically survive, though fish from water deeper than four hundred feet often suffer from disorientation and vision problems, compromising their ability to "move effectively, find refuge, and avoid predators upon release."[34] The barotrauma researcher Polly Rankin told me that she supported the use of descenders, but "avoiding capturing rockfish you can't retain is the best option."[35]

By the end of our ninety-minute test period, the crew had pulled up six more rockfish, along with one of the most impressive fish I have ever seen. Lingcod are like certain people we all know: more or less okay until they open their mouths. With people it's typically that they speak before they think. With lingcod, it's a dental issue. When a lingcod opens wide, canine-like fangs point downward along with numerous smaller teeth, paired with a host of equally sharp teeth on the bottom jaw. At the back of the mouth are what are known as pharyngeal teeth, reverse-facing daggers that help the fish grind its food. Between these formidable rows are another fang-like set, called vomerine teeth, which aid in holding prey, and finally there are three rows of what look like teeth but are merely very sharp gill rakers, bony protuberances that facilitate filter feeding.

With its mouth closed, the lingcod was still formidable looking because of his broad, flat head, wide mouth, and full, supermodel lips, which give the appearance of an animal able to chomp onto any human-sized body part. The one we caught was three feet long and weighed seventeen pounds. With their mottled skin of dark brown, gold, light brown, and pale white, lingcod are handsome. Steve and his volunteers considered them to be beautiful fish—and flavorful, too.

We then motored back north, past Elliott Bay to another good habitat spot west of Magnolia. This one, though, consisted of two gravel barges that sank in 1973, each about two hundred feet long and fifty feet wide.[36] "This is a bad spot for snags, so be careful," warned Steve before the fishers dropped their lines. This time they baited their lines with previously frozen herring and attached a lead weight to the seven-inch long fish. For each herring, Kelly employed two hooks, which gave the bait a more realistic swimming motion.

Over the boat went the lines, all of which snagged—sometimes against each other—periodically over the next ninety minutes. The fishers caught two additional species of rockfish: a quillback, with sinister-looking dorsal spines, and the darker and heftier black (*S. melanops*).

My favorite fish was the Pacific spiny dogfish, also known as a sand or mud shark, a sleek-looking beast with a cartoonish, human-like face, big eyes, smooth skin, pink lips, and a long snout with nostril-like openings. One of the dogfish looked a bit guilty, though I am not sure of what. Spiny dogfish can live to be one hundred years old. They don't reach sexual maturity until their thirties; when they reproduce, females gestate

Pacific spiny dogfish such as this one caught in Puget Sound in 2017 were historically harvested for their vitamin D content, which decimated their numbers. They primarily eat herring and sandlance. Photograph by the author.

for two years and give birth to live fish, mini versions of the parents. Biologists have found that the Puget Sound population is doing well. Kelly measured the ones we caught and tossed them back.[37]

Although we didn't fish with the sand dab on that June day in the Sound because of high winds, I went out again in April 2018 with Kelly, Steve, and another crew up to the San Juan Islands, where they baited lines with small flounder. "Time to measure the prisoners," said Kelly, as he placed the curious-looking fish on his measuring table. Like all flounders, the sand dab has evolved to live on the sea bottom by a unique process of development: as the fish mature, their bodies flatten so that one side always faces up, and the eye from the downward-facing side migrates to the upward side. To tell which side of a flatfish is right or left, look for the protruding lower jaw, and turn the fish so the lower jaw is downward. Whichever side the eyes are on indicates right or left. (Most flatfish species are right-sided or left-sided; a few species can be either.)

"Don't jig. Let 'em chew on it. He'll hook himself. Or at least that's the plan," said Steve. The idea was that lingcods, who eat, or at least latch onto, just about any fish that passes by, would attempt to consume the entire sand dab while being slowly reeled up to the surface. Steve calls these lingcods "clingons." Eventually Steve's plan worked: one of the crew pulled up a forty-one-inch clingon from 237 feet below the surface. Inside her mouth was a thirteen-inch sand dab, mostly intact, which Kelly wrestled out of the lingcod's grip. After he removed the hooks, we took photos of the fish and the proud fisher who caught her, and then Kelly tossed her back overboard.

By the end of the day, we had fished thirteen locations around the islands and caught only eleven fish: five quillbacks, two coppers, three lingcod, and a red Irish lord—a stunning, red-splashed, yellow-brown fish in the sculpin family. No one was upset by our limited success. Steve and Kelly and their helpers were having a great time. They joked. They rarely stopped fishing. They exclaimed over the different rockfish. They carefully returned them to the depths. They fantasized about eating them.

Preliminary data from the study show that using sand dabs for bait seems to be the best way of reducing rockfish bycatch when fishing for lingcod. But because they also caught a yelloweye rockfish, which is protected under the federal Endangered Species Act (ESA), Kelly suggested that recommendations for bait might be modified in areas where yelloweye are present. "I don't expect our data to change how the state regulates rockfish but see it more as an additional piece of data to help make an informed decision in a complicated process," he said.

Few fish in the Sound were as satisfying to catch as rockfish, says Dan Tonnes, who caught many in his youth in the early 1980s. "They filled a strong cultural niche by making it easy to introduce kids to fishing. They didn't have to get up early, the fish were easy to catch, and they tasted great. I am sad my kids cannot do that. They have lost that connection to Puget Sound."

•   •   •

Studies like Kelly's bycatch project originated with the April 28, 2010, placement of bocaccio (from the Italian for "big mouth"), canary, and yelloweye rockfish on the federal list of endangered and threatened species. The listing applied specifically to the populations of these species that live in the Puget Sound–Georgia Basin waterway, east of a line between Port Angeles and Victoria, British Columbia. That location was chosen because of the sill that rises up from the sea floor and restricts water movement and, potentially, the interchange between coastal and inland bocaccio and yelloweye.[38] According to the ESA, bocaccio and yelloweye east of the sill are known as a distinct population segment (DPS), separate from all other populations of those species. Southern resident killer whales, Puget Sound steelhead, Puget Sound Chinook, Hood Canal summer-run chum, and Puget Sound bull trout are also DPSs.

The federal listing prompted the development of a formal recovery plan by a team of state, federal, tribal, and academic biologists led by Dan Tonnes. The 267-page plan for Puget Sound–Georgia Basin bocaccio and yelloweye rockfish was published in October 2017. It begins with two sobering sentences. "Total rockfish abundance in Puget Sound has declined approximately 70 percent in the past 40 years. Yelloweye rockfish and bocaccio have declined to an even greater extent." It then addresses what has happened to the fish, describes their biology, and outlines steps to be taken to promote their recovery. The goal is to restore the two species "to the point where they no longer require the protections of the ESA."

As with all other species within the Sound, no one knows how many bocaccio and yelloweye rockfish inhabited the waterway prior to Euro-pean settlement. Rockfish show up only sporadically and in small num-bers in the archaeological and ethnographic records of Puget Sound.[39] Contemporary tribal biologists have told me that rockfish were caught and eaten only as a minor component of the diet. These findings did not surprise the Bear Creek archaeologist Bob Kopperl, because rockfish do not aggregate in the large numbers that would require people pooling together to harvest them. No tribe in Puget Sound proper currently has a management plan for rockfish.

Nor do many records exist following European settlement. An 1888 report from the US Commission on Fish and Fisheries mentions that Puget Sound rockfish cost three cents per pound, the same price as salmon and smelt but considerably less than halibut, which fetched a quarter per pound. By 1899, the commission devoted almost all of its one-hundred-page report to salmon, with no specific reference to Puget Sound's rock-fish. To his credit, the author, Richard Rathbun, offered this advice, which clearly was not heeded: "In the region to which this paper relates there may still be time to give the fisheries the full benefits of a wise pro-tection before any of its branches shall have been appreciably impaired, but action should not be long deferred, as a decrease once begun is hard to check."[40]

During the next seventy-five years, rockfish remained a minor spe-cies in the fishery. For example, in a 1956 state report on trawling, the total rockfish catch in Puget Sound accounted for only 45,000 pounds out of the 3.5 million pounds of all species caught.[41] Then came the Boldt decision, and rockfish began their brief rise in popularity followed by long-term decline, which ultimately resulted in the ESA listing of bocaccio and yelloweye, as well as the listing by the state of black, brown, canary, China, copper, greenstriped, quillback, redstripe, tiger, widow, and yellowtail rockfish as "species of concern."

At present, Washington State regulations prohibit targeting and retention of all species of rockfish by recreational anglers in Puget Sound. Nor can anyone fish for bottomfish in water deeper than 120 feet unless fishing for halibut or salmon. This restriction covers 64 percent of the Sound. Nontribal commercial fisheries must follow corresponding regulations that prohibit fishing for rockfish.

Despite these protections for rockfish in Puget Sound, they continue to die because of lost nets, crab pots, and prawn traps that litter the sea bottom. Dating mostly from the extensive fishing in the 1960s and after the Boldt decision, the derelict gear kills hundreds of thousands of marine invertebrates, fish, mammals, and birds, and may continue to do so for decades because the abandoned equipment is made of artificial materials, such as plastic and steel, that degrade slowly. Since 2002, however, and accelerated by the ESA listing, more than 5,900 nets have been cleared, leading to the restoration of more than 870 acres of habitat.

More than other animal species in Puget Sound, the ESA-listed rockfish, and to a lesser extent the eleven state species of concern, came under threat because of human actions that specifically targeted them—as opposed to human actions that have inadvertently harmful consequences, such as dams, disease, habitat degradation, global warming, introduction of invasive species, pollutants, and predation. For rockfish, though, biologists blame overfishing as the primary cause of the population crashes that followed the Boldt decision. Consequently, bocaccio and yelloweye rockfish now fall under a fundamentally different management regime than other rockfish species. Under the 2017 Rockfish Recovery Plan for the Puget Sound–Georgia Basin area, fish management takes a holistic approach, factoring in the connections between the two species and other species, fish and nonfish, within the ecosystem, as well as the ways people alter that ecosystem. In Puget Sound these interwoven factors include bycatch, degraded water quality and habitat, derelict nets, dredging, release of hatchery salmon, runoff, vessel traffic, and the big uncertainty, though it is certainly happening—climate change.[42]

One result of this ecosystem perspective is a stronger focus on kelp. Although rockfish have a well earned reputation as deep-dwelling, sedentary rock lovers, many species live more gregarious youths, spent in far less daunting habitat. In particular, schools of juveniles gather in the sunlight-filled kelp forests of the nearshore, along with juveniles of other species, including salmon. The small, slow rockfish require a safe nursery where they can find food, protection from predators, and shelter from strong currents. When they get older, the rockfish abandon these refuges as they transition to their adult deep-water habitat. Some species also take advantage of floating mats of dead bull kelp as a more mobile haven to facilitate the change to adulthood.

Researchers believe that the long-term decline in the abundance of kelp forests throughout Puget Sound could be another reason why most species of rockfish, not only the listed species, are not doing as well as in the past. This concern has led scientists to designate kelp as critical habitat for the conservation of rockfish and to develop a kelp recovery plan that centers on a more thorough study of the roles of kelp in the Puget Sound ecosystem. They hope that a better understanding of the relationship between kelp and rockfish will benefit not only rockfish but also the dozens of other species that live in the kelp for all or part of their lives, particularly Chinook salmon.

Known as ecosystem-based management, this more inclusive way of approaching the natural world is both a reflection and a catalyst of the changing relationship between Puget Sound and the humans who live, work, and govern here. This change is particularly notable in the case of rockfish. Unlike salmon and orca, they are not charismatic, iconic, or cute species that inspire human care and protection. Nor are they economically important or particularly popular with fishers. On the contrary, they are fish that required a public relations campaign simply to make people want to catch and eat them. Rockfish were so little known that people didn't even know what to call them.

We have now begun to recognize that the twenty-seven species of *Sebastes* have unique life histories, each having evolved to fill a specific niche and interact with its own species and other species in a distinct manner. Preserving the genetic diversity of rockfish will give this group of fishes a better chance to adapt to future environmental challenges.

The fundamental question for rockfish applies to all of the species whose populations have plummeted in Puget Sound: Are we too late? Biologists have reason to believe we are not. The example of Pacific ocean perch suggests that rockfish may be able to rebound and rebuild their populations if we humans are willing to constrain our actions. But constraint has to be tied to understanding. Biologists have learned from rockfish the same lesson they learned from herring: fisheries managers cannot operate in a vacuum, independent from or ignorant of the life histories of these fish and their connections to their world.

Humans, too, will surely benefit if, in addition to thinking more holistically about the Puget Sound ecosystem, we can exercise patience, trust, and time: patience, to allow scientists to study rockfish, because we still have so much we need to know about them and their relationships with Puget Sound's flora and fauna; trust, to accept what scientists tell us even if it's not what we want to hear; and time, because rockfish, and the rest of Puget Sound, will require decades to recover from our earlier actions.

We are lucky that rockfish live so long. Perhaps we can take inspiration from knowing that there may be rockfish who were born here before the signing of the treaties, swam under a pointy-ender from the mosquito fleet, survived artillerymen shooting mortars from Fort Flagler, heard the thrum of diesel-powered ferries, escaped the fishing excesses of the 1980s, and will benefit from our actions sometime in the future. That would certainly be a worthy destiny for these quintessential Puget Sound fish.

9

The Table Is Set

The narrow band between high and low tide is Puget Sound's most protean ecosystem, where the rhythms of existence fluctuate with the twice-daily expansion and contraction of our inland sea. For thousands of years, those pulses of water dictated life for the Sound's human inhabitants. Where people lived, how they traveled, and when they could find food all depended on knowing the tides and how they affected the movement and location of water, plants, and animals.

Today, understanding the tidal cycle of the Sound has little relevance to most residents' lives. We no longer worry much about the phase of the moon or how the tide might affect our next meal. This lack of awareness of the tidal rhythms is neither good nor bad: it's simply the reality of our lives and a reflection of our overall disconnect from the natural world around us.

Hoping to remedy my disconnect, at least in a minimal way, I decided to watch a tidal exchange at Seattle's Discovery Park. On August 10, 2017, I reached the beach at 6:30 a.m., when the tide had been ebbing for three hours. I established my base for the day at a driftwood tree trunk perfect for leaning against.[1] A dozen feet away, beyond a sloped cobble and sand beach, waves approached the shore so gradually and quietly that they seemed reluctant to arrive. Beyond, no feature broke the smooth surface.

The water continued to recede from the sloped beach out onto a terrace. By 7:00 a.m., the top of a boulder poked above the surface about sixty-five yards offshore. Closer in, three ends of a stump had breached, and within another hour, the water had retreated enough to expose more than a dozen boulders the size of a doghouse or larger, as well as seaweed-strewn fingers of cobbles and expanses of rippled sand. Farther out in the water, a steady stream of kelp moved north, carried by the ebbing current.

As the water retreated, I periodically abandoned my tree trunk to explore the world so recently revealed: barnacle-covered boulders and worm-covered barnacles; horse clam siphons and moon snail casings; crabs and crab tracks; anemones, logs, eelgrass, and kelp; ripple marks, pools, and channels; red algae and white bird poop; abandoned pier pilings and critter-filled tires; tube-worm towers and squiggly worm castings; great blue herons with fish in their bills and gulls with clams in their bills; squadrons of black-capped Caspian terns and a lone bald eagle harassed by gulls; and a variety of holes in the sand that hinted at another hidden world below.

At the bottom of the tide, at 10:34 a.m., the beach was more than a third of a mile wide. I observed only minimal change over the next hour, during what is known as slack water. Then the water began to advance at increasing speed, moving fastest between 1:30 and 2:00.[2] During this period, I walked out to the waterline, stopped, and watched as the water swelled toward shore. Twenty minutes later, the water was close to my knees, and the waterline had advanced more than one hundred feet. After another thirty minutes or so, the waterline was almost where it had been when I arrived eight hours earlier.

Watching that surge was humbling and exciting, fully revealing the tidal pulses that most Puget Sound residents, me included, fail to notice every day. Every twelve hours the Sound inhales and exhales, covering and uncovering a beautiful, evanescent world at the intersection of land and water.

•   •   •

According to one of the traditional sayings associated with Coast Salish people, "When the tide is out, the table is set." But it still took experience to be able to fill the plates, says Rosa Hunter of the Jamestown S'Klallam tribe. "When the tide is out, you don't just grab what's sitting on the surface. Assume they are dead. Clams are supposed to be dug."[3] No clam in Puget Sound is more challenging to dig than the region's most famous, the geoduck (pronounced "gooey-duck").[4]

Called the "prince of clams" by an anonymous *New York Times* writer in 1883, the geoduck is the largest burrowing clam in the world, native only to the west coast of North America.[5] The biggest can have nine-inch-long shells and weigh up to twenty pounds, though most top out at around eight pounds. They are some of Puget Sound's longest-lived marine residents, with ancient geoducks pushing two hundred years old.[6] They survive in part because they live out of reach of most predators, buried in soft sediment. As juveniles, they burrow down by sucking water in through a channel in their siphon and blasting it out the opposite end. This liquefies and displaces the sediment below them and allows them to pull themselves into this soft ground with their foot, or ambulatory muscle. There, two to three feet beneath the surface, they stay for the rest of their long lives. To eat, geoducks extend their muscular siphon up through the sediment into the water and filter feed on phytoplankton. They expel waste through a second channel in the "neck" (the wrinkled, flexible, beige to brown siphon). When alarmed, a geoduck can quickly retract its neck, often ejecting a spout of water, though the shell can never close fully over the siphon. This buried lifestyle provided the clam's common name, from the Lushootseed word gʷidəq, meaning "dig deep."[7] The scientific name, *Panopea generosa*, translates roughly to "big and all-seeing."[8]

Buried deep, the big bivalves are mostly out of sight of people and predators. Geoducks make an appearance—if you consider poking a pig-snout-like siphon tip out of the sediment an appearance—only at very low tides, which generally occur at night in winter and during the day in summer. (WDFW publishes a guide to when tides are good for digging geoducks; a typical year has about twenty-five good clamming days, all between May and August.) To obtain the dig-deep clams, harvesters had to know the right times; to persevere in digging when the siphon kept withdrawing out of reach; and to be willing to extend an arm, and sometimes more, into cold, mucky water.

A successful geoduck hunter extracted a savory length of meat "highly satisfactory to the daintiest epicure" and "suitable food for very good men of scientific proclivities," according to R. E. C. Stearns, who visited Olympia in June 1882.[9] Whether Stearns thought that lesser people would savor what he called the "boss clam of North America" is unclear. His close friend and fellow conchologist Henry Hemphill, who ate geoduck in 1881, considered them the "most delicious of any bivalves I have ever eaten, not excepting the best oysters," though he cautioned that the flesh was "too rich to permit of regular stuffing or gormandizing."[10]

• • •

For those who didn't want to go to the trouble of obtaining the inimitable geoduck, another tempting option was the two-inch-long, tear-drop-shaped Olympia oyster (*Ostrea lurida*), colloquially called an "Oly."[11] Found only on the west coast of North America and arguably at their most abundant in Willapa Bay on the outer Washington coast, and in the

A pile of sand, a shovel, and a geoduck in hand. Pride, joy, and astonishment, hunting for geoduck on the beach, ca. 1920–40. (Courtesy of UW Special Collections, Image UW5784)

South Sound, these bivalves were far easier to gather. Olys accumulated in great beds, or reefs, in the miles of tide flats in the Sound and Willapa Bay. At high tide, when they were submerged, they could be harvested by using long tongs. At low tide, procuring your next meal was as simple as walking across a beach, though you still had the challenge of extracting the meat from the shell.

Oysters are one of the few animals that people eat when their meal is still alive. To do so requires prying open, or shucking, the shell. When European settlers arrived, they brought with them thin-bladed but stout knives that made this task easier. Native people could have broken the end opposite the hinge, called the bill, inserted another shell and either forced apart the oyster's two shells or sliced the muscle that held them shut. It's doubtful whether they did. Ethnographic studies in Puget Sound, such as Marian Smith's work with the Puyallup and Nisqually people, confirm that no one ate oysters or any other shellfish raw, except perhaps barnacles.[12] William Elmendorf reported that Twana people on Hood Canal boiled or steamed oysters, often with clams, cooking them on hot rocks layered in a pit and covered with maple leaves, cedar boughs, and a mat.[13] Other groups preserved oysters for winter consumption by smoking them and stringing them on buckskin or sticks.[14]

Well known for its coppery flavor, the Olympia oyster barely makes a mouthful: the meat of an individual oyster weighs about 1.8 grams, or a bit less than a dime, and filling a gallon container with the meat requires harvesting 1,600 to 2,000 individual oysters. But when you eat one, you have a food that "judges of the article, have pronounced as the sweetest, and best flavored, that they ever tasted."[15]

Clearly the Coast Salish people living in Puget Sound have appreciated the metallic-tasting morsels for thousands of years. In 1899, the archaeologist Harlan Smith of the Jesup North Pacific Expedition documented dozens of shell heaps in the Sound. One of these middens stretched for half a mile and rose more than ten feet high. When Smith excavated a handful of the shell piles, he found oysters in each one, along with species such as mussels, sand dollars, giant Pacific sea scallops, and Pacific littleneck clams.[16] A more recent study, from 1993, noted that more than half of the midden sites in the South Sound included oysters, making it more widely distributed than any other mollusk.

Olympia oysters were still important to Indigenous people when European settlers arrived in the Olympia area and began taking an interest in the mollusks. One person mentioned in the early writings was Dick Jackson of the Squaxin Island tribe, whose descendant Tyler Johns is the operations manager for the tribe's commercial shellfish business. "We've been doing this forever, and that history inspires me," says Tyler. "Olympia oysters are very sensitive and really hard to keep alive, but I don't want to see them disappear. I want to do what's best for my tribe, and Olympia oysters are part of that."[17]

• • •

Although people have harvested other local shellfish—such as cockles, mussels, and littleneck, butter, and horse clams—for thousands of years, Olympia oysters and geoducks have become the most emblematic native mollusks in Puget Sound. They achieved their fame primarily through the commercial market, which began in the 1850s for Olympia oysters, but not until the 1980s for geoducks. Fans of these two bivalves contend that each deserves credit for the location of the state capital in Olympia: the geoduck because its abundance would provide "the source of future legislative suppers," and the oyster because it "created a warmth and friendly spirit" when served at public meetings deciding where to locate the capital.[18]

These shellfish are certainly good representatives of the Puget Sound story in that they illustrate the changing relationship between people and the natural resources of the waterway. Oysters exemplify the first half century or so of postcontact history, when non-Native residents viewed the plants and animals of the Sound as resources to be extracted. On May 13, 1859, the editor of the *Puget Sound Herald* summed up the newcomers' feelings when he referred to "oyster mines [he preferred this term to the conventional *beds*] of immense wealth all about us."[19] Like other resources, oysters were harvested with little regard for the environment, with predictable results. Nor was there much regard for the Indigenous people or their knowledge of the oysters and how to harvest them sustainably.[20] Geoducks represent the more recent use of natural resources, in that their harvesting is heavily regulated, with a focus on the ecosystem. In addition, the tribal nations of Puget Sound now have a critical role in the science and management of these keystone cultural resources. Residents, politicians, and scientists may not always succeed or live up to their ideals, but we at least attempt to encourage less harmful behavior than that of the early generations of newcomers.[21]

Puget Sound's settlers began to appreciate oysters when they figured out in the 1850s that there was a market for them. Most of those buyers lived in San Francisco, where many new residents had arrived from the East Coast with a passion for oysters. Portland residents also acquired a taste for them, and their newspapers contained advertisements promoting a "Ladies' Oyster & Coffee Saloon" and proclaiming, "Oysters! Oysters!! Is the Cry!"[22] The earliest harvests would have been wild Olys, replaced soon after by farmed, or cultivated, varieties as producers scaled up to meet demand.

In the last half of the nineteenth century, most of the United States, along with much of western Europe, was gripped by oystermania. Londoners in the 1880s alone accounted for seven hundred million oysters a year.[23] When the British author Charles Mackay visited the United States during this oyster-loving era, he wrote of "oysters pickled, stewed, baked, roasted, fried, and scolloped; oysters made into soups, patties, and puddings; oysters with condiments and without condiments; oysters for breakfast, dinner, and supper; oysters without stint or limit—fresh as the fresh air, and almost as abundant."[24] By 1880 oysters made up about 25 percent of the value of the products of the US fisheries industry. (In 2017, oysters accounted for 4 percent of the $5.4 billion total.)

The mollusk madness also gripped the new territory of Washington.[25] By the time of the first census, in 1860, the value of the oyster fishery in Washington Territory was $44,567, compared with a total of $17,450 for cod, mackerel, salmon, and white fish combined.[26] One year later, the territorial legislature enacted a law "to encourage the cultivation of oysters," which gave any citizen who planted oysters on oyster-free tidelands the right to claim that area. (This giveaway was not legal, however: at that time the federal government owned the tidelands, holding them in trust until the territory became a state.)

The ongoing popularity of Olys in Washington contributed to an unusual aspect of state law. Unlike most coastal states, Washington allows for private ownership of tidelands. In March 1895, the state legislature passed two laws, known as the Bush and Callow Acts, that allowed for the purchase of up to one hundred acres of state-owned tidelands at $1.25 per acre, as long as the land would be used for oyster planting and cultivation.[27] The acts' sponsors, Anderson S. Bush and William Callow, who represented oyster-farming districts in Willapa Bay and the South Sound, believed, like many in the trade, that ownership of the tidelands was essential if oyster farmers were going to invest in and develop them for oyster production.

This legislation, along with a ruling in 1899 that allowed for oyster dredging, did bolster the oyster industry, but it was too late, at least in Willapa Bay. In 1902, the Willapa Olympia oyster harvest peaked at 150,000 bushels before crashing to 2,400 bushels in 1914. (A bushel contained about 2,500 unshucked oysters.) Unregulated harvests of a finite crop, a new ability to dig out deeper beds, the substitution of motors for sails on harvesting boats (which made it easier to reach the beds), and harvesters' failure to return shells to the bay (which deprived new oysters of much-needed substrate) combined with several years of freezing weather to kill the Willapa Bay Olympia oyster industry.

All US oyster-producing areas, including the biggest—Long Island Sound, New York harbor, and Chesapeake Bay—suffered the same fate as Willapa. What started out as the harvesting of a local delicacy expanded into industrial fisheries, with consequent overharvesting, environmental degradation, and an industry crash. In the East, the commercial collapse dominoed from New York to New Jersey to Delaware to Maryland to South Carolina to Georgia, and finally to Mississippi and Louisiana. To counter each failure, regulators passed laws—the first in 1658, on Manhattan Island—that attempted to curtail the harvest. When regulation failed, growers began to import juvenile and adult oysters to reseed formerly copious beds. Few opted for the simplest way to boost the oyster population: reducing their harvest.

On the West Coast, a similar pattern developed, spreading north from San Francisco to Washington. In a 1901 report, the state fish commissioner, A. C. Little, wrote: "Until a few years ago it was not thought necessary to exercise any care in taking the oysters from the beds. The supply seemed almost unlimited, and it was supposed it would always remain so." Of course, it didn't, and the Olympia oyster has never recovered in Willapa Bay.

The other main contributor to the drop in oyster harvests was industrial pollution, which began in Puget Sound in 1927 with the opening of a sulfite pulp mill in Shelton, on Hammersley Inlet. Using a multistep chemical bath, the plant converted wood waste into paper and dumped the by-products, known as sulfite waste liquor (SWL), into Hammersley. Almost immediately, South Sound oyster farmers noticed a significant drop in the population of Olympia oysters. The larvae failed to set, and adult mortality rose.[28]

Despite efforts by oysters growers to stop the mills' discharge and state fisheries reports in 1931 and 1949 concluding that SWL was "the

For decades the Rayonier Pulp Plant in Shelton, pictured here in 1957, spewed toxic waste harmful to oysters, juvenile salmon, crabs, shrimp, and clams. As of 2019, the Washington Department of Ecology was still sending letters to Rayonier requesting a more thorough cleanup of the facility and its surroundings. Photograph by Leland J. Prater. (Courtesy of Leland J. Prater, Forest History Society, Durham, NC)

most probable cause of the alarming decline" in oysters, pulp mills continued to discharge their toxic wastes into the Sound for decades.[29] They were able to do so in part because the pulp owners and other resource extractors still held power in Puget Sound, according to a presentation by Daniel Jack Chasan at a 1991 conference.[30] He cited Washington State's general lack of "backbone to enforce its own deadlines" for the discharge permits, which were supposed to be renewed every five years. But the "focus suddenly changed" as the "environment became a national issue." A massive oil spill in Santa Barbara, California, in 1969 led to the signing of the National Environmental Policy Act and a similar state bill, both of which required environmental impact statements for major government actions.

With these laws and other federal and state regulations in place, industrial dumping into the Sound was gradually reduced. Although many industries did not agree with the regulations, they did change their practices, or else they shut down because they could not afford or chose not to bring their plants into compliance. Enhancing the effects of these changes were restoration and cleanup efforts designed to remove earlier pollutants. Because of the widespread historic discharge of toxins within Puget Sound, the cleanup has been slow and will never be finished or result in pristine conditions; but pollution from most industries in the Sound is less now than it was thirty years ago.

One of the first ways that Washington's oyster harvesters responded to lowered output was to follow the example of their eastern counterparts and attempt to cultivate nonnative oysters. They first tried importing the eastern oyster (*Crassostrea virginica*) and had moderate success until most of them died in 1919. Two years later, two Japanese American oyster farmers, J. Emy Tsukimato and Joe Miyagi, became the first to successfully import commercial quantities of what was initially known as the Japanese oyster (*Crassostrea gigas*), which was much larger than the Olympia, with an average shell size of six to eight inches. However, they ran up against local anti-Japanese sentiment, which led to the passage of Washington State's Alien Land Bill of 1921. The act barred nonwhite immigrants from buying, owning, or leasing land in the state, and Miyagi and Tsukimato were forced to sell their land and cede control of their oyster operations. Anti-Japanese bias also resulted in the new owners of these oyster beds, who were exclusively white, changing the name of the Japanese oyster to the Pacific oyster, the name by which it is known today.[31]

Despite the laws, Japanese immigrants, some of whom had brought with them oyster-harvesting knowledge and skills, remained essential to the growth of the local oyster industry as key workers in the harvests. Their jobs were not easy: they often worked at night and had to harvest in the winter. They did the challenging work of culling and opening oysters in frigid factories and typically lived in poorly made, poorly heated, floating houses anchored among the oyster beds. Ironically, Japanese immigrants had moved into the oyster trade because of laws banning the previous generation of oyster harvesters, who were Chinese immigrants. They, in turn, had replaced the Native workers, who had been the first group hired in the nascent industry as well as the first to be discriminated against.

By the beginning of World War II, six of the eight largest oyster companies in the state employed Japanese Americans almost exclusively. Their employment ended with the passage on February 19, 1942, of Executive Order 9066, the law that incarcerated 120,000 Japanese Americans in internment camps throughout the western United States. After the war, Japanese Americans returned to the oyster trade and helped make the imported species the dominant oyster, first around Willapa Bay then in Puget Sound. As of 2013, 94 percent of the oysters harvested in Washington were Pacific oysters.[32]

During all these years, few nonresidents expressed much interest in geoducks, though the geoduck lover Henry Hemphill proposed an

Two men harvesting oysters at low tide, ca. 1900–1920. First- and second-generation Japanese workers were the dominant labor force during the 1900s until World War II, when Japanese and Japanese Americans in the United States were forcibly removed to internment camps. (Washington State Historical Society, Image C1950.8.6)

elaborate plan to ship live ones to the East Coast in 1881. His attempt failed, as did other attempts by equally ambitious geoduck promoters. Geoducks remained a local food until the later twentieth century, when divers discovered geoducks living in much deeper water than anyone had previously suspected.

Robert and Margaret Sheats inaugurated the commercial harvest of geoducks in May 1970, when they dove to the sandy bottom of Thorndyke Bay on Hood Canal and pulled up fifty clams. Robert had recently retired as a diver for the US Navy from the base at Keyport. One of his jobs had been to locate errant torpedoes on the bottom of Puget Sound.[33] In 1960, he and other divers had found fields of geoducks deep below the low-tide line, which they reported to state fisheries biologists. Following several years of surveying the sea bottom, biologists estimated that more than sixty-three million geoducks lived deep in the Sound, enough to justify opening the fishery to commercial clam hunters.

After securing one of the first harvest permits, the Sheats family started Bubble Heads, Inc., and over the next two years hauled out 4,021 geoducks. Their plan was to sell the clams to local food markets and restaurants. Robert's son Carl told me they met with limited success: "Restaurants paid just twenty-five cents a pound. We found better luck selling them on the side of the road for a buck a pound."[34] Their partner in the company, Herman Kunz, tried canning the geoducks but found little desire for canned chunks of oversized mollusks. Nor did other commercial harvesters do well. In a 1972 report for the Department of Fisheries, the economic consultant Lee E. Erickson wrote that "this is not a profitable business yet, but the potential does exist."[35]

One reason that such a potential existed is that the giant clams are arguably the most abundant biomass in Puget Sound—calculated in 2018 to be at least 925 million pounds—as a result of their extravagant reproduction.[36] Like rockfish, the other long-lived denizens of Puget Sound, geoducks grow more fecund with age. Unlike the rockfish, however, geoducks can become sexually active as early as two years old, though most wait another year. They appear to have no reproductive senility; one male was found to still be producing sperm in his 107th year. Unfortunately, scientists had to kill him to learn this.[37]

Geoducks begin to develop what one biologist called "sex products" in early winter.[38] They continue to produce into early summer, with peak output in the Sound in April and May. Triggered by warming water, algal density, and perhaps more extreme tides, which provide a higher potential for greater dispersal, male geoducks eject free-floating sperm via their siphon in thirty-minute-long eruptions. Females release as many as twenty million eggs, which they can do multiple times in a single year.

When fertilization occurs, a shell about as wide as a very fine sand grain begins to form, along with a velum (from the Latin word for "sail"), a ciliated organ that aids in movement and eating. For the next several weeks, the larvae sail the current before settling down on the sea floor. The ideal spot consists of sand mixed with a bit of mud and pea gravel at least two feet deep, allowing a young geoduck to dig a safe refuge.

Life now becomes a race as the sand-grain-sized geoduck tries to find a suitable spot to burrow before other species make it a crunchy little meal. Young geoducks are aided in their pursuit of a good home by a "conspicuously large foot" with which they push themselves along the sea floor.[39] If the currents are too strong, young clams may anchor themselves by attaching thin guy wires, called byssal threads, to sand grains. They can also employ the threads as a sort of kite that raises them off the substrate and allows them to drift freely. (Spiders create similar threads, which allow them to float hundreds of miles through the air.) Geoducks soon abandon their peripatetic lifestyle and begin to bury themselves in the sediment. In Puget Sound, this can be as deep as 360 feet below the water surface, though the maximum densities of clams—greatest in the South Sound—occur at depths of 18 to 70 feet.

Shell growth is fastest during the clam's first decade, followed by another ten to fifteen years of much slower growth. After that, the shells become thicker but do not increase in length or width. A typical single shell weighs about half a pound; the biggest shells can reach almost two and a half pounds, for a total animal weight of more than eight pounds.

Buried two to three feet deep in the sediment and protected by their shells, geoducks may seem almost immune to attack. But otters dig up adult geoducks, and fish such as flounder, cabezon, halibut, and dogfish shark nibble exposed siphon tips. The biologist David Fyfe told me of diving in Barkley Sound and seeing a two-foot-wide giant pink sea star that had latched onto a geoduck's siphon with its tube feet. Exerting constant pressure on the siphon to hold it in place, the sea star had everted its stomach seven or eight inches into the sediment to consume the clam's meaty protuberance.[40] Fyfe said that the sea star feasted on the geoduck for more than a week. He doesn't know if the sea star ended up eating the entire siphon, but the geoduck would have had little chance of survival.

Mature geoducks have a pretty tranquil life, free from the daily concerns of most animals—avoiding predators, seeking out a safe home, finding food. About all they have to do is suck in water, eat, expel waste, and procreate. Over the course of a full lifetime—a bit more than a century—a single geoduck has the potential to generate more than a billion progeny. If you consider that the estimated number of geoducks in Puget Sound is 487 million individuals, the total number of potential offspring is staggering.

•   •   •

Like geoducks, oysters are "prolific to the point of indecency," wrote Eleanor Clark in her wonderful paean *The Oysters of Locmariaquer*.[41] Unlike them, however, Olympia oysters occur not as male and female individuals but as hermaphrodites. They typically begin life as male, then switch regularly between female and male phases, with each individual oyster having its own rhythm of sexuality. As one early biologist wrote, "All possible intergradations between the different phases . . . are found in young animals, so that it is frequently impossible to assign the individuals to any one of the principal phases of sexuality."[42]

Depending on environmental conditions, an Oly can reach sexual maturity as a male as early as the age of five months, when he discharges several hundred thousand sperm balls. Each tightly packed sphere consists of 250 to 2,000 sperm, heads glued together, tails wagging. Out in the sea, the glue dissolves, and the microscopic sperm swim away. Fertilization occurs when a female sucks the sperm into her gills and passes them to her mantle cavity, which holds her eggs. Ten to twelve days later, she expels her brood of 250,000 to 300,000 larvae, which, like geoduck larvae, soon sail away under power of a ciliated velum. If lucky, they land on a suitable substrate to which to attach themselves, known in the trade as cultch. Although old oyster shells are ideal, cultch can be any hard material, such as rock, wood, metal, or concrete slabs. Once it lands, the young oyster, or spat, uses its foot to obtain a purchase, then secretes a glue to bind itself in place for the remainder of its life.

After the spat attaches to cultch, it grows to a length of two inches or so in about three years, if it can avoid bad weather and predation. Olympia oysters can live for about ten years, but they cannot survive freezing or high temperatures. Nor do they live long when moon snails, red rock crabs, black scoters, or greater scaups find them. Since the 1920s, Olympia oysters have also had to contend with new scourges that arrived with the introduction of nonnative oysters. The two most worrisome are a parasitic flatworm and a carnivorous snail, both of which have a macabre feeding method. The flatworm drills a small hole to get inside the oyster shell, severs the adductor muscle that keeps the shell closed, then crawls inside, surrounds the oyster, and eats it alive. The snails also penetrate the shell by drilling, a process enhanced by secreting sulfuric acid. They then inject digestive enzymes into the oyster and slowly consume it over a week.

Like kelp, Olympia oysters can engineer their environment by converting normally soft, muddy intertidal habitat into stable reefs. These three-dimensional structures attract a host of other organisms and prevent erosion by attenuating wave energy. In addition, by filtering up to three gallons of water per day, each oyster cleans Puget Sound by removing suspended solids, nutrients, microbes, and phytoplankton, as well as by sequestering toxins such as PCBs and pesticides.

More than most Puget Sound marine organisms, Olympia oysters both adapt to and alter their environment. A recent study of three widely separated bays in Puget Sound found that oysters from each location had genetic and physical traits, such as growth, reproductive capacity, and temperature tolerance, that were specific to where they lived. The oysters, like herring, had evolved different life histories tailored to their homes. "We fully expected to see no local adaptation," says the University of Washington ecologist Brent Vadopalas, a coauthor of the study. "It was totally surprising, like something salmon would do."[43]

In comparison, geoducks showed little genetic differentiation from Baja California to Alaska. That does not mean geoducks are not well adapted or that they are not as essential to the ecosystem as oysters: "Just from a biomass point of view, they are very important in the overall scheme of things in Puget Sound, in their feeding and in their contribution to being a food source for other animals," says Lynn Goodwin, a retired WDFW biologist.[44]

•   •   •

After addressing sex among mollusks, the logical next subject is money. The key to financial success for geoduck harvesters was found in Asia, writes Craig Welch in Shell Games. He traces the expansion from local to international sales to Brian Hodgson, who had obtained one of the first geoduck permits in 1970. Hodgson had had limited sales to Puget Sound restaurants until one of his buyers, Carol Kondo, told of selling geoducks to Asian groceries. After learning that grocers sold the geoducks overseas, Hodgson and Kondo teamed up to market geoducks in Japan. Unfortunately for them, writes Welch, the pair "lacked the connections and cultural acumen to see the next big market . . . China."[45] Hodgson also lacked a belief in regulations and ultimately ended up in jail for geoduck poaching.

The first geoduck exporter to establish Chinese connections was Claude Tchao. As a child he had been taken to numerous banquets in Hong Kong, where hosts often tried to outdo each other with exotic foods. Tchao ended up in Vancouver, BC, amid a growing population of Hong Kong immigrants, and realized that geoducks, with their enhanced anatomy, were the perfect banquet food. In 1984, he began to ship the well-endowed clams directly to China. "It was only a matter of time before Washington divers and seafood brokers found this market, too," writes Welch. By 1994, the price of Washington geoduck had risen above four dollars per pound, after remaining below fifty cents a pound from 1970 to 1990. In 2018, the export value of Washington geoduck totaled $103 million, with 97 percent ending up in China or Hong Kong. No other state produces a remotely comparable number of geoducks.

In 2013, harvesters collected 3.1 million geoducks.[46] About one-third of the total was farmed on privately owned land in the intertidal zone of Puget Sound.[47] It is a labor-intensive process, at least in the initial and final phases of farming, and not for those who expect quick profits, as I realized after spending a long morning in Eld Inlet, about six miles northwest of Olympia. I was with Shina Wysocki, the owner of Chelsea Farms, on one of her farming beaches at low tide, where workers were preparing homes for new geoducks.

Ten or so people worked the sandy beach, stooping and standing, surrounded by a field of white PVC tubes. About twelve inches tall, four inches in diameter, and covered by netting held on by a rubber band, the tubes were lined up in long rows, spaced about a foot apart. The workers pushed them into the ground by standing on them and wriggling their feet until the tube top stood about five inches above the silty beach. Between high tides, a team of workers could place about five thousand tubes, said Shina.[48]

Within a week each of the tubes would become a home for four of the cutest little animals I have seen: baby geoducks. They were deposited by a diver at high tide, when water completely covered the tubes. Geoducks at the age of six months or so look like miniature replicas of their parents, with an appendage too big for their pinto-bean-sized shells. The feature that makes huge, phallic, adult geoducks unappealing to some people makes them charming when young and sitting in a nursery tank swinging their little siphons around. Touch one of the siphons, and it shrinks immediately. It's enough to make you forgive the adults' appearance.

The baby geoducks' small size makes them vulnerable to predators, which is why the tubes are covered by nets that stay in place for about six months. Even so, two of the four typically die. By the age of twelve

These farm-raised geoducks have just been extracted from their sandy homes, where they resided for the previous five to seven years. Each weighs about three pounds, typical for a farmed geoduck. Photograph by the author.

months, the young geoducks, now about the size of a kumquat, can survive with the protection of the tube alone. Another year passes before the clams, now the size of a lemon, have buried themselves into the sediment, away from predators. At this point, workers return to the beach, use their feet to loosen the tubes, and pull them up with pliers. The geoducks are left alone for the next three to four years as they grow to a weight of two to three pounds, with a shell the size of a baked potato.

For the harvest of the five- to seven-year-old geoducks, crews of two to three spend months extracting up to five hundred pounds of geoduck per day. Using a high-powered water hose, called a stinger, workers liquefy the sand, reach deep, and pull up the clam by its siphon. Fast workers can get their prey in as little as five seconds. The day I visited was part of a second sweep, lasting several weeks, when one or two harvesters seek out the last, hard-to-find geoducks. I did not envy Kevin, who was often prone on the cold beach, his arm and shoulder deep in the colder sand and water, using a stinger to release the well-anchored holdouts. He was typically taking longer than five seconds to remove them.

Farmed Pacific oysters have a life regimented by cultivators, too. Some cultivated Pacifics are produced in hatcheries to be nonreproductive, for better marketability during the summer months: reproductive oysters put more energy into eggs and sperm, which leads to less flavorful meat. No matter their sexual future, modern farmed oysters initially develop in hatcheries before being spread as seed onto cultch, most often old oyster shells or rows of plastic disks called coupelles. Some of the growing oysters are grouped together in mesh bags suspended on lines in the water, which move with the tides. This enables them to grow faster because there is usually more food higher in the water column. How fast they mature is specific to the location.

• • •

Not everyone supports commercial oyster and geoduck aquaculture. The most common complaint Shina hears is that the geoduck tubes detract from homeowners' water views. She responds that the tubes are visible only during part of the day and that they tend to get coated in green algae in less than a year. More fundamentally, Shina says, "It's a working waterfront issue. We need to get people to see that the Sound is not just a view, and to see it as a living ecosystem that people rely on for jobs and for food." Like other oyster and geoduck farmers, she tries hard to prevent the loss of tubes and nets and has looked for nonplastic alternatives to the PVC tubes. When she tried a biodegradable product, however, she found it didn't degrade. "I have a lot invested in Puget Sound, and I want it to be okay," she says.

Others who object to the farms cite ecological issues. They worry about plastic from the PVC tubes and the way the nets change the dynamics of the beach, and they argue that a monoculture is inherently less healthy and sustainable than a diverse natural ecosystem. One social and policy study of stakeholders also found that some respondents felt government scientists were biased in favor of aquaculture and thus questioned the accuracy of their research. The report cited one person who said that the government reports were "written to try to make a determination that favors aquaculture as opposed to really seeing the whole entire picture."[49]

I find this assertion hard to believe. When I interviewed state, federal, tribal, and academic biologists who work on aquaculture, all of them clearly expressed their concern about the environment and how people and industry affected it. I am sure that each has some bias—we all do— but they are scientists who take great pride in eliminating those biases to try to get to the underlying truths. They were upfront about where they lacked knowledge and recognized that they didn't have enough experimental data to fully explain all of the impacts of geoduck farming.

On the basis of current knowledge, biologists believe that geoduck and oyster aquaculture have minimal and temporary effects on the ecosystem. Overall biodiversity changes very little with geoduck aquaculture. The more complex structures created by the tubes and nets benefit some fish and larger invertebrates by providing additional habitat and creating a refuge that discourages flatfish and predatory moon snails. Some scientific models predict that the additional human and boat traffic involved with aquaculture could lead to a temporary decrease in bald eagle abundance, which may benefit other species, such as the migratory shorebirds often eaten by eagles. Researchers acknowledge that the results from their short-term studies on relatively small plots may fail to reveal cumulative long-term effects. But they also observe that because Puget Sound intertidal communities evolved in response to an ever-changing environment characterized by tidal fluctuations, shifting substrates, flooding, and thermal stress, intertidal organisms are adapted and resilient to disturbances, "including those of anthropogenic origin."[50]

The main concern with geoduck farming is the use of the plastic tubes, but even the Monterey Aquarium's Seafood Watch program, which produces the most respected fisheries-related environmental reports, concluded the issue is "surrounded by uncertainty." Regulations require cleanup of lost tubes, and studies have shown that PVC may be less prone to degrade or leach pollutants in the marine environment than on land. As one ecologist told me, geoduck farming "is not as bad as people claim, nor as good as the farmers claim."[51]

Biologists have also examined mollusk aquaculture as it compares to fisheries, livestock, and fish aquaculture. The most far-reaching study was published in 2018 and led by the University of Washington fisheries ecologist Ray Hilborn. He and his team reviewed 148 cradle-to-grave assessments that addressed energy use, carbon footprint, nutrient release, and acidifying compounds and found that the production methods with the lowest environmental impact were small pelagic fisheries (such as herring) and mollusk aquaculture. Beef production and catfish aquaculture were the worst, though Ray told me that the carbon footprint of our geoducks would go way up once they were flown to China.[52]

When I spoke with Brent Vadopalas, he made another insightful observation about geoduck and oyster farming: "People are comfortable with land agriculture but not with marine aquaculture." We are used to seeing cows and fields of wheat. We are used to encountering the land as a working landscape. We don't have that type of relationship with the sea. "Now that fewer people go clamming, more people around Puget Sound have lost that attachment to the water," says Brent.[53]

Ironically, the oldest evidence for managing the environment for food in Puget Sound and the Salish Sea comes from aquaculture rather than agriculture. (Agricultural practices, such as root and berry cultivation, cutting down trees and shrubs to create openings, tilling soil, and periodic landscape burning are probably of similar antiquity, but no physical evidence remains.) People built rock walls along the low-tide line of bays and inlets in order to stabilize beaches and develop terraces behind the wall where clams could become established. The early farmers of the sea enhanced the terraces by digging up the clams to aid sediment aeration, returning small clams to the gardens for subsequent harvest, removing predators, and transplanting clams from productive to unproductive spots, all of which contributed to the development of habitat that made clams a more accessible and sustainable food. Known as clam gardens, these sites offer some of the earliest evidence of food cultivation in the region: the oldest known clam garden dates to 3,500 years ago.

As of 2019, the Swinomish Tribe is planning to expand on this tradition by building and managing the first clam garden south of the Canadian border, says Jamie Donatuto, environmental community health analyst for the Swinomish Tribe. For her, clam gardens epitomize a sense of place and an active, respectful, and responsible connection to the land. She describes shellfish as a keystone cultural resource. This term connotes more than food: it encompasses community, heritage, and personal and emotional connections. In addition, clam gardens are about stewardship. They lead to increased productivity and biodiversity and may help reduce wave action from rising sea levels and mitigate other effects of climate change. "The clam garden is a Coast Salish technology that works to address issues of today," says Jamie.[54]

Donatuto's colleague, the biologist Courtney Greiner, has written that clam gardens may provide a local, place-based method to address one of the most significant modern ecological concerns: ocean acidification, or OA. This refers to the changes in ocean water chemistry generated by human-caused increases in atmospheric carbon dioxide (CO_2). When CO_2 is absorbed into the ocean, it lowers the concentration of carbonate ions in the water and reduces pH (makes the water more acidic). This phenomenon is harmful to shellfish because it not only decreases the availability of essential minerals that they incorporate into their shells (two forms of calcium carbonate) but also makes the water more corrosive to the shells once they form.

Because of the way global ocean currents transport water to Puget Sound, the waterway presently has CO_2 concentrations equal to what scientific models predict will be average worldwide levels in 2100, or perhaps even earlier. Although some scientists have suggested that this means that Puget Sound organisms are potentially preadapted to future conditions, most are now rejecting this hypothesis. "Our relatively high ambient levels of CO_2 do not mean that species can tolerate a consistent increase in CO_2. And OA doesn't happen on its own. Ocean temperatures are warming at the same time that OA is increasing," says Terrie Klinger, director of the School of Marine and Environmental Affairs at the University of Washington. "The evidence from laboratory studies suggests that species may be able to withstand an increase in temperature or acidity but not tolerate a simultaneous increase in both."[55]

Perhaps the most obvious effects of ocean acidification in Puget Sound are the challenges faced by shellfish larvae, particularly economically important animals such as mussels, clams, and oysters. In Hood Canal, for example, a major Pacific oyster hatchery began to suffer significant reductions in larval production between 2006 and 2008 because of the altered water chemistry. In response, the facility's owner, the Taylor Shellfish Company, began to buffer the water at the hatchery. Output has improved but has still not returned to earlier levels. Because Taylor is both the largest producer of farmed shellfish in the United States and a supplier to many local growers, both private and commercial, any impact to their hatchery ripples across the Sound.

OA also affects adult shellfish, particularly pteropods, swimming snails generally smaller than the end of your thumb. No longer able to absorb the calcium compounds they need to build strong shells, pteropods are vulnerable to being eaten away by the acidified water. Signs such as pitted and pocked shells worry ecologists because the changes due to OA have occurred faster than many predicted and also because of pteropods' role in the ecosystem. These "potato chips of the sea," as one ecologist calls them, act as a conduit for energy transfer, eating smaller zooplankton and being eaten by larger animals, including herring and salmon.[56] As OA increases, pteropods will become less viable and could go extinct in places. Although such a drastic change has not been predicted for Puget Sound, oceans without pteropods could precipitate a change in the local food dynamic.

Recent research also shows that fish have started to react to OA. A 2014 study reported that Atlantic herring embryos raised in more acidified water had stunted growth, compromised kidney development, and impaired metabolic function. When researchers increased the CO_2 concentration in the water, it further exacerbated growth and development problems. Salmon face a different problem: high amounts of carbon dioxide interfere with their neurosensory behavior, making young fish unable to detect their predators. Rockfish have also experienced sensory changes, which affect their ability to swim upright.

None of this bodes well for the future. Even if we could somehow stop all contemporary carbon emissions, ocean water would continue to acidify because of all the CO_2 already emitted into the atmosphere. Locally, there are ongoing attempts to counter OA. Courtney told me that because of both the chemical benefits of clam gardens (stabilizing the pH of the water) and their structural benefits, she sees them as a potential way to mitigate the increase in CO_2 on a small scale, as well as a way to help people connect to their local landscape. Studies are also taking place at the Puget Sound Restoration Fund's kelp farm at Hood Head to determine whether the fast-growing sugar kelp can sequester enough CO_2 to improve seawater chemistry. Even though researchers know that mitigation measures such as clam gardens and kelp forests have limited, local effects, they are a starting point, which also provides critical refuge habitat for juvenile rockfish and salmon.

Marine ecologists such as Terrie Klinger recognize that our ability to mitigate OA within Puget Sound is limited. For her, it is part of our future, and we will have to adapt. "We are going to have to learn to like new things: what we value culturally and what we eat. We are also going to have to learn to like things we now consider noxious, such as jellyfish and invasive species," says Terrie.[57]

Unfortunately, we, as a species and as Puget Sound residents, have a long history of having to adapt and revise our expectations downward. Ecologists sometimes refer to this phenomenon as the "shifting baseline syndrome," as we lower the standards of what we recognize as normal in an ecosystem. Typically, the shift results from our inability to perceive change, to learn from the past, and to recognize how human activity has diminished the natural world. In adjusting to this new, lower baseline, we tend to reduce the importance of other species by failing to recognize their historical abundance and how the ecosystem evolved in response to that abundance and diversity.

Shifting baselines can also result from a lack of data, particularly in Puget Sound. Because of the inherent challenges of a marine environment, it is hard to monitor changes in real time and to track how different species interact within diverse ecosystems. "I don't know that management of marine resources is as wrong as various people claim from time to time," says Jodie Toft, deputy director of the Puget Sound Restoration Fund. "We would make better decisions if it were easier to count animals underwater, but that part is tough."[58]

Within the Sound, all the species I have considered—kelp, rockfish, herring, and Olympia oyster—as well as salmon and orca have suffered

Oyster shells drying at the J. J. Brenner Oyster Company in Olympia, 1910, historically one of the largest Puget Sound oyster companies. These shells would have been ground for chicken feed. Photograph by Asahel Curtis. (Courtesy of the Washington State Historical Society, Image 1943.42.19971)

from shifting baselines. (Geoduck is the exception.) For the most part, we are simply trying to keep up, to stabilize their populations at their present levels, despite the fact that all were more abundant as well as more culturally important in the past. As our connection to these species has weakened, we have allowed their populations to diminish and turned our attention to other species. We now tend to focus on the well-being of salmon and orca. This is not a bad thing to do, but it prioritizes what is important to present-day Puget Sound citizens, not necessarily what is good for the ecosystem as a whole.

No ecologists suggest that we can return to earlier conditions, and most point out that we shouldn't try, in part because the ecosystem has changed too much. But we can be inspired by the past. We can keep in mind that salmon and orca historically relied on the abundance of species such as herring, kelp, and rockfish, along with the hundreds of other species that inhabit Puget Sound. Perhaps if we recognize this interdependence, we will have the vision and determination to restore the balance of life within the Puget Sound ecosystem.

•   •   •

Geoduck farming provides one-third of the state's marketable supply of the clams; the rest come from wild-stock harvesting, the practice initiated by Bubble Heads. The harvesting of most other marine animals, such as herring or sea urchins, occurs over a broad region, but geoduck harvests are regulated to occur at a specific location and to yield a specific quantity. "Geoduck are unusual for a marine species. They are more like a forest in that they are immobile and live so long," says Hank Carson, lead scientist for the WDFW Wild Stock Geoduck Fishery. "And we manage them as such."[59]

A geoduck harvest begins when WDNR, which owns the bottom-lands of Puget Sound, auctions the rights to acquire geoducks within specific tracts, examined and defined by state biologists. Four times a year, bidders gather together in a conference room, submit their bids and their $75,000 deposit checks in sealed envelopes, and wait patiently for each bid to be announced. On the day I watched, bids for the seventeen tracts up for auction ranged from $5.00 to $11.78 per pound of clams. By the end of the day, the state had taken in $4,584,524.[60] A month or so later, the winning bidders would be able to harvest their tracts.

Diving for geoducks is exhausting, says Jim Boure, a retired diver and now the harvest coordinator for Suquamish Seafood Enterprises, a company chartered by the Suquamish Tribe. Divers have to find the two-inch wide siphons on the sea bottom, eighteen to seventy feet down in cold water that can be clear or murky, depending on tides, currents, and weather. If no current is flowing, sediment stays in suspension, which is "like diving in chocolate milk," he said. "We call it brailling for geoduck." At the end of a day of diving, Jim said that he often went home, sat down to rest, and ended up sleeping through dinner.[61]

The day we talked, we were out on the tribe's geoduck boat in Agate Passage, north of Bainbridge Island, in part of their "usual and accustomed" shellfish harvest area. As with fishing, tribal rights to harvest shellfish in Washington were restored in a landmark court case, this one presided over by Judge Edward Rafeedie. On December 20, 1994, the Rafeedie decision resulted in a fifty-fifty split of the harvest between tribal and nontribal harvesters.[62] Prior to Rafeedie, no tribes had a commercial shellfish program; now they harvest clams, oysters, crab, sea cucumbers, and shrimp.[63]

The Rafeedie decision was about more than restoring Indigenous rights to historic shellfish harvesting grounds, says Danica Sterud Miller, a member of the Puyallup Tribe and professor of American Indian Studies at the University of Washington. "It was about culture and politics and what it means to be a nation." Danica centers her argument, in part, on the name *geoduck*. During the trial, the state argued that the deep-water habitat of geoducks meant that tribal people would have lacked the knowledge to harvest the clams. The tribes countered that *g*ʷ*idəq* is a Lushootseed word that has been absorbed into English, and its connotation of digging implies that it was Indigenous people who taught harvesting skills to the colonial settlers.

According to Danica, Coast Salish peoples base their hunting and fishing rights on specific relationships with specific locations. Through these relationships, they developed their traditional concept of sovereignty. The Rafeedie decision interprets the contemporary Western ideas of sovereignty through the lens of treaty rights and nationhood. "Rafeedie was about reaffirming our language, decolonizing the space, and reasserting our ability to self-determine. It was a profound moment," she says.

In addition to Jim, other people on the Suquamish boat included the captain and six divers, two of whom were getting ready to dive. Each had on a full wetsuit, a weight belt, thick rubber gloves, a spare air tank, and a head-covering face mask. They would be connected to the boat by an air hose, or umbilical line, as the divers called it. Before jumping into the water, they clipped to their belt an orange net, held open by a metal ring, and grabbed a black water hose that ended in a hollow plastic wand a couple of feet long—the same kind of stinger used in geoduck aquaculture. The weights helped the divers sink straight down, though they held onto the umbilical line to slow their descent and allow their ears and sinuses time to adjust to the increased pressure of water thirty feet deep.

On the bottom, divers had two goals: find the "ducks" and avoid each other. To facilitate both, the divers were in constant voice contact through an audio system on the boat. Most of the time we heard the divers' repetitive, Darth Vader–like breathing, punctuated by discussions about location—currents can carry a diver fifty to sixty feet away from the boat on the descent—and whether they had found any ducks. Occasionally they produced more colorful phrases, if their lines got tangled or something spooked them. Jim told me the scariest things he had seen were unexpected pieces of kelp drifting by, and another diver told me of

Amelia Sneatlum, great-grandniece of Chief Si'ahl (siʔaɬ, anglicized as *Seattle*), date unknown. Sneatlum told anthropologist Warren Snyder that as a young girl she dug clams with her mother at night—they were a food source, along with ducks, in winter, and she and her family sold the clams in Seattle. (Courtesy of the Suquamish Museum)

stepping on a giant skate, which shot out from under him. Joe Seymour, a Squaxin geoduck diver, said that he regularly saw dogfish shark—"just swimming muscles"—but they weren't bothersome.

To find a geoduck, a diver looks for a siphon, then jabs the wand into the sediment next to the clam. After two or three thrusts, the jets of water loosen the geoduck so that it can be grabbed by its neck, pulled out, and placed in the mesh bag. The diver then seeks out the next target. Joe said that digging up a geoduck shouldn't take more than about ten seconds—any more than that and it wasn't worth it.

The first diver took about thirty minutes to fill his bag and signaled those on board to lower a rope to winch the bag to the surface and send another one down. Once the bag was on board, the rest of the diving crew took out the ducks, wrapped a rubber band around the unbroken ones (the broken ones were separated out to be given to elder tribal members), and placed them in cages resembling milk crates. A bag weighs between 250 and 300 pounds. That day's order was for 2,200 pounds, about thirty-five cages. In 2017, Suquamish Seafoods sold 430,000 pounds of geoduck, 99 percent of which ended up in China.

By early afternoon, the crew had filled its quota, and the geoducks were offloaded and trucked to the Suquamish Seafoods' processing plant, an open warehouse below the company offices. To get them ready for shipment, a second crew transferred the product from the cages into an ice-lined plastic bag in a Styrofoam box inside a cardboard box. A full box weighs between forty-nine and fifty-one pounds. They were then labeled, put in a van, and driven to SeaTac Airport. The next morning they would be received by a Chinese wholesaler, who would put the geoducks into tanks in rooms that could hold up to fifty thousand pounds of geoducks. Although the big clams can live in the tanks for several months, most are shipped immediately to larger cities, either to markets or to restaurants, where they are held in another tank, often with a host of additional creatures, such as lobsters, crabs, and oysters.

What a strange fate for those Agate Passage geoducks. One day they are doing what comes naturally, hanging out in the sediment sucking in water, expelling waste, and bothering no one. The next day, they have acquired a huge carbon footprint and flown to China, where they will be purchased—for upwards of $150 per pound—and eaten, most often in a hot pot or stir-fry, but also raw, in sushi.

The globetrotting geoduck illustrates a local conundrum. Many residents of Puget Sound, like others in trendy locations, obsess over food and its origins, and yet one of our more common and unique foods is often overlooked. Although oyster bars are ubiquitous, no one has opened a geoduck bar. The only place I know that incorporates the name is the Geoduck Restaurant and Lounge in Brinnon, which seems more about attitude, with signs such as "Caution—Stampeding Geoducks," than about eating: geoduck isn't on the menu. Instead of celebrating the giant clam and its local abundance, we seem to suffer from a disconnect, not recognizing the cultural, economic, environmental, and nutritional opportunities of eating locally raised geoduck. I understand that geoducks' appearance does not endear them to everyone, but when you get down to it, is eating geoduck any less appealing than slurping slimy living oyster innards, as many locals happily do? At least geoducks are usually cooked, and in light of Ray Hilborn's observation, a local geoduck's carbon footprint is drastically reduced if it fails to board a plane to Asia. So eating local geoducks helps save the planet.

The disconnect between Puget Sound's human residents and the geoduck is paralleled by the lack of knowledge about our native oyster. Many locals do not realize that Olympia oysters are native and Pacific oysters are not, or that present populations of Olys are far lower than they used to be. Over the past two decades or so, however, the Puget Sound Restoration Fund has focused on trying to bridge that gap and gain recognition for our little local oyster. PSRF has set a goal for 2020 of reestablishing one hundred acres of Oly habitat in the Sound. Basing their work on a 1998 WDFW stock rebuilding plan for Olympia oysters, PSRF began with seeding efforts in 2000 in places such as Dogfish Bay, a ten-acre, sheltered cove across Liberty Bay from Poulsbo.

After testing a variety of methods, they had a lightbulb moment in 2004, says Betsy Peabody, when they were surveying a tideland in Liberty Bay with the WDFW biologist Brady Blake. They realized they needed to enhance the substrate. Instead of trying to seed the muddy bay, they teamed with the nearby Keyport naval base to fill two navy barges with Pacific oyster shells and spread about 1,000 cubic yards of shell in Dogfish Bay. "It was revelatory," says Betsy. Olys began settling on the nonnative oysters. By 2010, the population had become self-sustaining.[64]

Betsy told me this story as we motored in a fifteen-foot skiff from Poulsbo to Dogfish Bay with Brian Allen and Ryan Crim, PSRF's hatchery manager. "See that dark patch rising above the water line? That's the oyster beds," said Brian. When we got closer, the dark patch resolved itself into oyster shells, orders of magnitude more than I had ever seen. We landed, stepping onto a squishy surface of shells and mud. Fountains of water, or what Betsy called "little squirts," gave the appearance of a water-gun fight between buried combatants.

The PSRF team had come to survey the site to determine the density of Olympia oysters, which involved counting oysters within the boundary of a small, randomly tossed square made of PVC pipe. "I have one." "Look at the ridges on this one, they're gorgeous." "Hey, a golf ball." (Apparently people like to hit golf balls into mudflats. Fortunately, Olympia oysters aren't terribly picky and will colonize golf-ball surfaces.) "Ooh, look at that, an Oly on an Oly." It was muddy work that took experienced fingers and eyes to discern the Olympia oysters, particularly the smaller ones, from the Pacifics. And it was aromatic. "You know you're working the tideland when you have to turn your head to breathe," said Brian.

We were not alone in our interest in oysters. Moments before we arrived, seven great blue herons flew away from the beds, and throughout our stay gulls flew up and tried to break open shells by dropping them from above, though not when bald eagles coasted over the mudflats. The most active inhabitants were numerous, quarter-sized crabs sprinting to hiding spots under much larger Dungeness crab carapaces or moon snail casings. I also watched several varieties of snail meander between barnacles that had colonized the Pacific oyster substrate.

When PSRF first started to look for Olys in the Sound, the maximum density of the remaining natural beds was about seventy-five oysters per square meter, at the upper end of Case Inlet. Then they were invited to go up to the west side of Vancouver Island, where they discovered Olympia oyster beds with a density of seven hundred oysters per square meter. The visit was eye-opening, although they knew they could not approach those numbers in Puget Sound. Their current goal is to reach one hundred oysters per square meter in all of their restoration localities. In 2013, the density at Dogfish was 89 oysters per square meter; the figure jumped to 163 in 2017.

As we walked along, I felt guilty stepping on the oysters. "Yes, we are walking on a living structure, but that's what we are trying to get to," said Betsy. "To most eyes, this may look like mud and shells, but it's very significant to have reestablished this community." Before they began, Dogfish Bay had been a muddy, boot-sucking expanse mostly devoid of visible life forms. Now, it had a three-dimensional habitat of living and dead organisms, the Olympia oyster adult population was becoming denser, and larvae were spreading. In addition to their work at Dogfish Bay, PSRF and a group of collaborators have restored Olys to fifty-seven acres in the Sound, including Port Gamble Bay, Fidalgo Bay, Liberty Bay, and Squaxin Island. Additional funding will allow them to expand into Sinclair Inlet and Dyes Inlet.

If the historical harvesting of Olympia oysters characterized the exploitative manner in which early generations of Puget Sound residents regarded natural resources, and if geoduck harvesting is more in line with modern concerns about sustainability, fragility, and protection, the work of PSRF and others who focus on restoration work within the Sound illustrates a third way to view resources. In addition to sustaining what we have, they are working to restore what has been lost. For Betsy and many people like her, focusing on restoration provides an essential link between the past and the future. "Olympia oysters represent a historical abundance in a place that fed people for generations," said Betsy. "Yes, the habitat has dwindled, but that abundance can inspire us as we work toward a goal of restoration."

She knows that Puget Sound's Olympia oysters will never return to pre-1860 conditions, but she believes we can still work to make the native oysters part of our living shorelines once again. In some places, particularly in Hood Canal, they have begun to return on their own. And when the Swinomish have established their clam gardens, the connections between past and present and community and culture will be further strengthened and spread.

By returning foods such as Olympia oysters to Puget Sound, Betsy and others focused on restoration are not only helping to restore habitat, they are helping to restore community. They are sowing reminders of the past, of stories, and of long-standing connections to place through local foods, all of which build resilience and offer hope for those who use that knowledge to try to create a better future.

Although Olympia oysters are not yet abundant enough to harvest, Betsy told me that it gives her a sense of security and a great feeling of hope to know that she lives in a place that can still feed her. In Betsy's worldview, which I am guessing many people share, harvesting shellfish is one of the classic Puget Sound experiences. Indeed, of the many natural resources in the waterway, few are as accessible as oysters and clams and mussels. Nor do many other resources give you the special opportunity of ingesting the essence of the Sound, its water, its sediments, and the deep history of evolution embodied in these delicious bivalves. When the tide is out, the table will be set.

10

᛫Homebodies

Like many residents of Puget Sound, I grew up surrounded by images of salmon and orca. I learned about them in grade school, saw them countless times in advertisements, and read about them in the newspaper. I worried about them and wondered if they would survive what we had done to Puget Sound. But it wasn't until I worked on this book that I learned what seems to be an often overlooked aspect of their lives: they are homebodies.

Used by some as a pejorative term to describe the less adventurous, *homebody* also conveys a sense of belonging, of being placed where one feels whole, has connections, and has established enduring relationships and ways of living. Salmon and orca are indeed wanderers, well known for their long-distance travels, but they always return to Puget Sound. The southern resident orca's home base is the San Juan Islands, where they exploit the unique subsurface topography to hunt for salmon. And, they don't arrive randomly; their arrival occurs at precisely the time when Chinook salmon, their favorite food, are at maximum abundance.

Salmon are even more focused when they return home. As the ecologist Phil Levin told me, "Salmon are very narcissistic. It's all about their stream."[1] After swimming for thousands of miles on an ocean journey lasting several years, salmon follow the Earth's magnetic field and chemical clues back to the Sound and their natal stream. They then work their way upriver, find a suitable spot, spawn, and die, completing one of Puget Sound's most essential circles of life.

This long-term dance of salmon and orca with their homewaters began roughly fifteen thousand years ago, when the Sound first became an inland arm of the Pacific Ocean. Although researchers don't know what orca ate when they first arrived here, they hypothesize that they began eating salmon in response to a need for an abundant, easily accessible, highly nutritious meal. (The food preferences of orca rival human idio-syncrasies: one group prefers penguins, another specializes in minke whales, some relish Pacific sleeper sharks, some focus on herring, and an Argentinian population of orca beach themselves to hunt elephant seals.) After the first Puget Sound orca developed a taste for salmon, parents taught it to their offspring, leading to a hunting technique specifically adapted to the local geology and ecology. No other population of orca outside the Salish Sea has the same adaptations as the southern residents.

Some researchers further suggest that this population's preferential consumption of Chinook salmon (the recommended daily allowance of salmon for an adult male orca is about 325 pounds) may have an evolu-tionary effect on behavior. When juvenile orca learn to hunt for salmon from their parents, it solidifies their membership in a community with unique social structures, morphology, and behavior, and reduces inter-action with other groups. This is the situation with the southern resident orca and another local ecotype, known as transient orca, which neither mingle nor interbreed. Over time, the reproductive isolation of the resi-dent orca could result in the evolution of a new species.

At present these two groups of orca, the residents and the tran-sients, coexist within the Sound, though with opposite population trends. From 1975 to 1990, the West Coast population of transient orca annually increased about 10 percent, though its growth has subsequently slowed to about 2 percent. The most recent status report estimated that there were more than five hundred individuals, which is probably at the limit of the carrying capacity for the ecosystem, though not all of these animals make their way into Puget Sound during their travels between southern California and southeastern Alaska.

In contrast to the transients, the southern residents' population was down to only seventy-three individuals in December 2019, the lowest number in more than three decades. Divided into the J, K, and L pods, which consist of extended family groups that stay together for their entire lifetimes and are led by matriarchal females, they also migrate between Alaska and Canada and reside primarily in the Salish Sea from late spring through fall. The southern resident population suffered greatly in the 1960s and early 1970s from the demand for the capture of live individu-als for aquariums. In one disturbing and unregulated event in Penn Cove, on the east side of Whidbey Island, some forty orca were netted. As the public watched, many orcas died and many more suffered as the nets separated the tightly knit, highly social family groups. By the time live capture was banned in 1977, more than three hundred orca had been caught in the Salish Sea. Of the forty-seven Puget Sound orca that ended

On August 8, 1970, Seattle Marine Aquarium owner Ted Griffin and his partner Don Goldsberry organized a roundup and capture of orcas at Penn Cove, trapping between ninety and one hundred animals. Four babies died. At the time, no regulations existed for whale captures. (Courtesy of the Orca Network)

up in aquariums, only one, Lolita, remains alive, trapped in her tank at Miami's Seaquarium.

With the banning of live capture, the southern resident population began to rebound, reaching a peak in 1995 of ninety-eight orca. Its steady descent since then led in 2005 to the federal listing of the southern residents as an endangered species. In contrast, the northern resident orca, which live primarily around northern Vancouver Island and southeast Alaska and have a similar salmon-based diet, have more than doubled in number since 1974, and the population now stands at 309 individuals. The main difference is that their environment is far more intact, with fewer people, less vessel traffic, fewer pollutants, and abundant salmon. In 2008, federal biologists released an orca recovery plan that called for cleanup of pollutants and contaminants, stricter guidelines for commercial and recreational whale watching, abatement of vessel noise, and habitat improvement. These recommendations were echoed by those of the Southern Resident Orca Task Force in 2019. Both plans also emphasized the recovery of salmon, particularly Chinook.

Like orca, the Puget Sound Chinook salmon have adapted superbly to the waterways' unique ecosystem during the fifteen thousand years they have lived here, traveling from their birth stream through the deltas to protected shorelines and out to the Pacific Ocean. In the past, when they returned from their one- to five-year adventure north along the Canadian coast, Chinooks, also known as kings or tyees (a Chinook Jargon term meaning "chief"), could weigh more than 125 pounds and reach a length of five feet, though on average they came home at a more svelte 40 pounds.

Within the Sound, all of these habitats were once abundant. Along the shores of the many rivers, dense stands of trees provided shade and stabilized stream banks. Trees that fell into the water created calm pools and logjams. The logjams further enhanced the riparian ecosystem by moderating water velocity and sediment movement, thus creating good spawning areas. Out on the deltas and shorelines, washed-up logs accumulated and provided similar benefits. Abounding in the nearshore area were great schools of forage fish—herring, sand lance, and surf smelt— that also exploited the shelter offered by kelp forests and eelgrass beds. Bordering the Sound and providing additional habitat were more than one hundred square miles of wetlands. And when the salmon died after spawning, sea-derived nutrients in their bodies became sustenance for land and river dwellers.

Unfortunately, Puget Sound's Chinook salmon share another characteristic with the southern resident orca. In 1999, all the naturally spawned populations found in streams and rivers that flow into the Sound and the Strait of Juan de Fuca, from the Elwha River eastward, were listed as threatened under the Endangered Species Act. Biologists cited three main factors for the Chinook's steep population decline: habitat degradation, unsustainable harvesting, and the negative influence of hatcheries. In the years since, climate change and poor ocean conditions, such as rising temperature, altered salinity, and declining prey availability, have had further negative effects.

It is the inextricable links to each other and to the Puget Sound ecosystem that I have found most compelling about southern resident orca and Chinook salmon. Through their complementary evolution, these homebodies have forged relationships that have allowed them to thrive for thousands of years. By better understanding these relationships between wild species and place, we strengthen our connections to our homewaters and to those other species that live below the beautiful blue surface of the Sound. In addition, if we want to work toward the restoration of a sustainable Puget Sound, we are surely going to have to understand not only the relationships between these species but also the relationships between us and them.

· · ·

As indicated by the find of a 12,500-year-old salmon bone at Bear Creek, people and salmon have a relationship that stretches back nearly to the origin of Puget Sound. One of the more unusual aspects of that relationship is how little effect the predator, people, had on the prey, salmon. The archaeological record shows that people everywhere have tended to deplete their food supplies. Probably the best-known example is the arrival of people in North America and the rapid extinction of charismatic megafauna such as camels, giant beaver, mammoths, mastodons, and saber-toothed cats. In contrast, despite their long-term mass harvesting of salmon, the people of the Salish Sea regulated their catch. Not only did they always take the same proportion of salmon relative to other fish, but they didn't turn to other food resources to supplement dwindling salmon populations. In other words, the Coast Salish residents harvested salmon sustainably throughout periods of social and environmental change during which they could easily have exhausted their main food resource.

The archaeologists Sarah Campbell and Virginia Butler assert that such consistency was a hallmark of the region's Indigenous people.[2] They write that although the early human population around the Salish Sea was tiny in comparison to today's, overexploitation of resources was a distinct possibility. Estimates suggest that the Northwest Coast had the second-highest population density in North America at European contact, which could imply consumption rates comparable to twentieth-century annual commercial salmon harvests. In addition, the weirs and traps on rivers that early fishers set up were so efficient that they could easily have destroyed a specific river run of salmon, particularly Chinook and sockeye. Expanding populations with highly skilled hunters typically result in unsustainable harvests.

Campbell and Butler conclude that food resources were not exhausted here as they were in many other regions because Coast Salish social "institutions, beliefs, and rituals," such as the first salmon ceremony, cultivated behavior that moderated the timing and extent of the salmon harvest.[3] These practices probably developed slowly, in tandem with population growth and environmental change over thousands years of residence in the Salish Sea. They were still the defining cultural characteristics of Coast Salish people when George Vancouver arrived in 1792 and remain so today.

Campbell and Butler argue that, as in so many other contexts, the history of salmon harvesting in Puget Sound offers lessons for the present. They recommend that modern salmon fisheries managers move away from "isolated technological fixes" and a single-minded focus on increasing salmon populations. Instead, managers should address the "broader social and ecological context of the problem," as well as making a "greater investment in activities that foster direct connections among people, fish, and other resources." One way to strengthen these cultural ties is to focus on urban streams and habitat recovery. When salmon find

Emma (Napoleon) Capoeman, Lizzie Capoeman, and Sarah Sotomish, date unknown, preparing to bake salmon over an open fire using ironwood sticks to splay out the fish. (Courtesy of the Suquamish Museum)

CHAPTER 10

a home in our neighborhoods, as they have done thanks to restoration efforts in several Seattle-area streams, people can have encounters with live salmon instead of merely consuming them at the dinner table or seeing them as a marketing icon. These relationships, the archaeologists contend, are essential to salmon recovery.[4]

· · ·

Throughout the time that people adapted to salmon in Puget Sound, the salmon were changing as well. Evolutionary biologists have concluded that by about six million years ago, the salmon genus *Oncorhynchus* had evolved into species such as pink, chum, and sockeye, but evolution did not stop there.[5] During the Pleistocene, particularly after the retreat of the Puget lobe and the formation of modern Puget Sound, flooding, landslides, and volcanic eruptions, as well as sea level rise and postglacial rebound, continued to create habitat change that forced salmon to adapt. The isolation, specialization, and genetic divergence that resulted ultimately led to the evolution of the modern salmon lineages.

The differences among the various lineages in the Sound include variations in the time they spend in river, estuary, and ocean waters, as well as the timing of their seasonal migrations. At one extreme are pink salmon, which migrate within a few days of emerging from their redd. They move rapidly from fresh- to saltwater, stay in the ocean for two years, and return to spawn between June and September. At the other end are Chinook, whose migratory patterns and life stages vary so much that it is hard to pin down exactly how long they may spend in any one place.

As with Puget Sound herring, rockfish, and Olympia oysters, the diverse life history of Chinook salmon confers resilience to ecological change and disturbance. If environmental conditions lead to the deaths of some fish in a population before they complete their life cycles, others, who migrate and reproduce at different times and in other conditions, may survive and maintain the population. In contrast, the resilience of pink salmon is based on their incredible fecundity, as well as their predilection, despite the general reputation of salmon as always returning to their natal stream, to stray and spawn in new territory.

These diverse behavior patterns are another example of the portfolio effect. Biologists argue that this has been central to salmon success throughout their existence. And, once again, the big question has to be asked about human impacts. Have their effects on salmon overwhelmed the resilience conferred by the portfolio effect? The NOAA fisheries biologist George Pess, who has studied salmon throughout the Pacific

Northwest, believes it is not too late. As an example, he cites how salmon with varying life histories have repopulated the Elwha River. Between 2011 and 2014, the National Park Service removed two dams on the river, which had been erected between 1914 and 1927, opening up more than seventy miles of riparian habitat. "This isn't the first time these fish have been bottlenecked by a barrier. They certainly were following the last ice age. They were able to return now because they have been doing this for thousands of years," says George.[6]

But he cautions that fisheries managers have to adapt as well. Instead of focusing simply on preserving the existing types of salmon populations, managers should think about preserving, enhancing, and restoring evolutionary processes as well. George recognizes that these are not easy processes to manage. Therefore, he and his colleagues have written, the best general strategy is to build it—or in some cases, destroy it—and salmon will come.[7] Remove culverts and dams. Replace agricultural and industrial lands with forests. Take out or set back levees and diking. Restore floodplain ecosystems. Reconnect habitats. Such conservation and restoration efforts will ultimately result in more natural evolutionary processes, which in turn will allow the natural resilience of salmon to drive successful restoration of their populations. "If we give the fish the chance, they can reawaken what they know. We just have to be better," says George.[8]

Perhaps nowhere is this focus on ecological processes and relationships better illustrated than with salmon hatcheries, a primary tool of Pacific Coast fisheries managers since the 1870s. The first to propose them was Spencer Baird, commissioner of fish and fisheries for the US Fish Commission, in an 1875 letter to the Oregon state legislature about Columbia River fisheries. Baird clearly stated that excessive fishing, dam building, habitat destruction, and stream pollution (primarily with industrial refuse) would drive salmon to extinction. In order that "this threatened evil [extinction] may be averted," he recommended laws to regulate when and how many salmon could be caught. Baird was skeptical of this approach, though, because regulations "cannot be enforced except at very great expense and with much ill feeling."[9]

"A still better procedure" would be "artificial multiplication of fish," which would "not only maintain the present supply of fish indefinitely, but . . . increase it if desired," he wrote.[10] Based on what Baird had seen at the first hatchery on the Pacific coast, which opened in 1872 on the McCloud River, north of Redding, California, he believed that human control of fishery production would be relatively inexpensive. More important, hatcheries would also be far more efficient at producing salmon than the natural spawning process was; managers would be able to propagate so many fish that no one would ever have to worry about the harm caused by dams, overfishing, or habitat degradation.

Within a decade of Baird's letter, fish propagation had become well established, and by the end of the century, it was central to salmon management in Washington and Oregon. Between 1896 and 1928, Washington State and federal hatcheries cranked out 4,458,052,578 salmon eggs, fry, fingerlings, and adults.[11] Yet these billions of salmon did not do what Baird had hoped. Within Puget Sound, salmon numbers kept falling, primarily because of the canning industry, the main consumer of the fish. What had begun in 1877 with a cannery at Mukilteo that produced 4,800 cases, each containing 48 one-pound cans of fish, peaked in 1913 as a major Puget Sound industry producing more than 2.5 million cases. Seven years later, the total pack had dropped to 168,306 cases.[12] In addition to fishing pressures, pollution from pulp mills and other sources, impairment of the hydrologic cycle through dams and irrigation, and habitat degradation all contributed to the long-term decline of salmon in Puget Sound.

John Cobb, the founder and director of the University of Washington's College of Fisheries, was one of the first to express his concerns with what he called the "almost idolatrous faith" in hatcheries. He wrote in a 1916 report: "While it is an exceedingly difficult thing to prove, the consensus opinion is that artificial culture does considerable good, yet the very fact that this can not be conclusively proven ought to be a warning to all concerned not to put blind faith in it."[13] In addition to citing bad practices such as damming and industrial pollution, Cobb asserted that the best way to conserve fisheries was to enact and enforce laws that allowed fish unmolested access to their spawning grounds.

Cobb may have been a lone voice in questioning hatcheries, but he was not alone in worrying about the impact of people on fish. Authors of state and federal fisheries commission reports from the 1890s onward consistently noted that unrestrained harvests could not continue without consequence. They understood that people also harmed salmon through actions that had no direct connection to harvesting. In order for salmon to thrive, they had to be able to complete their life cycle in clean, cold water, and the hydroelectric and natural-resource extraction industries seemed to be doing all they could to prevent this from happening.

Why did we allow all this damage to occur? Few people have written as effectively and forcefully about this issue as Jim Lichatowich. He worked as a salmon researcher for more than four decades before writing his landmark *Salmon without Rivers: A History of the Pacific Salmon*

Crisis, essential reading for anyone interested in the full story of salmon. (The other indispensable book is Bruce Brown's *Mountain in the Clouds: A Search for the Wild Salmon.*)[14] For Jim, the problem boils down to money and the commodification of salmon. Instead of concerning themselves with ecological processes and relationships, managers have instead focused on expanding fisheries and providing fish for sport, commercial, and subsistence interests.

Driving this entire economically based practice is the hatchery system. For almost 150 years, Baird's view has prevailed: artificial propagation of fish could always generate adequate salmon populations, regardless of anything humans might do to reduce their chances. By relying on hatcheries, managers could overlook environmental threats to salmon. According to Jim, it was wrong then, and it is wrong now, to try to substitute hatcheries for conservation.[15] If fisheries managers were correct, he asks, then why have salmon been extirpated from 40 percent of their range and barely survived in most of the remainder?

The problems of hatchery fish are many. They are smaller, less productive, more susceptible to disease, and more aggressive toward other salmon, yet also less likely to evade predators. They also compete with wild salmon for limited food resources and can dilute or eliminate valuable genetic traits by breeding with wild fish. And numerous studies have shown that hatchery fish can reduce the abundance of wild salmon in stocked streams. But few problems trouble Jim more than the long-term disregard for salmon life histories and their unique adaptations to place. To managers, salmon were viewed as industrial parts that could be interchanged at random and fit into any niche: an egg from an Alaskan sockeye could be raised at a hatchery in Oregon and released as a fry in a Washington stream. In the end the result was the same—salmon begat salmon—and that was what mattered. To be fair, writes Jim, early hatchery operators did not understand the importance of life histories, but subsequent generations of managers, despite better information, failed to adequately assess and evaluate the effects of swapping salmon around without consideration of geography and ecology. Nor have they implemented the recommendations offered by more recent studies. "My feeling is that they have been generally ignored," he says.

Jim believes that hatcheries managers don't fully acknowledge the complexities of salmon and their adaptation to place. "They claim with more research to be able to produce a 'wild salmon,' but that's an impossibility. Wild salmon are the product of a huge range of environmental relationships, some good and some bad, and hatcheries cannot duplicate these relationships. Yes, they have made improvements in hatcheries, but they are mostly doing a better job of something we shouldn't have done in the first place, focusing on economics at the expense of conservation," he says. He worries about the future, too. Citing a 1987 Oregon Department of Fish and Wildlife study that showed far lower survival rates for hatchery fish relative to wild ones following a change in ocean conditions, Jim told me that this is an "indication that we can't rely on hatchery fish to bring salmon through climate change. The only hope is to have populations with diverse life histories."

Jim acknowledges that hatcheries can sometimes benefit salmon populations, but only in unusual situations. Specifically, he cites a project on the Columbia River run by the Wild Fish Conservancy, where an experimental fish trap allowed the selective harvest of hatchery fish and the release of wild ones. The project was similar to Kelly Andrews's study to reduce bycatch of rockfish, looking at ways techniques and technology might be used to preserve threatened species.

Hatcheries can be part of the tool kit of change but not the central tool. In taking this tactic, writes Jim, managers must prioritize a conservation-based approach that addresses ecosystem relationships throughout the entire life cycle of salmon, from natal stream to estuary to ocean and back. By definition, this approach requires addressing problems ranging from overfishing to dams to pollutants to habitat degradation.

Such fundamental changes in management are not new ideas: researchers have recognized them for decades. But putting them into effect is going to require a long-term vision and commitment, says Jim. More and more though, biologists emphasize that for salmon conservation efforts to succeed, they must acknowledge and promote genetic and life-history diversity, the singular factors that have given salmon resilience for thousands of years.

• • •

Life-story diversity has also been critical to the relationship between salmon and the southern resident orca. During the thousands of years that they have cohabitated in the Sound, orca have evolved to favor Chinook, but their feeding patterns and preferences are complex. Orca don't feed in a single location at any given time of year; nor do they repeat their previous year's menu preferences. And the timing and patterns of Chinook migration also vary. Orca will eat chum, coho, steelhead, pink, and the occasional sockeye salmon as well as Chinook: as one biologist told me, "Orca don't have a refrigerator, so they eat what is around them." Put another way, the southern residents have evolved to take advantage of the diverse life histories of different salmon species and stocks. It's a classic example of the portfolio effect of not limiting yourself to a single resource.

In Puget Sound, moreover, we have two orca populations with very distinct life-history traits. The more celebrated southern residents are known for their appetite for salmon, complex dialect, and large matrilineal pods. The transients eat marine mammals exclusively, tend to be more socially fluid, hunt in small groups, and rarely vocalize when hunting.[16] Transients also have a much higher toxic load because of their diet of seals and sea lions; the toxins bioaccumulate in the mammals from their diet of herring and, to a lesser degree, salmon.

In recent years, biologists have come to realize that the label *transient* is misleading, implying that these orca are comparable to well-regarded, out-of-town family members who drop in for a visit, grab a meal, and subsequently head back to their own haunts. Transients are no less local than the southern residents and no less important to the health of the ecosystem: they simply evolved to eat a less culturally and ecologically renowned food and have most likely been swimming into Puget Sound for as long as it has existed. Both groups are skilled, top-tier predators who not only feed in Puget Sound but also grace our waters with their beauty and intelligence.

As in so many situations, we didn't have the knowledge to understand the differences between the two ecotypes until very recently. The orca researcher Ken Balcomb, who has been a leader in identifying local orca from photographs, has said that if he started his identification project now, he'd probably label the transients as the residents, because they are around more often. Reflecting their better understanding of the two ecotypes, researchers have now started to refer to the transients as Bigg's orca, in honor of Michael Bigg, who did pioneering studies on the local orca populations before he died in 1990.

One notable aspect of our understanding of Bigg's orca is our relationship with their mammalian food base of harbor seals, Steller sea lions, and California sea lions (collectively called pinnipeds, meaning "flipper footed"). Historically, Puget Sound's commercial fishers didn't like these sleek fish eaters, which led to the state establishing a three-dollar bounty per pinniped.[17] In an early and prescient study of harbor seals in 1944, the biologists Victor Scheffer and John Slipp wrote about these killings. "Blame for the decline in a local fishery is often directed at the harbor seal, whereas it rightfully belongs to selfish or thoughtless practices of man, such as overfishing, the damming of streams, pollution by industrial wastes, and so on."[18]

Pinnipeds continued to suffer until 1972 and the signing of the Marine Mammal Protection Act (MMPA), which prohibited the taking of all marine mammals in US waters. Since then, Washington's seal population has ballooned from around five thousand to more than thirty thousand, though it appears to have leveled off or declined since 2000. Within Puget Sound proper, the most recent surveys have found about three thousand seals. (The sea lion population totals about 2,500 for the entire state.) With increased food resources, numbers of Bigg's orca increased; in 2017, observers reported a record number of them in the Salish Sea.

To mix a metaphor, seals and sea lions have again become scapegoats in Puget Sound. To some, the increased population of these mammals represents a threat to Chinook salmon. They point to studies showing that harbor seals' consumption of Chinook increased from 68 to 625 metric tons between 1970 and 2015, or roughly twice what the southern resident orca consume and six times the average annual haul of commercial and recreational fisheries. Because of these numbers and the seals' preference for Chinook smolt, there has been a push to return to the historical solution of culling.

If culling were permitted—various groups are looking at ways to get special permission to circumvent the MMPA—what would happen to the Bigg's orca? Researchers have a strong idea: by the end of the long era of killing seals and sea lions to protect the salmon fishery, the Bigg's population was drastically reduced. "One problem is that everyone's baseline comes from when we were shooting the seals and sea lions," says Joe Gaydos of the SeaDoc Society. "No one knows what is a normal population and what their effect would be on the salmon." At a May 2019 workshop that brought together salmon and pinniped scientists and managers from around the Salish Sea, the researchers noted that they had made considerable advancement in understanding how pinnipeds affect the ecosystem but still had many unanswered questions. Were their pinniped population estimates accurate? Were pinnipeds merely opportunists responding to the teeming pulses of hatchery fish, who would turn elsewhere if they had other choices? Would some other predator fill the gap if harbor seals were somehow eliminated? Without the answers to basic questions such as these, providing good management recommendations will be problematic.

Although our lack of knowledge about pinnipeds and a host of other organisms may impede the finding of innovative, science-based solutions to restoring salmon and orca, it should not prevent us from acting. We know what the broad solutions are to the present situation in the Sound.

Biologists have been listing them since the time of Spencer Baird. Don't take too much. Don't degrade habitat. Don't pollute the water. Stop the waste. Be responsible.

Sadly, for an equally long time, people have been ignoring these admonitions. We have continued to build dams that prevented fish from reaching their natal streams, dumped all manner of industrial, personal, and agricultural contaminants into streams and the Sound, and harvested salmon, and herring, rockfish, and Olympia oysters, as if the supply were endless. Following decades of human population growth and shrinking animal and plant populations, the results are as clear and as utterly predictable as when Baird wrote of "this threatened evil" of extinction nearly 150 years ago.

If we won't listen to the human experts, perhaps we will listen to Tahlequah and her family of southern resident orcas and to countless other species making similar, though less well-heeded, calls. Their collective chorus is sounding a clear alarm. We need to figure out what direction we want to go: Is Puget Sound a place whose society matches its scenery, in which its residents collaborate and make the hard choices on moving forward on restoration and sustainability, or is it a society that follows its worst instincts from the past?

Anyone who has doubts as to whether restoration can work can draw inspiration from what has happened when we have focused on environmental needs and not on economic ones. Probably the best-known example is salmon recolonizing the Elwha River watershed following removal of the Elwha and Glines Canyon Dams. This has further resulted in beavers returning to the river; the development of new, habitat-enhancing logjams; and record numbers of herring swimming in the river's mouth. Inspiration can be drawn, too, from the population increase among Pacific ocean perch after harvesting was stopped; from Dogfish Bay, where active restoration is making it possible for Olympia oysters to return and spread into their former habitat; and from legislation that has mostly ended the dumping of pollutants, such as sulfite waste liquor from pulp mills. In each situation, deep genetic memories and the resilience they confer are resulting in the recovery of plants and animals. I find it hard not to be inspired and cheered by such loyalty to place.

There is one central difference between the historical degradation of Puget Sound and the present situation: climate change and its influence on every aspect of the ecosystem. To name just a few of its effects, ocean acidification is leading to weaker shell construction in oysters. Warmer saltwater is restricting kelp growth, and warmer stream water is inhibiting salmon growth. Rising sea levels are increasing wave erosion, leading to degraded shorelines and intertidal habitat. Reduced snowfall limits water availability in streams.

The fact that the flora and fauna of Puget Sound have previously survived environmental upheavals does not mean that individual species will survive the present deviations or that the ecosystem has enough resilience to counter human actions. Climate change poses two unprecedented environmental challenges. The first is its rapid pace. In contrast to change on a geologic timescale, which afforded time for a commensurate evolutionary response in living creatures, the present round of climatic change is occurring on a human timescale. We don't know whether the local species can survive this collision of chronologies. The second is the problem of cumulative effects: as with the consequences of ocean acidification, some animals may be able to tolerate one change but not multiple changes. Although species can demonstrate amazing resilience, we may simply be piling up too many assaults against them.

Climate change certainly has the potential to overwhelm every human good intention in Puget Sound and to lead people to conclude that it is not even worth trying to address the complex issues that the Sound faces. But we cannot abrogate our responsibility to improve these homewaters. The issues are too important, the place too beautiful, the ecosystem too deserving. We owe it to our fellow residents to work toward a better future.

•　•　•

In the months following Tahlequah's period of mourning for her calf, it was clear that she had moved people to act. You could read it in online comments, hear it in the calls for action, see it in Governor Jay Inslee's establishment of the Southern Resident Orca Task Force. All of these responses were attempts to address our collective grief and, I think, to move toward healing the environment and our relationships with it and its denizens. Puget Sound residents know that this will be a long-term process requiring us to change our ways, to give up practices and objects we cherish, to spend vast amounts of money, and—perhaps hardest of all in this political climate, but also the most satisfying—to collaborate as a community.

At this moment of reckoning, when the fate of Puget Sound is in our hands, I am reminded of a conversation I had with Jamie Donatuto of the Swinomish Tribe and the Swinomish elder Larry Campbell. As we chatted, they kept returning to the theme of developing a sense of place through long-term cultural and social connections to the environment. In Jamie's work on sense of place, she has found that those connections motivate people to be more responsible. Her advice was simple: "Be present on the land. Engage with the goal of actually learning, and therefore caring about the place where you live. We have so many people moving here, if we cannot convince them that their actions have amplifying effects on everybody and everything else in the area, we're sunk."

Jamie is correct. Each of us plays a role in the future of Puget Sound and has the potential to create a positive legacy. Perhaps I am naive, but I believe that that potential resides in each of us, as surely as the geology and ecology of Puget Sound reside in the herring and geoduck and Olympia oysters and salmon and orca and rockfish that have passed on their innate connections to place for untold generations. If we can allow our relationship to Puget Sound to flourish, as the wilder species have done, then surely we can create a better future for all who live here.

ACKNOWLEDGMENTS

One of the great pleasures of writing a book is spending time talking to people about their fields of research. Even more fun is when they let me go out in the field with them. Fortunately for me, this book involved dozens of interviews and days of field time, during which I filled more than seven field notebooks. All the people below have brought their areas of research to life for me and helped me get to know Puget Sound, its history and science, and its connection to the greater world.

I sincerely thank each of you for your time. Please know that although I didn't include information from every interview, each of you helped shape this book. I couldn't have written it without you: Ken Ames, Bill Angelbeck, Kyle Antonelis, Joe Baar, Ken Balcomb, Russel Barsh, Kevin Bartoy, Dick Beamish, Brady Blake, George Blomberg, Dick Blumenthal, Matthew Booker, Randy Bouchard, Robert Boyd, Ray Buckley, Jeremy Buddenhagen, David Buerge, Kathryn Bunn-Marcuse, Virginia Butler, Meg Chardsley, Eric Cheney, Trevor Contreras, Claire Cook, Dale Croes, BJ Cummings, Joth Davis, Ryan Desrosiers, David Dethier, Megan Dethier, Robert De Wreede, Jon Erlandson, Tim Essington, Brian Ferguson, John Findlay, Tessa Francis, David Fyfe, David Giblin, Barry Gough, Dave Grant, Correigh Greene, Cheryl Greengrove, Courtney Greiner, David Hansen, Brad Hanson, Alexandra Harmon, Paul Hershberger, Ray Hilborn, Bob Hitz, Mark Holmes, John Incardona, Steven Jeffries, Orlay Johnson, Grant Keddie, Claire Keller-Scholz, Dorothy Kennedy, Terrie Klinger, Chris Krems, Phil Levin, Nate Mantua, Katherine Maslenikov, Mike McHugh, Kevin McNeel, Jay Miller, Kristen Munk, Nicole Naar, Jan Newton, Jay Orr, Wayne Palsson, George Pess, Ted Pietsch, Melissa Poe, Polly Rankin, Josh Reid, Jeff Rice, Jonathan Scordino, Dave Secord, Jamey Selleck, Anne Shaffer, Ole Shelton, Si Simenstad, Margaret Siple, Hugh Spitzer, Jodie Toft, Nancy Turner, Russ Vetter, Robin Waples, Jon Waters, James West, Chantel Wetzel, Todd Wildermuth, Greg Williams, Todd Woodard, Bill Woodward, and Sandy Wyllie-Echeverria.

I also extend an extra thank-you to those who took me out in the field or let me into their labs. It was an honor and pleasure to see you in your element: Brian Allen, Kelly Andrews, Julie Barber, Jennifer Blaine, Ben Budka, Henry Carson, Phill Dionne, Paul Dorn, Jacob Gregg, Micah Horwith, Lindy Hunter, Rick Keil, Bob Kopperl, Audrey Lamb, Shawn Larson, Dayv Lowry, James McArdle, Marsha Morse, Tom Mumford, Betsy Peabody, Dan Penttila, Eleni Petrou, Blain Reeves, Todd Sandell, Hugh Shipman, Bethany Stevick, Nick Tolimieri, Michael Ulrich, and Shina Wysocki.

I have also been fortunate to work with many people who provided images to me either at no cost or at reduced rates. I deeply appreciate your generosity: Becky Andrews, Bill Angelbeck, Mark Berhow, Jen Burke, Cherie Christensen, Terry Donnelly, Paul Dorpat, Roy Fletcher, Howard Garrett, Su Kim, Eben Lehman, Adam Lindquist, Beth Matta, Kevin McNeel, Marsha Morse, Tom Mumford, Laura Murphy, Matthew Parsons, Lydia Sigo, and Robert Warren.

During my years of writing, I have learned how easy it is to misinterpret, misread, or misrepresent what I have learned, so I am deeply appreciative to those who read chapters and checked for errors: Kelly Andrews, Helen Berry, Joe Gaydos, Bob Kopperl, Dennis Lewarch, Jim Lichatowich, Tom Mumford, Jennifer Ott, Laura Phillips, Todd Sandell, Richard Strickland, Coll Thrush, Dan Tonnes, and Brent Vadopalas. Any mistakes, of course, are mine.

I have also been fortunate to talk with many tribal members. I sincerely hope that I have been respectful in telling the stories I have been privileged to hear in our discussions and correspondence. Charlotte Basch (Puyallup), Will Bill Jr. (Muckleshoot), Jim Boure (Suquamish), Larry Campbell (Swinomish), Jamie Donatuto (Swinomish), Tony Forsman (Suquamish), Marco Hatch (Samish), Rosa Hunter (Jamestown S'Klallam), Bill James (Lummi), Tyler Johns (Squaxin), Warren King George Jr. (Muckleshoot), Danica Miller (Puyallup), Steven Mullen Moses (Snoqualmie), Adam Osbekoff (Snoqualmie), Joe Seymour Jr. (Squaxin), Lydia Sigo (Suquamish), and Zalmai Zahir (Sioux/Puyallup).

I live and work on the unceded land of the dxʷdəwʔabš (Duwamish) and Coast Salish peoples. I acknowledge and honor with gratitude the land itself and those who have inhabited it since time immemorial.

To the City of Seattle Office of Arts and Culture and 4Culture: Thanks for financial support. We are so blessed in this community to have public agencies that support artists and historians.

Thanks to my writer pals and good friends who always listened and offered sage advice: Tony Angell, Skip Berger, Lang Cook, Carol Doig,

Lyanda Lynn Haupt, John Horning, David Laskin, Lynda Mapes, Jeff Moline, Andy Nettell, Steve Olson, Jennifer Ott, the Unspeakables, Scott Wanek, and Emily White.

Thanks to the University of Washington Press for their ongoing support for me and their support of local writers through the Pacific Northwest Writers Fund, and especially to Erika Büky for her thoughtful copy editing and to Andrew Berzanskis for editing suggestions, words of encouragement, and keeping the process moving steadily forward.

To Marjorie Kittle: as you well know, I couldn't have done this without you.

NOTES

PREFACE

1 Lisa Benton-Short, *The Presidio: From Army Post to National Park* (Boston: Northeastern University Press, 1998), 4–5.

CHAPTER 1: BIRTH OF A NAME

1 T. T. Waterman, "The Geographical Names Used by the Indians of the Pacific Coast," *Geographical Review* 12, no. 4 (April 1922): 178.

2 T. T. Waterman, *Puget Sound Geography*, edited and with additional material from Vi Hilbert, Jay Miller, and Zalmai Zahir (Federal Way, WA: Lushootseed Press, 2001), 18–19.

3 This concept of saltwater versus freshwater is still relevant to Puget Sound residents. In 2017, I was on a boat with the sport fisherman Steve Kesling and biologists studying lingcod and rockfish. Several times during the day, Kesling mentioned "fishing on the salt." He was not referring to a specific location but rather drawing a contrast to the inland lakes and rivers and, by association, to freshwater fish.

4 Conversation with Warren King George Jr., October 5, 2017.

5 Waterman, "Geographical Names," s.v. "x̌ʷəlč," 185.

6 Conversation with Dennis Lewarch, January 4, 2017.

7 Edmond S. Meany, *Vancouver's Discovery of Puget Sound: Portraits and Biographies of the Men Honored in the Naming of Geographic Features of Northwestern America* (New York: Macmillan, 1907), 230.

8 Vancouver, quote in Meany, *Vancouver's Discovery*, 147.

9 Puget Sound Water Quality Authority, *Puget Sound Water Quality Management Plan* (Seattle: Puget Sound Water Quality Authority, 1987), 1–2.

10 Puget Sound Water Quality Authority, *Puget Sound Water Quality Management Plan*, xv.

CHAPTER 2: BIRTH OF A PLACE

1 Technically they are active volcanoes, meaning they have occasional seismic or geothermal activity or show evidence of eruptive activity in the past ten thousand years, though some are mostly dormant.

2 In contrast to their southern neighbors, which consist of glacially derived sediments less than two million years old, the San Juan Islands are made of

thin slivers of igneous, metamorphic, and sedimentary rock up to 540 million years old that were sutured onto the North American continent during plate tectonic collisions between 84 and 100 million years ago. One sign of this geology is that none of the southern islands rises more than 580 feet above sea level, whereas the San Juans top out at 2,407 feet on Mount Constitution, because of the harder rock.

3 Conversation with Richard Strickland, July 10, 2017.

4 If you have seen rising boils, or large, smooth, round bubbles of water, over the sills at Admiralty Inlet or the Tacoma Narrows, you have seen the turbulence causing the water to mix.

5 William W. Elmendorf and A. L. Kroeber, *The Structure of Twana Culture* (Pullman: Washington State University Press, 1992), 37.

6 Conversations with Hugh Shipman, October 27, 2016, and May 16, 2019.

CHAPTER 3: PEOPLING PUGET SOUND

1 My account is based on archaeological materials, as opposed to the oral histories, stories, and legends told by the Native people who inhabit Puget Sound. In these stories, the people have always been here: they did not migrate here from someplace else. I focus on the Bear Creek site because it is the oldest thoroughly excavated archaeological site in Puget Sound and the best scientific illustration of how people began to populate this region soon after the ice retreated.

2 By about 12,800 years ago, most of the great Pleistocene beasts were extinct in the Pacific Northwest. Columbian mammoths do not appear to have returned after the glacial retreat; the youngest fossil remains for them come from Victoria, British Columbia, and are dated at 17,500 years before the present.

3 Robert E. Kopperl, ed., *Results of Data Recovery at the Bear Creek Site (45KI839), King County, Washington*, vol. 1 (Seattle: SWCA Environmental Consultants, 2016), 289.

4 Conversation with Robert Kopperl, May 12, 2017.

5 Arthur C. Ballard, "Mythology of Southern Puget Sound," *University of Washington Publications in Anthropology* 3, no 2 (1929): 74, 80. Ballard was an amateur anthropologist who collected these stories in the 1910s and 1920s.

6 Timothy J. Beechie, Brian D. Collins, and George R. Pess, "Holocene and Recent Geomorphic Processes, Land Use, and Salmonid Habitat in Two North Puget Sound River Basins," *Geomorphic Processes and Riverine Habitats* 4 (2001): 37–54.

7 Sarah K. Campbell and Virginia L. Butler, "Archaeological Evidence for Resilience of Pacific Northwest Populations and Socioecological System over the Last ~7,500 Years," *Ecology and Society* 15, no. 1 (2010), www.ecologyandsociety.org/vol15/iss1/art17. Elk and deer didn't disappear but became much less common.

8 One unique strategy developed by Coast Salish people in the Salish Sea and utilized in the San Juan Islands was reef net technology. A net was held between two canoes and anchored underwater by rocks in a path where salmon migrated.

9 The first quote is from Thomas Manby's journal, in *With Vancouver in Inland Washington Waters: Journals of 12 Crewmen, April–June 1792,* ed. Richard W.

Blumenthal (Jefferson, NC: McFarland, 2007), 194. The second quote is from Edmond S. Meany, *Vancouver's Discovery of Puget Sound: Portraits and Biographies of the Men Honored in the Naming of Geographic Features of Northwestern America* (New York: Macmillan, 1907), 124.

10 Vancouver, quoted in Meany, *Vancouver's Discovery*, 108.

11 Cole Harris, "Voices of Disaster: Smallpox around the Strait of Georgia in 1782," *Ethnohistory* 41, no. 4 (Autumn 1994): 618.

12 All quotes are from Samuel Purchas, *Hakluytus Posthumus; or, Purchas His Pilgrimes: Contayning a History of the World in Sea Voyages and Lande Travells by Englishmen and Others*, vol. 14 (New York: Macmillan, 1906), 415–18.

13 J. C. Beaglehole, *The Journals of Captain James Cook on His Voyages of Discovery*, vol. 3, part 1 (Cambridge: Cambridge University Press, 1967), cxxi (emphasis in original).

14 Barry Gough, *Juan de Fuca's Strait: Voyages in the Waterway of Forgotten Dreams* (Madeira Park, BC: Harbour, 2012), 93. Born in 1769, Frances Trevor Barkley was seventeen when she accompanied her husband on his expedition beginning in 1786. She became the first European woman to reach the shores of British Columbia, and the first woman to circumnavigate the globe as a woman; the Frenchwoman Jeanne Baret traveled the globe disguised as a man on Louis Antoine de Bougainville's expedition between 1766 and 1769.

15 George Vancouver, *A Voyage of Discovery to the North Pacific Ocean and Round the World*, vol. 1 (London: G. G. and J. Robinson, 1798), xviii.

16 Peter Puget, quoted in Blumenthal, *With Vancouver in Inland Washington*, 24.

17 Vancouver, quoted in Meany, *Vancouver's Discovery*, 157.

18 This species of lily was originally named *Hookera coronaria* but is now known as *Brodiaea coronaria*.

19 C. P. Newcombe, ed., *Menzies' Journal of Vancouver's Voyages: April to October, 1792* (Victoria, BC: William H. Cullin, 1923), 42, 40.

20 Vancouver, quoted in Meany, *Vancouver's Discovery*, 131.

21 Vancouver, quoted in Meany, *Vancouver's Discovery*, 137.

22 Puget, quoted in Blumenthal, *With Vancouver in Inland Washington*, 34, 36.

23 In contrast to present-day residents, who say they go "down" to Olympia and "up" to Port Townsend, Puget called the area around what is now Olympia the upper Sound. Most early visitors and settlers also thought of the Sound this way. They were not directionally challenged: they were viewing the landscape with a nautical mindset. Sailing south into Puget Sound takes you to the end, or upper reach, of the waterway.

24 Vancouver, quoted in Meany, *Vancouver's Discovery*, 137.

25 Vancouver, quoted in Meany, *Vancouver's Discovery*, 131; Archibald Menzies, quoted in Blumenthal, *With Vancouver in Inland Washington*, 74.

26 Menzies, quoted in Blumenthal, *With Vancouver in Inland Washington*, 87; Vancouver, quoted in Meany, *Vancouver's Discovery*, 155.

27 Menzies, quoted in Blumenthal, *With Vancouver in Inland Washington*, 85.

28 Menzies, quoted in Blumenthal, *With Vancouver in Inland Washington*, 83.

29 Menzies, quoted in Blumenthal, *With Vancouver in Inland Washington*, 85, 71, 85.

30 Puget, quoted in Blumenthal, *With Vancouver in Inland Washington*, 32.

31 Vancouver, quoted in Meany, *Vancouver's Discovery*, 128.

32 T. C. Elliott, "Journal of John Work, November and December 1824," *Washington Historical Quarterly* 3, no. 3 (July 1912): 198–228.

33 The most curious wildlife they found was a "shapeless animal with long toes joined together in the middle," or what we would call a sea star. John Work, quoted in Elliott, "Journal of John Work," 212.

34 Edmond S. Meany, ed., "Diary of Dr. W. F. Tolmie," *Washington Historical Quarterly* 23, no. 3 (July 1932): 224.

35 The HBC eventually formed the Puget's Sound Agricultural Company, which operated farms and ranches until 1870.

36 Richard G. Beidleman, "Early Fur Returns from the Pacific Northwest," *Journal of Mammalogy* 39, no. 1 (February 1958): 146.

37 George Simpson to John McLoughlin, July 10, 1826, and July 9, 1827, quoted in Barry Gough, "The Hudson's Bay Company and the Imperialism of Monopoly: A Review Article," *BC Studies* 18 (Summer 1873): 70–78. Although these observations predate the HBC's establishment of Fort Nisqually, the HBC had not changed its policies when it established itself in Puget Sound. Gough argues that the HBC's trading policy was to "insulate the [Columbia] river's north bank from traders and settlers." He further states that the HBC was not completely rapacious and did establish "quotas in order to protect the beaver," but their policy still focused on profits over the effects on the environment.

38 Alexandra Harmon, *Indians in the Making: Ethnic Relations and Indian Identities around Puget Sound* (Berkeley: University of California Press, 1998), 15.

39 Harmon, *Indians in the Making,* 43.

40 Augustus A. Gould, *United States Exploring Expedition, during the Years 1838, 1839, 1840, 1841, 1842, under the Command of Charles Wilkes, U.S.N.,* vol. 12 (Boston: Gould and Lincoln, 1862), 3.

41 William Tolmie to James Douglas, November 14, 1848, Journal of Occurrences 1846–1852, Box 2, Puget Sound Agricultural Company, Acc. 5033-001, University of Washington Special Collections, Seattle.

42 Robert E. Fricken, *The Forested Land: A History of Lumbering in Western Washington* (Seattle: University of Washington Press, 1987), 31.

43 David Michael Goodman, *A Western Panorama, 1849–1875: The Travel Writings and Influence of J. Ross Browne on the Pacific Coast, and in Texas, Nevada, Arizona and Baja California, as the First Mining Commissioner and Minister to China* (Glendale, CA: Arthur H. Clark, 1966), 58.

44 A. S. Mercer, *Washington Territory: The Great North-West, Her Material Resources, and Claims to Emigration* (Utica, NY: I. C. Childs, 1865), 17.

45 Jim Lichatowich, *Salmon without Rivers: A History of the Pacific Salmon Crisis* (Washington, DC: Island Press, 1999), 66.

46 Harris, *Voices of Disaster,* 618; Robert Boyd, in *Handbook of North American Indians,* ed. Wayne Suttles (Washington, DC: Smithsonian Institution, 1990), 135.

47 Harmon, *Indians in the Making,* 58.

48 Richard White, "The Treaty at Medicine Creek; Indian-White Relations on Upper Puget Sound, 1830–1840" (master's thesis, University of Washington, 1972), 52.

49 "Report of Mr. George Gibbs to Captain Mc'Clellan, on the Indian Tribes of the Territory of Washington, March 4, 1854," in I. I. Stevens, *Explorations and Surveys to Ascertain the Most Practicle and Economic Route for a Railroad from the Mississippi River to the Pacific Ocean, Report of Explorations for a Route for the Pacific Railroad, near the Forty-Seventh and Forty-Ninth Parallels of North*

Latitude from St. Paul to Puget Sound (Washington, DC: Government Printing Office, 1855), 423.

50 Report of the Commissioner of Indian Affairs, Accompanying the Annual Report of the Secretary of the Interior, for the Year 1858 (Washington, DC: Wm. A. Harris, 1858), 225.

51 J. Ross Browne, "Indian War in Oregon and Washington Territories," 35th Congress, 1st session, Ex. Doc. 38, House of Representatives, January 25, 1858, 4.

52 Harmon, Indians in the Making, 79.

53 Alexandra Harmon, "Lines in the Sand: Shifting Boundaries between Indians and Non-Indians in the Puget Sound Region," Western Historical Quarterly 26 (Winter 1995): 446.

54 Russel Lawrence Barsh, "Ethnogenesis and Ethnonationalism from Competing Treaty Claims," in The Power of Promises: Rethinking Indian Treaties in the Pacific Northwest, ed. Alexandra Harmon (Seattle: University of Washington Press, 2008), 217.

55 Clarence B. Bagley, "Transmission of Intelligence in Early Days in Oregon," Quarterly of the Oregon Historical Society 12, no. 4 (December 1912): 356.

56 These figures are based on census data from 1860 and 1890 for counties bordering greater Puget Sound.

CHAPTER 1: DEFENDING PUGET SOUND

1 Peter Puget, quoted in Bern Anderson, "The Vancouver Expedition: Peter Puget's Journal of the Exploration of Puget Sound, May 7–June 11, 1792," Pacific Northwest Quarterly 30, no. 2 (April 1939): 177–217.

2 Paul Kane, Wanderings of an Artist (London: Longman, Brown, Green, Longmans, and Roberts, 1859), 232.

3 Edward Curtis, The North American Indian, vol. 10, The Kwakiutl (Seattle: Edward Curtis, 1915), 98.

4 R. Brian Ferguson, Warfare, Culture, and Environment (Orlando, FL: Academic Press, 1984), 309. In contrast to Puget Sound, northern Indigenous people did have chiefs.

5 Ferguson, Warfare, Culture, and Environment, 5.

6 Conversation with Brian Ferguson, December 18, 2017.

7 Bill Angelbeck, "Conceptions of Coast Salish Warfare, or Coast Salish Pacifism Reconsidered: Archaeology, Ethnohistory, and Ethnography," in Be of Good Mind: Essays on the Coast Salish, edited by Bruce Granville Miller (Vancouver, BC: UBC Press, 2007), 260.

8 Alan Lyle Bryan, "An Archaeological Survey of Northern Puget Sound," Occasional Papers of the Idaho State University Museum 11 (1963): 76.

9 Kenneth D. Tollefson, "In Defense of a Snoqualmie Political Chiefdom Model," Ethnohistory 43, no. 1 (Winter 1996): 155.

10 Bryan, "An Archaeological Survey," 79.

11 Coll Thrush, Native Seattle: Histories from the Crossing-Over Place (Seattle: University of Washington Press, 2007), 220.

12 Donald Mitchell, "Predatory Warfare, Social Status, and the North Pacific Slave Trade," Ethnology 23 (1984): 39–48. Mitchell recognized that potlatches predated the monetizing of slaves. He wrote that accumulating goods for a

potlatch could take years, "but it is clear from our sources that at least some leaders shortened the process considerably through predation" (40–41).

13 Ferguson, *Warfare, Culture, and Environment*, 269; Jeremy Buddenhagen, "Tsemsyaenhl-get: Sixteen Battles in the Military History of the Nine Allied Tsimshian Tribes" (master's thesis, University of Victoria, 2017), 183.

14 June McCormick Collins, "Growth of Class Distinctions and Political Authority among the Skagit Indians during the Contact Period," *American Anthropologist* 52, no. 3 (July–September 1950): 337.

15 Herbert C. Taylor Jr., "The Fort Nisqually Census of 1838–1839," *Ethnohistory* 7, no. 4 (Autumn 1960): 406.

16 Robin Fisher, *Contact and Conflict: Indian-European Relations in British Columbia, 1774–1890*, 2nd ed. (Vancouver, BC: UBC Press, 1992), 16.

17 Edmond S. Meany, *Vancouver's Discovery of Puget Sound: Portraits and Biographies of the Men Honored in the Naming of Geographic Features of Northwestern America* (New York: Macmillan, 1907), 151.

18 Charles Wilkes, *Narrative of the United States Exploring Expedition during the Years 1838, 1839, 1840, 1841, 1842* (Philadelphia: Lea and Blanchard, 1845), 481.

19 Marian W. Smith, *The Puyallup-Nisqually* (New York: Columbia University Press, 1940), 151.

20 Conversation with Will Bill Jr., January 9, 2018.

21 Alexandra Harmon, *Indians in the Making: Ethnic Relations and Indian Identities around Puget Sound* (Berkeley: University of California Press, 1998), 37.

22 They are also known as the southern Kwakiutl, Lekwiltok, Euclataws, and yəkwiɬtax. The name *Laich-Kwil-Tach*, which I have substituted in the quotations, is the spelling in their own Kwak'wala language; hence they are considered to be Kwakwa̲ka̲'wakw people. Their home territory includes Quadra Island and the Campbell River on Vancouver Island. The story of the battle comes from a variety of sources, including Edward Curtis, *The North American Indian*, vol. 9, *Salishan Tribes of the Coast; The Chimakum and the Quilliute; The Willapa* (Seattle: Edward Curtis, 1913), 33–34; Bill Angelbeck and Eric McLay, "The Battle at Maple Bay: The Dynamics of Coast Salish Political Organization through Oral Histories," *Ethnohistory* 58, no. 3 (Summer 2011): 359–92; and William W. Elmendorf, *Twana Narratives: Native Historical Accounts of a Coast Salish Culture* (Seattle: University of Washington Press, 1993), 34–35.

23 Angelbeck and McLay, "The Battle at Maple Bay," 369.

24 Angelbeck reports that the poisons may have been extracts of human brains, though he adds that the knowledge of poisons was typically secret.

25 Curtis, *The North American Indian*, 34.

26 Elmendorf, *Twana Narratives*, 149.

27 Curtis, *The North American Indian*, 34.

28 Angelbeck and McKay, "The Battle at Maple Bay," 376.

29 Conversation with Will Bill Jr., January 9, 2018.

30 The colony of British Columbia was established in 1858 but did not include Vancouver Island until 1866. British Columbia became part of Canada in 1871.

31 Captain George Stoneman, a cavalryman, and Lieutenant W. H. C. Whiting of the Corps of Engineers made the most extensive survey. They make an interesting and exemplary pair of military men in Puget Sound. They graduated

from West Point a year apart, Whiting ranking first in his class in 1845 and Stoneman thirty-third in 1846. Stoneman's roommate was Thomas "Stonewall" Jackson. Whiting joined the Corps of Engineers and surveyed in Texas and the South. When the Civil War started, he quit the Corps and joined the Confederates. He died of dysentery in March 1865. Stoneman joined the cavalry and spent time in the American West and California. He, too, fought in the Civil War, for the Union, and was governor of California from 1882 to 1886. Stoneman might be best known from the Band's song "The Night They Drove Old Dixie Down": "Virgil Caine is the name, and I served on the Danville train/ Till Stoneman's cavalry came and tore up the tracks again."

32 Unless specifically stated, all military reports mentioned in this chapter appear in part or whole in the following summary document: *Letter from the Secretary of War, Transmitting, in Response to Senate Resolution of March 27, 1888, reports relative to Fortifications upon Puget Sound*, 50th Congress, 1st Session, Ex. Doc. No. 165 (Washington, DC: Government Printing Office, 1888).

33 *Letter from the Secretary of War*, 74.

34 Totten Inlet honors Totten's son George, a member of the Wilkes expedition.

35 Mary Margaret Thomas, "Science, Military Style: Fortifications, Science, and the U.S. Army Corps of Engineers, 1802–1861" (PhD diss. University of Minnesota, September 2002), 9.

36 *Letter from the Secretary of War*, 23.

37 *Letter from the Secretary of War*, 4.

38 "The Russian Purchase," *Daily British Colonist and Victoria Chronicle*, May 16, 1867, partially quoted in Barry M. Gough, *The Royal Navy and the Northwest Coast of North America, 1810–1914: A Study of British Maritime Ascendancy* (Vancouver, BC: University of British Columbia Press, 1971), 215.

39 *Letter from the Secretary of War*, 55.

40 *Letter from the Secretary of War*, 53.

41 *Letter from the Secretary of War*, 60.

42 *Letter from the Secretary of War*, 16.

43 *Letter from the Secretary of War*, 19. George Vancouver named Marrowstone Point because he thought the glacial sediments looked like "a rich species of marrow stone." Vancouver, quoted in Meany, *Vancouver's Discovery*, 99. He appears to have not known the correct usage of the term, as most people of the era preferred *stone marrow*, or *lithomarge*, an early name for soft, clay-like minerals formed by weathering.

44 House Memorial 8, "Praying for the Erection of Fortifications on Puget Sound," in *Laws of the Washington Territory Enacted by the Legislative Assembly, Tenth Biennial Session, 1885–6* (Olympia: Thomas H. Cavanaugh, 1886), 536.

45 Watson Squire (WA), "Fortification Appropriation Bill," *Congressional Record* 23, 6204 (July 15, 1892).

46 Gough, *The Royal Navy and the Northwest Coast*, 234.

47 Most of the details about the forts come from David M. Hansen's thoroughly researched *Battle Ready: The National Defense System and the Fortification of Puget Sound, 1894–1925* (Pullman: Washington State University Press, 2014).

48 Charles C. Morrison, *Modern Guns and Mortars*, Artillery Circular 1, Series of 1893, 1895 (Washington, DC: Government Printing Office, 1895), 196.

49 John Evans, "Worden, Casey and Flagler Form Trio of Grim Defenders," *Seattle Times*, July 27, 1913.

50 John W. Gulick, "Armor and Ships: A Brief Resume of Twenty Years' Progress and Its Effect on Coast Defenses," *Journal of the United States Artillery* 38, no. 3 (November–December 1912): 276.

51 Meany, *Vancouver's Discovery*, 89.

52 This would have been the total firing capacity, or weight of shells, if all the artillery at the three forts had been fired simultaneously (which never would have happened).

53 This conflict, known as the Pig War, centered on an American settler who killed a British pig. It escalated because of poor decisionmaking, particularly posturing by George Pickett, who posted a note claiming exclusive American jurisidiction. This provoked James Douglas, governor of the Crown Colony of British Columbia. Calmer leaders eventually settled the dispute without the use of force. Two years later, Pickett resigned his position to fight for the Confederacy in the Civil War.

54 William C. Endicott, *Report of the Board on Fortifications or Other Defenses Appointed by the President of the United States Under the Provisions of the Act of Congress* (Washington, DC: Government Printing Office, 1886), 11.

55 Like other dollar estimates, this figure is calculated from Measuringworth.com, using the economy cost valuation.

56 The US military still has a strong presence in Puget Sound, including navy facilities at Whidbey Island, Everett, Bremerton, and Indian Island, as well as the most daunting, Naval Base Kitsap, which is the third largest navy base in the United States and home to the country's third largest collection of nuclear weapons. The other large facility is Joint Base Lewis-McChord, south of Tacoma. What has changed is that none of these bases focuses on local protection. Instead, they are part of the US military's plans for protecting the entire country.

CHAPTER 5: THE MARITIME HIGHWAY

1 The US Coast Guard defines a ferry as a "vessel that is used on a regular schedule—(1) To provide transportation only between places that are not more than 300 miles apart; and (2) To transport only—(i) Passengers; or (ii) Vehicles, or railroad cars, that are being used, or have been used, in transporting passengers or goods."

2 These figures are based on the following ferry runs: Anderson-Ketron, 217,152; Bremerton Foot Ferries, 607,755; Decatur, 3,625; Guemes, 389,805; Hat, 12,211; Herron, 36,866; Jetty, 39,675; Lummi, 199,973; Vashon Water Taxi, 224,023; West Seattle Water Taxi, 375,931; Washington State Department of Transportation, 24,460,045.

3 The Herron and Hat Island folks were kind enough to let me on their ferries for the purposes of this book, but their services are private, and they generally don't let nonmembers on without permission.

4 John Rockwell, "Extracts from the Report of Sub-assistant John Rockwell, U.S. Coast Survey," *Report of the Superintendent of the Coast Survey, Showing the Progress of the Survey during the Year 1855* (Washington, DC: A. O. P. Nicholson, 1856), 174–75.

5 Donald G. Shomwell, *Shipwrecks, Sea Raiders, and Maritime Disasters along the Delmarva Coast* (Baltimore: Johns Hopkins University Press, 2007), 5.

6 Lester B. Knight and Associates, *Working Conditions Report*, September 19, 1971, 5. Held by the Maritime Museum, San Francisco.

7 Isaac I. Stevens, "Narrative and Final Report of Explorations for a Route for a Pacific Railroad near the Forty-Seventy and Forty-Ninth Parallels of North Latitude from St. Paul to Puget Sound, 1855," in *Reports of Explorations and Surveys, to Ascertain the Most Practicable and Economical Route for a Railroad from the Mississippi River to the Pacific Ocean*, vol. 12, book 1 (Washington, DC: Thomas H. Ford, 1860), 281.

8 Bill Durham, *Indian Canoes of the Northwest* (Seattle: Copper Canoe Press, 1960), 39.

9 John Meares, *Voyages Made in the Years 1788 and 1789, from China to the North West Coast of America* (London: Logographic Press, 1791), 156.

10 Richard Blumenthal, *Charles Wilkes and the Exploration of Inland Washington Water: Journals from the Expedition of 1841* (Jefferson, NC: McFarland, 2009), 12.

11 The painting is usually on display at the Seattle Art Museum.

12 T. T. Waterman and Geraldine Coffin, "Types of Canoes on Puget Sound," *Indian Notes and Monographs* (New York: Museum of the American Indian, 1920), 14, 15. The Bierstadt painting is at the Rainier Club, a private club in Seattle. The date when it was painted is unknown. The Nootkan style of canoe was also known as a Chinook or Tsimshian canoe.

13 Waterman and Coffin, "Types of Canoes," 17; Marian W. Smith, *The Puyallup-Nisqually* (New York: Columbia University Press, 1940), 289.

14 Smith, *Puyallup-Nisqually*, 289. I have not found any other report that describes canoe use by women, but, as one cultural historian said to me, "Most early ethnographic reports weren't written by women."

15 Ben Fitzhugh and Junko Habu, eds., *Beyond Foraging and Collecting: Evolutionary Change in Hunter-Gatherer Settlement Systems* (New York: Kluwer Academic, 2002), 32.

16 Waterman and Coffin, "Types of Canoes," 22.

17 This comparison is based on an average flow rate of 85,000 cubic feet per second at Niagara Falls and a volume of 1.26 cubic miles of water entering the Sound at high tide.

18 Noel McGary and John H. Lincoln, *Tide Prints: Surface Tidal Currents in Puget Sound* (Seattle: University of Washington Press, 1977). McGary and Lincoln based their work on a 1:40,000 scale model of the Sound built out of concrete in 1950 and still in use today. The model uses a plunger to accurately simulate tides. Dyes added to the water indicate saltwater and freshwater flows and allow an easy way to see tidal movement at the surface and along the bottom.

19 Natalie Andrea Roberts, "A History of the Swinomish Tribe" (PhD diss., University of Washington, 1975), 30.

20 Often listed as the first steamer in the Pacific Ocean, the *Beaver* was in fact preceded by the *Rising Star* (1822) and *Telica* (1825), which operated in South America; the *Forbes* (1830) and *King-fa* (1832) in China; and the *Sophia Jane, Surprise*, and *William the Fourth* in Sydney, Australia, in 1831.

21 Sir George Simpson, *Narrative of a Journey round the World during the Years 1841 and 1842* (Philadelphia: Lea and Blanchard, 1847), 112.

22 *Columbian*, November 19, 1853. At the time, both Seattle and Alki (or Alki Point, as it is generally now known), were considered to be two separate settlements.

23 *Pioneer and Democrat* (Olympia), April 29, 1854.

24 Gordon R. Newell, *Ships of the Inland Sea: The Story of the Puget Sound Steamboats* (Portland, OR: Binfords and Mort, 1951), 10.

25 *Pioneer and Democrat*, September 16, 1854.

26 Newell, *Ships of the Inland Sea*, 79. The boat was the *Capital*. Heading across the tide flats at Olympia, the wooden scow appeared ready to explode because of a lack of water in the boiler, so the captain abandoned the flat-bottomed vessel, which continued forward of its own accord. It eventually beached itself, but the side wheel kept spinning and propelled the *Capital* through the mud until it hit pilings and finally ran out of steam pressure.

27 Jim Faber writes in *Steamer's Wake* (Seattle: Enetai, 1985) that the "accepted version" of the term comes from a newspaper article that refers to boats in Elliott Bay as a "swarm of mosquitos." I looked extensively in Seattle newspapers for this reference and never found it. That doesn't mean that someone long ago didn't use the phrase, but I suspect this origin story is apocryphal.

28 Baar has acknowledged that his list was not complete, though he doubted that there were 2,500 boats in the fleet. Correspondence with Joe Baar, October 3, 2017.

29 The *Old Settler* eventually decayed on the tide flats under a Seattle wharf. Its engine was taken out to power a printing press.

30 Hazel Heckman, *Island in the Sound* (New York: Ballantine, 1969), 112.

31 Email correspondence with Joe Baar, October 19, 2017.

32 Ida and Vern Bailey, *A Scrapbook of History: Brinnon* (Bremerton, WA: Perry, 1997), 21.

33 The *Admiral Pete* also makes a run between Annapolis and Bremerton. The Annapolis dock is merely a long pier jutting into Sinclair Inlet, about a mile east of Port Orchard's dock. You walk down it, the boat pulls up, you get on, and it returns to Bremerton. That process is how I envision how most people interacted with the innumerable small mosquito-fleet vessels: simple and practical.

34 The city of Benicia, California, purchased the *City of Seattle* in 1913 for the Benicia-to-Martinez ferry run east of San Francisco. It operated through World War II before ending up in Sausalito, where it is now a boutique lodging. In 1906, the *State of Washington* became the first ferry to carry an automobile—a Stanley Steamer—according to M. S. Kline and G. A. Bayless, *Ferryboats: A Legend on Puget Sound* (Seattle: Bayless, 1983), 83.

35 Carolyn Neal and Thomas Kilday Janus, *Puget Sound Ferries: From Canoe to Catamaran* (Sun Valley, CA: American Historical Press, 2001).

36 Newell, *Ships of the Inland Sea*, 190.

37 Neal and Janus, *Puget Sound Ferries*, 82.

38 "Wallgren Taken in Ferry Trap," *Seattle Times*, October 16, 1948.

39 The state supreme court eventually decided that the state lacked the authority to sell bonds in order to purchase the Black Ball ferries.

40 "Ferries to Disappear from Sound—Langlie," *Seattle Times*, March 8, 1950.

41 Washington Toll Bridge Authority, *Report to the Governor and the State Legislature of the State of Washington on the Subject of Bridging Puget Sound in the Vicinity of Seattle*, Washington (Olympia, WA: State Printing Plant, December 1, 1952), 12. The numbers come from Measuringworth.com.

42 Washington Toll Bridge Authority, *Second Preliminary Report on the Engineering and Economic Phases of Bridging Puget Sound in the Vicinity of Seattle,*

Washington (Olympia, WA: State Printing Plant, February 7, 1951). As yet, no one has built such a tube anywhere in the world.

43 "Langlie Issues Statement on Ferry Purchase," *Seattle Times*, December 31, 1950.

44 The original Black Ball Line no longer exists. The present-day Black Ball ferry between Port Angeles and Victoria, BC, was formed from a subsidiary of the original Black Ball that was established in 1936.

45 "Langlie Issues Statement on Ferry Purchase."

46 Conversation with Marsha Morse, December 6, 2017.

47 Conversation with Will Bill Jr., January 9, 2018.

CHAPTER 6: FORESTS IN THE SOUND

1 Kelp occupies its own taxonomic order, Laminariales (meaning "flat blade"), which includes just under 150 species.

2 Conversation with Tom Mumford, June 24, 2017.

3 This is yet another sound named for a British explorer, Francis Barkley.

4 The species name honors the prolific kelp researcher William Setchell, a professor at the University of California, Berkeley, from 1895 to 1934. One of his principal specimen suppliers was Nathaniel Gardner, who, as a first-year schoolteacher on Whidbey Island, wrote to Setchell in 1897 about the local seaweeds "I understand you are interested in the marine flora of the Pacific coast. . . . Will you identify specimens if I will send some to you?" Letter from N. L. Gardner to W. A. Setchell, April 26, 1897, University of California, Berkeley, Jepson Herbaria. I am grateful to Tom Mumford for sharing a copy of this letter.

5 This is the lone species of kelp collected by Lewis and Clark, on the Washington side of the Columbia River mouth on November 17, 1805. A specimen of it is in the Lewis and Clark collection at the herbarium of the Academy of Natural Sciences at Drexel University in Philadelphia.

6 The scientific name is often translated as "mermaid's bladder," though a more mythologically correct name would be "sea nymph's bladder," as the Nereids, the daughters of Nereus, were nymphs, not mermaids. The species name *luetkeana* honors the Russian sea captain and explorer Friedrich Benjamin von Lütke (also written as Fëdor Petrovič Graf Litke), who led an Arctic expedition in 1826–28. In 1827, the expedition botanist, Karl Heinrich Mertens, created the new name "in honour of our worthy Commander, who daily shows himself more zealous in favouring our Natural History labours." "Two Scientific Botanical Notices by the late Dr. Henry Mertens," *Botanical Miscellany* 3 (1833): 1–11.

7 Recently Jonathan Scordino, a marine biologist for the Makah Tribe, compared fishing with čibu·d and fishing with contemporary hooks and found that using čibu·d led to more selective catching of halibut, an important consideration when trying to prevent bycatch of threatened species. The downside was that the halibut catch with čibu·d was smaller, but, as he told me, "The hook was just one part of the package of knowledge that would have been shared by fathers and grandfathers." Conversation with Jonathan Scordino, April 9, 2018. Such traditional ecological knowledge would have included where, when, and how to fish.

8 James Swan, "The Indians of Cape Flattery," *Smithsonian Contributions to Knowledge* 220 (1869): 40.

9 Nancy J. Turner, *Ancient Pathways, Ancestral Knowledge: Ethnobotany and Ecological Wisdom of Indigenous Peoples of Northwestern North America,* vol. 1 (Montreal: McGill-Queen's University Press, 2014), 370. One way to distinguish slaves from people of higher rank was that slaves never had deformed heads.

10 Boas also edited accounts collected by George Hunt that include an elaborate description of head binding and shaping. "The kelp head-band is kept on for twelve days at a time, until the girl is twelve months old. It is a little different when the child is a boy, for then the kelp head-band is tied for ten days, and is taken off after eight months." Franz Boas, "Ethnology of the Kwakiutl, based on data collected by George Hunt," *Bureau of American Ethnology, 35th Annual Report,* part 1 (1921): 671.

11 Franz Boas, "The Jesup North Pacific Expedition," *Memoir of the American Museum of Natural History,* vol. 5, part 2, edited by Franz Boas (New York: American Museum of Natural History, 1902), 405–7, 419.

12 Conversation with Jon Erlandson, March 22, 2018.

13 George Steller, who spent months studying his eponymous beast in the Arctic in 1741, described the sea cow as so docile that a "man could move about them without danger and select at ease the one of the herd he desires to strike." "De Bestiis Marinis, or, The Beasts of the Sea," translated by Walter and Jennie Miller, in David Starr Jordan, *The Fur Seals and Fur-Seal Islands of the North Pacific Ocean,* part 3 (Washington, DC: Government Printing Office, 1899), 198.

14 Jon M. Erlandson, Todd J. Braje, Kristina M. Gill, and Michael H. Graham, "Ecology of the Kelp Highway: Did Marine Resources Facilitate Human Dispersal from Northeast Asia to the Americas?," *Journal of Coastal Archaeology* 10, no. 3 (2015): 405.

15 Turner, *Ancient Pathways,* 74.

16 The spores bear hair-like flagella called flimmers, which aid in movement.

17 Conversation with Anne Shaffer, March 22, 2018.

18 Dorte Krause-Jensen and Carlos M. Duarte, "Substantial Role of Macroalgae in Marine Carbon Sequestration," *Nature Geoscience* 9 (October 2016): 737–43.

19 Jon Waters of the University of Otago in New Zealand, who was involved in the study, wrote to me that colonization could have taken place more recently, "though I suspect it was quite quick after the ice retreated." Email correspondence with Jon Waters, April 16, 2018; R. Nikula, C. I. Fraser, H. G. Spencer, and J. M. Waters, "Circumpolar Dispersal by Rafting in Two Subantarctic Kelp-Dwelling Crustaceans," *Marine Ecology Progress Series* 405 (April 2010): 221–30.

20 "Urchin Barrens: Aka the Trouble with Tribbles," Echinoblog, http://echinoblog .blogspot.com/2013/07/urchin-barrens-aka-trouble-with.html, accessed May 28, 2019. Craig R. Johnson, Sam C. Banks, Neville S. Barrett, Fabienne Cazassus, Piers K. Dunstan, Graham J. Edgar, Stewart D. Frusher, et al., "Climate Change Cascades: Shifts in Oceanography, Species' Ranges and Subtidal Marine Community Dynamics in Eastern Tasmania," *Journal of Experimental Marine Biology and Ecology* 400 (2011): 17–32.

21 Email correspondence with Joe Gaydos, October 2, 2019.

22 Charles Darwin, *The Voyage of the Beagle*, ed. Leonard Engel (New York: Doubleday, 1962), 240.

23 George Davidson to Alexander Bache, September 18, 1854, "Loose Papers Removed from 1851–1854 Letterbook," Bancroft Library, MSS C-B 490, carton 1, vol. 1. Emphasis in original.

24 Modern UCGS maps continue to depict kelp beds with squiggles.

25 Davidson to Bache, emphasis in original.

26 "Companies Will Develop Sound Potash Industry," *Seattle Times*, October 2, 1913.

27 Conversation with Betsy Peabody, July 16, 2018.

28 Conversation with Brian Allen, April 25, 2018.

CHAPTER 7: THE SILVER WAVE

1 Pacific herring, which inhabit the Pacific Ocean from southern California to Japan, are known scientifically as *Clupea pallasii*. The Latin word *clupeus*, meaning "shield," is a reference to the scales covering the body. Like many scientific names, this one has an international pedigree. The specimen that inspired the scientific name was collected in Kamchatka in the 1730s or 1740s, acquired by the German zoologist Peter Simon Pallas later in the century, and bequeathed on his death to his Swedish friend Karl Rudolphi. It was then given to the German director of the Berlin Zoological Museum, Martin H. C. Lichtenstein, who provided the fish to the French ichthyologist Achille Valenciennes, who finally published his description of it in 1847.

2 Conversation with Paul Hershberger, September 17, 2018.

3 Calanoid copepods are the preferred food of herring. With a torpedo-shaped body and gangly antennae often more than half the length of the body, these microscopic crustaceans may be the most numerous group of multicellular organisms on Earth.

4 Conversation with Tim Essington, March 29, 2017.

5 Conversation with Ole Shelton, March 16, 2017.

6 *Century Dictionary and Cyclopedia* (New York: Century, 1897), s.v. "snuff-taker."

7 Unlike salmon, female herring do not die after spawning and can lay eggs for many years. The figure of three hundred million is from A. S. Hourston and C. W. Baegele, "Herring on Canada's Pacific Coast," *Canadian Special Publications of Fisheries and Aquatic Sciences* 48 (1990): 5. Herring spawning numbers in the Sound are now far lower.

8 Throughout the British Isles, herring were long known as "silver darlings."

9 Erika K. Lok, Daniel Esler, John Y. Takedawa, Susan W. De La Cruz, W. Sean Boyd, David R. Nysewander, Joseph R. Evenson, and David H. Ward, "Spatio-temporal Associations between Pacific Herring Spawn and Surf Scoter Spring Migration: Evaluating a 'Silver Wave' Hypothesis," *Marine Ecology Progress Series* 457 (June 2012): 148.

10 Email correspondence with Jeff Rice, December 11, 2019.

11 A 1982 study in British Columbia estimated that a major storm had washed ashore eggs in densities of 152 million per cubic yard. D. E. Hay and D. C. Miller, "A Quantitative Assessment of Herring Spawn Lost by Storm Action in French Creek, 1980," *Canadian Manuscript Report of Fisheries and Aquatic Sciences* 1636 (1980): 3.

12 Some herring do not migrate, says Eleni Petrou. Carbon isotope analysis indicates that herring spawning near Port Orchard, Port Madison, and Squaxin Pass stay in the Sound, whereas the carbon signature of Quilcene Bay fish does not indicate whether they stay or travel out of the Sound.

13 John Keast Lord, *The Naturalist in Vancouver Island and British Columbia*, vol. 1 (London: Richard Bentley, 1866), 101.

14 Gregory G. Monks, "Prey as Bait: The Deep Bay Example," *Canadian Journal of Archaeology* 11 (1987): 119.

15 Iain McKechnie, Dana Lepofsky, Madonna L. Moss, Virginia L. Butler, Trever J. Orchard, Gary Coupland, Fredrick Foster, Megan Caldwell, and Ken Lertzman, "Archaeological Data Provide Alternative Hypothesis on Pacific Herring (*Clupea pallasii*) Distribution, Abundance, and Variability," *Proceedings of the National Academy of Science* 111, no. 9 (March 2014): E812.

16 Thomas F. Thornton, Virginia Butler, Fritz Funk, Madonna Moss, Jamie Hebert, and Tait Elder, *Herring Synthesis: Documenting and Modeling Herring Spawning Areas within Socio-ecological Systems over Time in the Southeastern Gulf of Alaska*, North Pacific Research Board Project 728 (Anchorage: North Pacific Research Board, June 2010), 49.

17 Robert E. Kopperl, "Herring Use in Southern Puget Sound: Analysis of Fish Remains at 45-KI-437," *Northwest Anthropological Research Notes* 35, no. 1 (Spring 2001): 6.

18 William W. Elmendorf and A. L. Kroeber, *The Structure of Twana Culture* (Pullman, WA: Washington State University Press, 1992), 38, 44, and 53.

19 The name Herring's House comes from interviews conducted in the early 1900s by T. T. Waterman. It is found in Coll Thrush, *Native Seattle: Histories from the Crossing-Over Place* (Seattle: University of Washington Press, 2007), 234.

20 Lord described "shoal after shoal" of herring entering traps set up on the mudflats of Puget Sound. He felt that the area was ripe for bountiful harvests for the right investor with "judiciously appl[ied] capital, skilled labour, and good management." Lord, *The Naturalist*, 103, 104, 106.

21 Elmendorf and Kroeber, *Twana Culture*, 76.

22 David M. Buerge, *Chief Seattle and the Town That Took His Name* (Seattle: Sasquatch, 2017), 16.

23 No discussion of herring would be complete without mentioning pickled herring and red herring. Classic pickled herring, long a staple food of European Jews, involves marinating the fish with raw onions in vinegar and sugar. The tradition continued when immigrants arrived in America. As with many familiar phrases, there is an energetic debate about the origin of the term *red herring* to designate a distraction or deception. Some people point to Thomas Nash's 1599 book *Nashes Lenten Stuffe*, where he wrote that a red herring was a strongly cured and smoked herring, next to which, "to draw on hounds to a scent, to a red herring skin there is nothing comparable." The *Oxford English Dictionary* claims that the journalist William Corbett coined the term when he wrote in 1807 of a "political red-herring." Either way, red herrings stink; whether you want to eat one or mislead someone with it is up to you.

24 The gulls were Heerman's and glaucous-winged. Rhinoceros auklets were probably there, too. They are well known for creating baitballs by diving below the fish and generating bubbles (what one biologist labeled "killer

bubbles") that keep the fish in tight groups, or shoals. Individual auklets then shoot through the ball and catch the fish.

25 Because the populations of sand lance and surf smelt are hard to monitor by conventional means, state biologists do not know whether their numbers are up, down, or stable. They suspect populations are shrinking, mostly because the fishes' spawning habitat continues to be shrunk and degraded by shoreline development. This trend is worrying because of the importance of sand lance and surf smelt to the Puget Sound ecosystem. Although rarely mentioned in Puget Sound ethnographic studies, these fish would have been hard to miss, says Dan Penttila, a retired WDFW biologist who studied the Sound's forage fish for more than three decades. Native people "should have harvested them in various sorts of nets as they appeared on beaches, perhaps at the very doorsteps of their longhouses in some cases." Email from Dan Penttila, August 23, 2018.

26 J. P. Hammond, "Fish in Puget Sound," *Bulletin of the United States Fish Commission* 6, no. 13 (Washington: Government Printing Office, Sept. 11, 1886), 195–96.

27 W. M. Chapman, M. Katz, and D. W. Erickson, "The Races of Herring in the State of Washington," *Biological Report* No. 38A (Olympia: Department of Fisheries, November 1941), 18.

28 The dogfish shark harvest lasted for a few years in the 1930s and 1940s. By the late 1940s, the West Coast dogfish fishery centered on Puget Sound, and the *Seattle Times* proclaimed Seattle the "vitamin A-D capital of the world." Wallace V. McKay, "Seattle, Vitamin A-D Capital of the World," *Seattle Times*, June 29, 1947.

29 Heather A. Stout, Richard G. Gustafson, William H. Lenarz, Bruce B. McCain, Donald M. VanDoornik, Tonya L. Builder, and Richard D. Methot, "Status Review of Pacific Herring (*Clupea pallasii*) in Puget Sound, Washington," *NOAA Technical Memorandum NMFS-NWFSC-45* (Washington, DC: US Department of Commerce, March 2001).

30 Conversation with Eleni Petrou, August 27, 2018.

31 Luke A. Rogers, Anne K. Salomon, Brendan Connors, and Martin Krkosek, "Collapse, Tipping Points, and Spatial Demographic Structure Arising from the Adopted Migrant Hypothesis," *American Naturalist* 192, no. 1 (July 2018): 59; Alec D. MacCall, Tessa B. Francis, Andre E. Punt, Margaret C. Siple, Derek R. Armitage, Jaclyn S. Cleary, Sherri C. Dressel, et al., "A Heuristic Model of Socially Learned Migration Behaviour Exhibits Distinctly Spatial and Reproductive Dynamics," *ICES Journal of Marine Science* 76, no. 2 (March-April 2019): 598–608.

32 The model is not perfect, in that some fish make mistakes and go to new spawning areas, and some fish return without any "help" from elders.

33 Conversation with Margaret Siple, August 20, 2018.

34 Margaret C. Siple, Andrew O. Shelton, Tessa B. Francis, David C. Lowry, Adam P. Lindquist, and Timothy E. Essington, "Contributions of Adult Mortality to Declines of Puget Sound Pacific Herring," *ICES Journal of Marine Science* 75, no. 1 (2018): 319–29.

35 Conversation with James West, September 13, 2018.

36 Teresa M. Mongillo, Gina M. Ylitalo, Linda D. Rhodes, Sandie M. O'Neill, Dawn P. Noren, and M. Bradley Hanson, "Exposure to a Mixture of Toxic Chemicals: Implications for the Health of the Endangered Southern Resident

Killer Whales," *NOAA Technical Memorandum NMFS-NWFSC-135* (Washington, DC: US Department of Commerce, November 2016), 8.

37 People who drive electric vehicles are not excluded from this category. The manufacturing of car tires uses oil that contains PAHs. During regular driving, tires wear down and produce dust with PAHs in it.

38 Conversation with John Incardona, September 5, 2018. If you're wondering how to gauge how fast a fish swims, here's how his team did it: "We basically put them on a fish treadmill, a small tank where we could test swimming speed. It was a bit of a problem because single fish freaked out. Herring are schooling fish, and being alone means you have a better chance of getting eaten."

39 John does not dismiss the potential for a future spill, saying that with single-hulled tankers, a spill is an accident waiting to happen. He also warns about bunker fuel, which he describes as the dregs of the refining process, which is heavy and thick and used primarily by cargo ships. His research after the 2008 *Cosco Busan* spill in San Francisco Bay showed that sunlight increased the toxicity of the spilled oil to herring embryos. "Puget Sound is much clearer than San Francisco Bay, so the potential for damage here could be far worse," he says.

40 Jeff Burkey, *Updated Estimate of the Annual Average Volume of Treated and Untreated Stormwater Runoff from Developed Lands in King County*, Technical Memorandum (Seattle: King County Water and Land Resources Division, November 28, 2018).

41 Conversation with Tessa Francis, March 23, 2017.

42 Conversation with Correigh Green, September 14, 2018.

43 Conversation with Phil Levin, September 21, 2018.

CHAPTER 8: OLD FISH AND NEW LAWS

1 The total number of species comes from Theodore Pietsch and James Orr, *Fishes of the Salish Sea: A Compilation and Distributional Analysis,* NOAA Professional Paper NMFS 18 (2015). One other member of the rockfish family is also found in Puget Sound. Shortspine thornyheads, in the genus *Sebastolobus*, are deep dwellers that produce eggs instead of live young.

2 Conversation with Shawn Larson, October 15, 2018. If you want to see rockfish, go to the Seattle Aquarium. Along with octopuses and sea otters, rockfish are one of the institution's three iconic species, says Shawn.

3 "This process, called sexual selection, differs from natural selection, commonly known as 'survival of the fittest.' Under sexual selection, if a mutation results in a color variation, such as yellow instead of red, and yellow females only mate with yellow males, the trait can become rapidly fixed in the population because the yellow individuals have a lower effective population size. This can lead to rapid reproductive isolation and ultimately a new species. It has been proposed that this might have occurred when black and yellow rockfish differentiated from the closely related gopher rockfish." Correspondence with Russ Venter, August 13, 2020. In addition, in many fish species that reproduce by mating, the female chooses the male, though it is not known if this is the case with rockfish.

4 I based Bob Hitz's account on a blog post he wrote, "1966 and the Soviet Fishing Fleet Appears off the Oregon Coast," Carmel Finley blog,

https://carmelfinley.wordpress.com/2012/10/15/1966-and-the-soviet
-fishing-fleet-appears-off-the-oregon-coast, October 14, 2012, along with a
conversation with Bob on November 9, 2018, and email correspondence on
November 14, 2018.

5 Chantel R. Wetzel, Lee Cronin-Fine, and Kelli F. Johnson, *Status of Pacific
Ocean Perch* (Sebastes alutus) *along the US West Coast in 2017* (Portland, OR:
Pacific Fishery Management Council, 2017), 37.

6 In 1943, the US Fish and Wildlife Service published *Food from the Sea* to promote underutilized shellfish and fish. One of the chosen species was the rose-
fish, or rockfish (*Sebastes marinus*). With its firm flesh and "rich and agreeable
flavor," the rockfish, the report said, was rapidly becoming a popular fish and
sure to be one that cooks would want to add to their repertoire. The author
added, "The housewife who experiments with new fish species and new
methods of preparation banishes mealtime monotony and provides delightful
taste surprises for her family." That author was a relatively unknown aquatic
biologist, Rachel L. Carson.

7 Renaming fish is a regular practice in the fishing industry. A classic example
is the slimehead, better known by its new name, orange roughy.

8 Some people argue that the act was more about kicking out foreigners and
allowing in Americans, who would basically exploit the resource in the same
way, than about conservation.

9 P. M. Washington, R. Gowan, and D. H. Ito, *A Biological Report on Eight Species
of Rockfish* (Sebastes spp.) *from Puget Sound, Washington,* Northwest and
Alaska Fisheries Center Processed Report, April 1978.

10 The following paragraphs about Dick Beamish are based on an unpublished
account of his discovery that he sent to me, as well as his responses to several
follow-up questions sent on October 14, 23, 25, and 30, 2018.

11 Conversation with Kristin Munk, October 17, 2018.

12 Not everyone believed Beamish's numbers. Some thought he had simply
misinterpreted the data, but others did not want to accept that "the biological
understanding used to manage rockfish was mostly wrong," wrote Beamish.
Another biologist told me of being at a meeting where a colleague said to
him, "A fish living to be a hundred years old? We should hold a wake when
somebody catches one!"

13 K. P. Jochum, J. A. Schuessler, X. H. Wang, B. Stoll, U. Weis, W. E. G.
Müller, G. H. Haug, M. O. Andreae, and P. N. Froelich, "Whole-Ocean
Changes in Silica and Ge/Si Ratios during the Last Deglacial Deduced from
Long-Lived Giant Glass Sponges," *Geophysical Research Letters* 44 (November
2017): 11,555.

14 Ronald S. Petralia, Mark P. Mattson, and Pamela J. Yao, "Aging and
Longevity in the Simplest Animals and the Quest for Immortality," *Ageing
Research Review* 16 (July 2014): 67. Dr. Daphne Faustin, one of the world's
experts on sea anemones, told me she thought that our local *Metridium
farcimen* and species in the genus *Anthopleura* clearly "outlive humans,"
though she couldn't say by how much. Email correspondence with Daphne
Faustin, November 16, 2018.

15 The ancient geoduck was collected by WDFW divers from thirty feet of
water at Richmond Beach, a few miles north of Seattle, on April 15, 2015.
The 173-year-old clam was born one year after Captain Wilkes and the US

Exploring Expedition became the first known US citizens to visit Puget Sound. A 2003 study found that sea urchins could live for around two hundred years. Thomas A. Ebert and John R. Southon, "Red Sea Urchins (*Strongylocentrotus franciscanus*) Can Live over 100 Years: Confirmation with A-Bomb ¹⁴Carbon," *Fishery Bulletin* 101, no. 4 (July 2003): 915–22.

16 P. A. Larkin, "An Epitaph for the Concept of Maximum Sustained Yield," *Transactions of the American Fisheries Society* 106, no. 1 (January 1977): 1.

17 First discussed in the 1930s, the concept of maximum sustainable yield was not formally adapted by federal managers until the Magnuson-Stevens Act.

18 Conversation with Dan Tonnes, November 27, 2018.

19 Wetzel, Cronin-Fine, and Johnson, *Status of Pacific Ocean Perch,* 36, 37. These quantities are based on landings for Oregon, California, and Washington.

20 *Rebuilt* is an official designation meaning that the stock has recovered and can be fished again.

21 Washington State Attorney General Slade Gorton defended the state's position.

22 The full name of the decision is *United States of America, Plaintiff, Quinault Tribe of Indians on Its Own Behalf and on Behalf of the Queets Band of Indians, et al., Intervenor-Plaintiffs, v. State of Washington, Defendant, Thor C. Tollefson, Washington State Department of Fisheries, et al., Intervenor-Defendants.*

23 "Boldt Decision as Controversial Today as 3 Years Ago," *Daily News* (Port Angeles, WA), January 19, 1977.

24 The US Army Corps of Engineers had the authority to block the coal port because it is responsible for protecting the nation's oceans, rivers, lakes, streams, and wetlands. Any work in, over, or under these waters requires a permit from the Corps.

25 One biologist I spoke with pointed out that WDFW is funded by fishing license sales. With restrictions on salmon fishing, "the state would have lost money, so they needed to encourage people to continue to fish and to buy licenses," he said.

26 Doug Olander, "The Season Never Ends for Quillbacks," *Washington Fishing Holes,* November 1983, 17.

27 Some anglers also used names found more commonly in California, such as barriga blanca (Spanish for "white belly"), serena (from the Italian for its serene appearance), tambor (from the Portuguese for drum, in reference to the extended belly when they are first brought to the surface), rasher (or racha, Portuguese for cleft in the rocks), and priest fish.

28 Conversation with Ray Buckley, October 29, 2018.

29 James E. West, Raymond M. Buckley, and Daniel C. Doty, "Ecology and Habitat Use of Juvenile Rockfishes (*Sebastes* spp.) Associated with Artificial Reefs in Puget Sound, Washington," *Bulletin of Marine Science* 55, nos. 2–3 (1994): 345.

30 Raymond M. Buckley, "Marine Habitat Enhancement and Urban Recreational Fishing in Washington," *Marine Fisheries Review* 44, nos. 6–7 (June–July 1992): 30.

31 One of the better-known boathouses from that era evolved into Ray's Boat-house restaurant (no relation to Ray Buckley) in Seattle.

32 Phillip S. Levin and Aaron Dufault, "Eating up the Food Web," *Fish and Fisheries* 11 (2010): 307–12. Rockfish also pop up on menus from this era. For instance, Café Pinceau in Edmonds served a tomato rockfish creole with

pan-fried yelloweye. I have also recently eaten a rockfish taco, which came from fish caught in Oregon. I later found out it might have been rougheye rockfish, which meant I could have been eating a fish born in the 1800s. This did not seem right.

33 Edward T. Roche and Bruce Halstead, *The Venom Apparatus of California Rock-fishes (Family Scorpaenidae),* State of California Department of Fish and Game, Fish Bulletin 156, 1972, 46; *Fishing Holes* (May 1990): 11.

34 Polly S. Rankin, Robert W. Hannah, Matthew T. O. Blume, Timothy J. Miller-Morgan, and Jerry R. Heidel, "Delayed Effects of Capture-Induced Barotrauma on Physical Condition and Behavioral Competency of Recompressed Yellow-eye Rockfish, *Sebastes ruberrimus,*" *Fisheries Research* 186, no. 1 (February 2017): 266.

35 Email correspondence with Polly Rankin, October 3, 2018.

36 The two barges foundered on November 8, 1973. They were intended to carry gravel north from Steilacoom through the Hiram M. Chittenden Locks to Kenmore at the north end of Lake Washington.

37 A Canadian report from 1986 includes this comment about spiny dogfish: "To a commercial or sport fisherman along the west coast of Canada and the United States, a dogfish is a dogfish and if it needs adjectival adornment at all, the word or words would be out of place in polite literature." K. S. Ketchen, "The Spiny Dogfish (*Squalus acanthias*) in the Northeast Pacific and a History of Its Utilization," *Canadian Special Publication of Fisheries and Aquatic Sciences* 88 (1986): 3.

38 In January 2017, NOAA delisted canary rockfish because biologists determined that fish in the inland waters and those on the outer coast were not separate populations. Unlike yelloweyes, canaries are wanderers who may travel hundreds of miles per year.

39 The few ethnographic reports include Harriet Turner, *Ethnozoology of the Sno-qualmie* (n.p.: Harriet Turner, 1976); Wayne Suttle, *Economic Life of the Coast Salish of Haro and Rosario Straits* (New York: Garland, 1974); and Erna Gunther from the Makah, in Erna Gunther Papers, Accession 0614 005, University of Washington Special Collections.

40 Richard Rathbun, "A Review of the Fisheries in the Contiguous Waters of the State of Washington," in *Report of the Commissioner for the Year Ending June 30, 1899,* US Commission of Fish and Fisheries (Washington, DC: Government Printing Office, 1900), 331.

41 D. L. Alverson, A. T. Palmen, and N. Pasquale, *Report on the 1955 Trawl Investigations (Confidential)* (Olympia, WA: Department of Fisheries, April 12, 1956), 32.

42 Although the plan addresses these concerns, developing an administrative framework is more complicated. The main issue that concerns biologists is governance. One of the strengths of the Magnuson-Stevens Act, says Dan Tonnes, is that it stipulates that regulatory methods should be transparent, that regulators should use the best available science, and that discussions should bring all the stakeholders together. The language in the Rockfish Recovery Plan highlights these issues, but the Endangered Species Act itself lacks the regulatory teeth to guarantee that they will be followed. As an example, Dan says that bycatch is more rigorously monitored on the coast under the MSA than in the Sound under the ESA. Dan's concerns do not mean

that there isn't good fisheries management in the Sound; the problem is that managers often do not have the authority that might help to bypass political issues. Nor do the weaknesses of the ESA imply that the Rockfish Recovery Plan will not succeed. They mean that the citizens of Puget Sound have a greater responsibility to remain vigilant and aware of the politics and the science of the waterway.

CHAPTER 9: THE TABLE IS SET

1   High tide on my day at the beach was 11.26 feet at 3:33 a.m., and low tide was −2.78 feet at 10:34 a.m.

2   A NOAA website showed that the tide rose less then a foot in the first hour after low tide. During the peak tidal flow, it rose 1.59 feet in thirty minutes. Tidal aficionados adhere to the "rule of twelfths" to describe the speed of tidal change through the cycle. In the first hour, the water level changes one-twelfth of the total tidal range; in the second hour, one sixth; and in the third and fourth hours, one-fourth (three-twelfths) per hour.

3   Conversation with Rosa Hunter, April 23, 2018.

4   There have been numerous spellings, including *gwiduc, goeduck, gooeyduck,* and *gweduck.* Another curious spelling was *Gowey's duck,* after John F. Gowey, mayor of Olympia, US consul to Japan, and a duck hunter, who supposedly produced a few specimens when he returned from a hunting trip without a true duck. The name *geoduck* first appeared in print in an 1881 letter written by Henry Hemphill, who sent a specimen to the Academy of Natural Sciences and described it as resembling a "fat plump duck." He had acquired it near Olympia and wrote that the "Indians on the Sound call them Quenux." Henry Hemphill, "On the Habits and Distribution of the Geoduck, A Clam of the Pacific, with Suggestions as to Its Introduction into the Atlantic Coast of the U.S.," *Bulletin of the United States Fish Commission* (Washington, DC: Government Printing Office, 1881), 200.

5   *New York Times,* February 23, 1883.

6   Because geoducks live for so long and don't move for most of their lives, researchers have begun to study the clams as an indicator of climate change. The annual growth rings reflect marine conditions such as sea-surface temperatures, says Bryan Black, who studies geoducks at the Laboratory of Tree-Ring Research at the University of Arizona in Tucson. His primary work has focused on cross-matching growth-ring chronologies from different trees and locations in order to create a long-term chronicle of change. "We believe that geoducks could be the key to understanding climate history over the past few centuries in the Pacific Ocean," he says. Conversation with Bryan Black, January 15, 2019.

7   Geoduck shells do not appear in the archaeological record. This may be because despite their size, the shells disintegrate easily and therefore are hard to distinguish, or possibly because they were processed on beaches at low tide and would have washed away rather than ending up in middens. The archaeologist Ryan Desrosiers, who has been studying the shell structure of geoducks to determine whether they have a signature crystalline structure that can be distinguished in middens, told me that no geoducks had been positively identified in Salish Sea middens. There may be one from a dig

at Mukilteo, but Ryan had not had a chance to examine it when we corresponded in January 2019.

8 The scientific name, *Panopea generosa*, comes from Augustus A. Gould, a nineteenth-century conchologist. He based his original scientific description on a shell from the Nisqually flats. Whoever collected it was part of the Wilkes expedition, which spent time at Fort Nisqually in the summer of 1841. The French naturalist François Jean-Baptiste Menard de la Groye created the genus *Panopea*, naming it after Panopeia, one of fifty daughters of Nereus, the old man of the sea. Her name means "all-seeing."

9 R. E. C. Stearns, "The Edible Clams of the Pacific Coast and a Proposed Method of Transplanting Them to the Atlantic Coast," *Bulletin of the United States Fish Commission* 3, no. 23 (October 19, 1883): 358.

10 R. E. C. Stearns, "The American Fisheries Society," *Science* 5, no. 120 (May 22, 1885): 423; John A. Ryder, "The Geoduck," *Scientific American* 46, no. 17 (April 29, 1882): 264; Hemphill, "On the Habits and Distribution," 200.

11 *Ostrea* is the ancient Roman name for oysters. *Lurida* means wan, sallow, or ghastly of hue.

12 Marian W. Smith, *The Puyallup-Nisqually* (New York: Columbia University Press, 1940), 243.

13 William W. Elmendorf and A. L. Kroeber, *The Structure of Twana Culture* (Pullman, WA: Washington State University Press, 1992), 124 and 132.

14 Hermann Haeberlin and Erna Gunther, "The Indians of Puget Sound," *University of Washington Publications in Anthropology* 4, no. 1 (September 1930): 24. They don't indicate which Native peoples smoked oysters.

15 Item of interest, *Columbian*, October 30, 1852, 2.

16 Harlan I. Smith, "Archaeology of the Gulf of Georgia and Puget Sound," *Memoir of the American Museum of Natural History* 11, part 6 (1907): 303–441.

17 Conversation with Tyler Johns, April 11, 2019.

18 "One Almost Feels He Is Kidding Us," *Olympia Daily Recorder*, July 28, 1917; E. N. Steele, *The Rise and Fall of the Olympia Oyster* (Elma, WA: Fulco, 1957), 33.

19 "Oyster Mines," *Puget Sound Herald*, May 13, 1859.

20 Shellfish were included in the treaties, but in practical terms settlers showed little concern for Native rights and knowledge of shellfish.

21 Unfortunately, poaching of geoduck by various means is a big problem. Because all harvests are regulated, some divers illegally augment their harvest by collecting geoducks just outside their assigned tract or even farther afield while reporting that they came from the assigned tract. Some simply misreport or fail to report how much they harvest. Since buyers want the best, divers dump poor-quality geoducks and report only the ones they keep. The problem is so pervasive that it skews any quantity estimates by state biologists that are based on surveys.

22 *Morning Oregonian* (Portland), October 25, 1862.

23 George B. Goode, *The Fisheries and Fishery Industry of the United States*, section 2 (Washington, DC: Government Printing Office, 1887), vi, vii.

24 Charles Mackay, *Life and Liberty in America: or, Sketches of a Tour in the United States and Canada in 1857–8* (Philadelphia: Harper and Brothers, 1859), 23.

25 Captain Doane's Oyster House opened in 1881. Its signature meal was oyster pan roast, made with Olys, a sizable chunk of butter, ketchup, Tabasco sauce,

old-fashioned pepper sauce, Worcestershire sauce, and salt. The concoction was then poured over toast and served on a platter with pickles, and coffee or beer to wash it down. It cost thirty-five cents.

26 *The Fisheries: Statistics of the United States (including Mortality, Property, &c.,) in 1860* (Washington, DC: Government Printing Office, 1866), 550–51.

27 Anderson Bush, an oyster grower, represented Pacific County. William Callow came from Mason County and was involved in logging.

28 Oyster growers tried repeatedly to stop the discharge through lawsuits. In 1957 and 1964, oyster companies brought suit against Rayonier, Inc., the owner of the Shelton pulp plant. Citing insufficient evidence, the judge in both cases dismissed the plaintiffs' claims without allowing the suits to proceed. The judge was George H. Boldt.

29 In 1962 at least eight mills operated in greater Puget Sound. D. L. McKernan, V. Tartar, and R. Tollefson, *An Investigation of the Decline of the Native Oyster Industry of the State of Washington, with Special Reference to the Effects of Sulfite Pulp Mill Waste on the Olympia Oyster* (Ostrea lurida), Washington Department of Fisheries Biological Report 49A (1949), 115–65.

30 Daniel Jack Chasan, "Puget Sound: The Public's Perspective," in *Puget Sound Research '91, Proceedings*, ed. Timothy Ransom (Olympia, WA: Puget Sound Water Quality Authority, 1991), 23.

31 Little additional information about Miyagi and Tsukimato has been published. What I was able to find comes from E. N. Steele, *The Immigrant Oyster* (Ostrea gigas)*: Now Known as the Pacific Oyster* (Olympia: Warren's Quick Print, 1964); and Kathleen Whalen Fry's "Transforming the Tidelands: Japanese Labor in Washington's Oystering Communities before 1942," *Pacific Northwest Quarterly* 102, no. 3 (Summer 2011): 132–43.

32 Olympia oyster harvests lasted longer in Puget Sound because cultivators augmented their tide-flat farms with concrete and wood dikes, which trapped water and increased oyster production. Oyster growers further altered the habitat by filling and leveling the area behind the dikes. By 1957, more than four hundred acres in the South Sound had been diked.

33 The navy began testing and servicing torpedoes at Keyport in 1914 and continues to do so.

34 Conversation with Carl Sheats, January 18, 2019.

35 Lee E. Erickson, *Economic Studies on the Geoduck Clam Industry in Washington, Olympia* (Olympia, WA: State of Washington, Department of Fisheries, December 15, 1972), 16. The number of geoducks harvested by Bubble Heads also comes from this report.

36 The original estimate of 63 million geoducks represented the harvestable clams. In 2019, the harvestable number was 194 million. The number keeps rising because of increased surveys, which provide a better understanding of numbers and lead to new areas opening up for harvest.

37 N. A. Sloan and S. M. C. Robinson, "Age and Gonadal Development in the Geoduck Clam *Panopea abrupta* (Conrad) from Southern British Columbia, Canada," *Journal of Shellfish Research* 4, no. 2 (1984): 133.

38 C. Lynn Goodwin, "Observations of Spawning and Growth of Subtidal Geoducks," *Proceedings of the National Shellfish Association* 65 (1976): 52.

39 Sandra Tapia-Morales, Zaul Garcia-Esquível, Brent Vadopalas, and Jonathan Davis, "Growth and Burrowing Rates of Juvenile Geoducks *Panopea generosa*

and *Panopea globosa* under Laboratory Conditions," *Journal of Shellfish Research* 34, no. 1 (2015): 63.

40 Conversation with David Fyfe, February 19, 2019. A sea star can push its stomach out of its mouth and into or around what it wants to eat.

41 Eleanor Clark, *The Oysters of Locmariaquer* (New York: Pantheon, 1964), 72.

42 Wesley R. Coe, "Development of the Gonads and the Sequence of the Sexual Phases in the California Oyster (*Ostrea lurida*)," *Bulletin of the Scripps Institute of Oceanography*, Technical Series 3, no. 6 (March 26, 1932): 125.

43 Conversation with Brent Vadopalas, January 10, 2019.

44 Conversation with Lynn Goodwin, February 26, 2019. While working for the state from 1967 until 1994, he did some of the pioneer studies on geoduck.

45 Craig Welch, *Shell Games: A True Story of Cops, Con Men, and the Smuggling of America's Strangest Wildlife* (New York: Harpers Perennial, 2010), 55. During this period in the mid-1970s, wild-stock geoduck harvests peaked at 8,708,000 pounds, with an average sale price of $0.17 per pound. From 2010 to 2015, the average wild stock harvest was 4,705,333 pounds, at an average price of $10.07 per pound.

46 Getting the details on volume and values of harvested geoducks is not easy. The 3.1 million figure comes from 2013, when 6.2 million pounds were harvested. (The average weight of a harvested geoduck is two pounds.)

47 State biologists developed this process of tube-based farming not for aquaculture, but as a way to supplement wild-stock harvests, fearing that too many geoducks might be taken after the state commercialized geoduck diving. Lynn Goodwin and others tried more than one hundred experiments, transplanting eighteen million clams onto recently harvested beds, with no success. "All the juveniles were being eaten," he says. Eventually, he and others figured out the process of using plastic tubes to protect the vulnerable youngsters, though it was impractical for restocking the wild beds. "There wasn't a lot of interest at first. . . . Most of the shellfish companies were busy producing clams and oysters. It wasn't until my third talk or so that they got involved. Part of the problem was the time involved, because they could harvest in two to three years, whereas geoducks are more like five to ten," says Hal Beattie, who managed the WDFW facility. Conversation with Hal Beattie, February 26, 2019.

48 Conversation with Shina Wysocki, May 31, 2018.

49 C. M. Ryan, P. S. McDonald, D. S. Feinberg, L. W. Hall, J. G. Hamerly, and C. W. Wright, "Digging Deep: Managing Social and Policy Dimensions of Geoduck Aquaculture Conflict in Puget Sound, Washington," *Coastal Management* 45, no. 1 (2017): 81.

50 Glenn R. Vanblaricom, Jennifer L. Eccles, Julian D. Olden, and P. Sean McDonald, "Ecological Effects of the Harvest Phase of Geoducks Aquaculture on Infaunal Communities in Southern Puget Sound, Washington," *Journal of Shellfish Research* 34, no. 1 (2015): 183.

51 Conversation with Lynn Goodwin, February 26, 2019.

52 Ray Hilborn, Jeannette Banobi, Stephen J. Hall, Teresa Pucylowski, and Timothy E. Walsworth, "The Environmental Cost of Animal Source Foods," *Frontiers in Ecology and the Environment* 16, no. 6 (August 2018): 329–35.

53 Conversation with Brent Vadopalas, January 10, 2019.

54 Conversation with Jamie Donatuto, April 30, 2019.

55 Conversation with Terrie Klinger, April 17, 2019.

56 Conversation with Meg Chardsley, March 21, 2017.

57 Conversation with Terrie Klinger, April 17, 2019.

58 Conversation with Jodie Toft, March 8, 2019.

59 Conversation with Hank Carson, May 29, 2018.

60 The range in bids reflected the quality of the tracts, which state biologists had evaluated before publishing a list of tracts available for harvest. Each bidding round took about four minutes, followed by sixteen minutes of quiet chat among the bidders. Unsuccessful bidders got their deposit checks back. Winners then had thirteen days to pay the remainder of their bid. They also had to pay four dollars to the state for every pound they harvested. Harvesting could begin on either April 8 or May 23, depending on the tract.

61 Conversation with Jim Boure, May 10, 2018.

62 Following the logic of the 1974 Boldt decision, Judge Edward Rafeedie restored tribal rights to shellfish under the "usual and accustomed" clause of the treaties signed in the 1850s.

63 In 2017, tribes harvested 2.6 million pounds of littleneck and Manila clams, 2.9 million pounds of crab, 272,387 pounds of sea cucumbers, 393,632 pounds of shrimp, and 2.6 million pounds of geoduck.

64 Conversation with Betsy Peabody and Brian Allen, June 26, 2017.

CHAPTER 10: HOMEBODIES

1 Conversation with Phil Levin, March 7, 2017.

2 Virginia L. Butler and Sarah K. Campbell, "Intensification and Resource Depression in the Pacific Northwest of North America: A Zooarchaeological Review," *Journal of World Prehistory* 18, no. 4 (December 2004): 327–405; Sarah K. Campbell and Virginia L. Butler, "Archaeological Evidence for Resilience of Pacific Northwest Salmon Populations and the Socioecological System over the Last ~7,500 Years," *Ecology and Society* 15, no. 1 (2010), www.ecologyandsociety.org/vol15/iss1/art17.

3 Campbell and Butler, "Archaeological Evidence."

4 Campbell and Butler, "Archaeological Evidence."

5 Only one species of salmon, *Salmo salar,* exists on the geologically stable east coast of the United States.

6 Conversation with George Pess, December 5, 2019.

7 Robin S. Waples, Tim Beechie, and George R. Pess, "Evolutionary History, Habitat Disturbance Regimes, and Anthropogenic Changes: What Do These Mean for Resilience of Pacific Salmon Populations?" *Ecology and Society* 14, no. 1 (2009) www.ecologyandsociety.org/vol14/iss1/art3/.

8 Conversation with George Pess, December 5, 2019.

9 "Salmon Fisheries in Oregon," *Morning Oregonian*, March 3, 1875, 1.

10 "Salmon Fisheries," 1.

11 John N. Cobb, "Pacific Salmon Fisheries," appendix 13, *Report of the United States Commissioner of Fisheries for the Fiscal Year 1930 with Appendices* (Washington, DC: Government Printing Office, 1931), 668–69. On Puget Sound, the first state-run salmon hatchery opened in August 1896 on the Baker River, a tributary of the Skagit River.

12 The cannery business bounced back somewhat, but its production exceeded a million cases only once in the subsequent five decades.

13 John N. Cobb, "Pacific Salmon Fisheries," appendix 3 to the *Report of the U.S. Commissioner of Fisheries for 1916* (Washington, DC: Government Printing Office, 1917), 94.

14 Most of my discussion of Jim's work is based on Jim Lichatowich, *Salmon without Rivers: A History of the Pacific Salmon Crisis* (Washington, DC: Island Press, 1999), as well as Jim Lichatowich, *Wild Pacific Salmon: A Threatened Legacy* (St. Helens, OR: Bemis Printing, expanded July 2018 version); Bruce Brown, *Mountain in the Clouds: A Search for the Wild Salmon* (New York: Simon and Schuster, 1982).

15 All quotes from Lichatowich are from a conversation with him on December 9, 2019.

16 Researchers report that solid relationships do occur between transient mothers and their firstborn sons. And transients have their own complex dialect, different from the one used by residents. Although they do not usually vocalize while hunting, they do so after a kill.

17 The state legislature passed its first legislation offering a bounty in 1903. The bounties were $1 for a seal and $2.50 for a sea lion. In 1947, the amount was raised to between $3 and $10 for both seals and sea lions.

18 Victor B. Scheffer and John W. Slipp, "The Harbor Seal in Washington State," *American Midland Naturalist* 32, no. 2 (September 1944): 413. Sixteen years earlier Victor's father, Theophilus Scheffer, had written essentially the same thing.

FURTHER READING

Ballard, Arthur C. "Mythology of Southern Puget Sound." *University of Washington Publications in Anthropology 3*, no. 2 (1929).

Beaglehole, J. C. *The Journals of Captain James Cook on His Voyages of Discovery.* Vol. 3, Part 1. Cambridge: Cambridge University Press, 1967.

Benedict, Audrey DeLella, Cloud Ridge Naturalists, and Joseph K. Gaydos. *The Salish Sea: Jewel of the Pacific Northwest.* Seattle: Sasquatch Books, 2015.

Blumenthal, Richard W., ed. *Charles Wilkes and the Exploration of Inland Washington Waters: Journals from the Expedition of 1841.* Jefferson, NC: McFarland and Company, 2009.

——. *With Vancouver in Inland Washington Waters: Journals of 12 Crewman, April–June 1792.* Jefferson, NC: McFarland and Company, 2007.

Brotherton, Barbara. *S'abadeb / The Gifts: Pacific Coast Salish Art and Artists.* Seattle: University of Washington Press, 2008.

Brown, Bruce. *Mountain in the Clouds: A Search for the Wild Salmon.* New York: Simon and Schuster, 1982.

Buerge, David M. *Chief Seattle and the Town That Took His Name.* Seattle: Sasquatch Books, 2017.

Clark, Eleanor. *The Oysters of Locmariaquer.* New York: Pantheon Books, 1964.

Cummings, BJ. *The River That Made Seattle: A Human and Natural History of the Duwamish.* Seattle: University of Washington Press, 2020.

Durham, Bill. *Indian Canoes of the Northwest.* Seattle: Copper Canoe Press, 1960.

Elmendorf, William W. *Twana Narratives: Native Historical Accounts of a Coast Salish Culture.* Seattle: University of Washington Press, 1993.

Elmendorf, William W., and A. L. Kroeber. *The Structure of Twana Culture.* Pullman: Washington State University Press, 1992.

Faber, Jim. *Steamer's Wake.* Seattle: Enetai Press, 1985.

Fricken, Robert E. *The Forested Land: A History of Lumbering in Western Washington.* Seattle: University of Washington Press, 1987.

Gough, Barry. *Juan de Fuca's Strait, Voyages in the Waterway of Forgotten Dreams.* Madeira Park, BC: Harbour Publishing, 2012.

——. *The Royal Navy and the Northwest Coast of North America, 1810–1914: A Study of British Maritime Ascendancy.* Vancouver: University of British Columbia Press, 1971.

Hansen, David M. *Battle Ready: The National Defense System and the Fortification of Puget Sound, 1894–1925.* Pullman: Washington State University Press, 2014.

Harmon, Alexandra. *Indians in the Making: Ethnic Relations and Indian Identities around Puget Sound.* Berkeley: University of California Press, 1998.

————. "Lines in the Sand: Shifting Boundaries between Indians and Non-Indians in the Puget Sound Region." *Western Historical Quarterly* 26 (Winter 1995).

————. *Reclaiming the Reservation: Histories of Indian Sovereignty Suppressed and Renewed*. Seattle: University of Washington Press, 2019.

Heckman, Hazel. *Island in the Sound*. New York: Ballantine Books, 1969.

Hilbert, Vi, trans. and ed. *Haboo: Native American Stories from Puget Sound*. Seattle: University of Washington Press, 2020.

Lichatowich, Jim. *Salmon without Rivers: A History of the Pacific Salmon Crisis*. Washington, DC: Island Press, 1999.

Meany, Edmond S. *Vancouver's Discovery of Puget Sound: Portraits and Biographies of the Men Honored in the Naming of Geographic Features of Northwestern America*. New York: Macmillan, 1907.

Morgan, Murray. *Puget's Sound: A Narrative of Early Tacoma and the Southern Sound*. Seattle: University of Washington Press, 1979.

Neal, Carolyn, and Thomas Kilday Janus. *Puget Sound Ferries: From Canoes to Catamaran*. Sun Valley, CA: American Historical Press, 2001.

Neiwert, David. *Of Orcas and Men: What Killer Whales Can Teach Us*. New York: Overlook Press, 2015.

Newcombe, C. P., ed. *Menzies' Journal of Vancouver's Voyages: April to October, 1792*. Victoria, BC: William H. Cullin, 1923.

Newell, Gordon R. *Ships of the Inland Sea: The Story of the Puget Sound Steamboats*. Portland, OR: Binfords and Mort, 1951.

Pietsch, Theodore Wells, and James Wilder Orr, illustrated by Joseph R. Tomelleri. *Fishes of the Salish Sea: Puget Sound and the Straits of Georgia and Juan de Fuca*. 3 vols. Seattle: University of Washington Press, 2019.

Smith, Marian W. *The Puyallup-Nisqually*. New York: Columbia University Press, 1940.

Stewart, Hilary. *Indian Fishing: Early Methods on the Northwest Coast*. Vancouver, BC: Douglas and McIntyre, 1996.

Suttle, Wayne. *Economic Life of the Coast Salish of Haro and Rosario Straits*. New York: Garland Publishing, 1974.

Thrush, Coll. *Native Seattle: Histories from the Crossing-Over Place*. Seattle: University of Washington Press, 2007.

Turner, Harriet. *Ethnozoology of the Snoqualmie*. N.p.: Harriet Turner, 1976.

Turner, Nancy J. *Ancient Pathways, Ancestral Knowledge: Ethnobotany and Ecological Wisdom of Indigenous Peoples of Northwestern North America*. Vol. 1. Montreal: McGill-Queen's University Press, 2014.

Vancouver, George. *A Voyage of Discovery to the North Pacific Ocean and Round the World*. Vol. 1. London: G. G. and J. Robinson, 1798.

Waterman, T. T., and Geraldine Coffin. *Types of Canoes on Puget Sound*. New York: Museum of the American Indian, Heye Foundation, 1920.

Welch, Craig. *Shell Games: A True Story of Cops, Con Men, and the Smuggling of America's Strangest Wildlife*. New York: Harpers Perennial, 2010.

Wilkes, Charles. *Narrative of the United States Exploring Expedition during the Years 1838, 1839, 1840, 1841, 1842*. Philadelphia: Lea and Blanchard, 1845.

Workman, David. *We Are Puget Sound: Discovering and Recovering the Salish Sea*. Seattle: Braided River, 2019.

INDEX

be-shó-we (black cod), 94
bias, anti-Japanese, 162
Bierstadt, Albert (*Sunrise on Mt.
    Tacoma*), 69, 211n12
Bigg, Michael, 194
Bigg's orca, 194–95. *See also* orca
Bill, Will, Jr. (Muckleshoot Indian
    Tribe), 54, 56, 88
Binns, Archie, 77–78
bioaccumulate, 127
biofuel, 93
biomarker gene, 129
bison, 22
bivalve, 156–58
Black Ball Line ferry, 82, 83*fig.*, 84–85,
    212n39, 213n44
black cod (be-shó-we) (sablefish), 94
Black River, 37, 116
Blake, Brady (WDFW), 180
Bligh, William, 34
bloom, 122
blue light, 98
bluffs, 16–17, 51*fig.*, 79
Boas, Franz, 94, 96, 117, 214n10
boat angler reef, 143
boathouse culture, 143, 220n31
bocaccio rockfish, 135; Bocaccio
    Recovery Plan and, 140; ESA and,
    149–51
Boldt, George H., Judge, 141, 224n28
Boldt decision, 141–43, 150–51,
    226n62. *See also United States vs.
    State of Washington*
bones, mammal and bird, 22, 49,
    115–16
Bostons, 32, 43–44, 46
bottles, kelp, 96
Boure, Jim, 176–77
Boyd, Robert (Portland State Univer-
    sity), 29–30, 43
bridge, floating, 84
Britain, 32–33, 36–40, 46, 56–57, 64
British Columbia: establishment of,
    208n30; estuarine ecosystem of,
    8; threats from, 56; as Union Jack
    sandwich, 64
Broughton, William, 34
brown rockfish, 134. *See also* rockfish
    (*Sebastes*)

Browne, J. Ross, 43, 45
brush weir, 117, 121–22
Bryan, Alan, 50
Bubble Heads, Inc, 164, 176, 224n35
Buckley, Ray (WDFW), 142–44
Budd Inlet, 40, 41*fig.*
Buerge, David, 35, 117
bull kelp (*Nereocystis luetkeana*):
    anatomy of, 91; blade of, 98*fig.*;
    ecological role of, 93–98, 100–101,
    152; as fishing line, 94; restoration
    and recovery of, 106–7
bulrush (*Hookera coronaria*) (*Brodiaea
    coronaria*), 34, 205n18
Burton Acres, 116, 125
Bush, Anderson S., 160, 224n27
Bush, George Washington, 40–42
Bush Act, 160
Butler, Virginia, 187–88
bycatch, 144, 149, 151, 213n7, 221n42
byssal thread, 165

C

Calamity Point, 75
calanoid copepod, 215n3
calcium carbonate, 172
California sea lion, 194. *See also* pinni-
    ped (flipper footed)
Callow, William, 160, 224n27
Callow Act, 160
camas bulb, 10, 44
Campbell, Larry (Swinomish Tribe),
    197–98
Campbell, Sarah, 187–88
Canal de Lopez de Haro (Haro
    Strait), 33
canning industry, salmon, 191, 226n12
canoe: styles of, 68–72, 70*fig.*, 73*fig.*,
    88, 211n17; war and, 54–56
Cape Flattery, 7, 48, 102
Capoeman, Emma (Suquamish people),
    188*fig.*
Capoeman, Lizzie (Suquamish people),
    188*fig.*
Captain Doane's Oyster House, 223n25
carbon: emissions of, 174; herring
    spawning and, 216n12; kelp and,
    98, 100–101, 108–9, 113
carbon dating, 21

carbon dioxide (CO2), 172–73
carbon footprint, 171, 179
Carlisle II (passenger ferry), 80–81
carnivorous snail, 166–67
Carr, Overton, Lieutenant, 40
Carr Inlet, 40
Carson, Hank (WDFW), 176
Cascade Mountains, 9, 22
Case, Augustus, 40
Case Inlet, 181
cedar: canoe making and, 69, 71, 88; herring eggs and, 117; old-growth forests of, 10; as tree of life, 29
Chasan, Jack, 162
Chasina, F/V (trawler), 119
Chehalis River, 25, 37
Chelsea Farms, 168
Cherry Point: as coal port, 141; spawning biomass at, 124–25; toxins around, 127
chief: as defined by treaty process, 45
Chinook salmon (king) (tyees), 24; ecological change and, 189–90; orca and, 131, 183, 186–87
Christiansen, Lillie, 79–80
Chromista kingdom, 90–91
chum salmon (dog), 24, 150
čibu·d (fishing hook) (Makah tribe), 94, 95*fig.*, 213n7
City of Seattle (side-wheeler), 81–82, 212n34
clam garden, 172, 174, 182, 219n15
Clark, Eleanor (*Oysters of Locmari-aquer*), 166
climate change, 12, 27, 101, 103, 122, 172, 186–87, 193, 196–97, 222n6
clingon, 148
Clinton, George, 76
CO2 (carbon dioxide), 172–73
Coast Salish people: canoe styles of, 69–71, 70*fig.*; food harvest and, 29; HBC and, 38; land impact of, 36; location of, 5*map*; oysters and, 158; of Puget Sound, xii; relationship to landscape of, 3–4; reservations and, 45–47; smallpox and, 29–31, 204n8; sustainable salmon harvest and, 187–88; warfare and, 49–50; x̌ʷəlc (Whulge) as, 3

Cobb (ship), 135
Cobb, John (UW College of Fisheries), 191
Coffin, Geraldine, 69, 70*fig.*, 71, 211n12
coho salmon (silver), 24, 140, 193
Cold War politics, 135–36
Collins, June McCormick, 53
Columbia River: fisheries on, 190, 193, 213n5; as graveyard of Pacific, 68
Columbian editorial, 75, 211n22
Commencement Bay, 7, 35
commercial fish harvest, 142
commercial fishing: bans on, 144; fish stock and, 139–40; resource extraction jobs and, xiii
commuter, 65–66
Contreras, Trevor, 16
Convention for the Mutual Abandonment at Nootka, 33
Cook, James, 7, 32
Cook, L. F., 76
copper rockfish, 134, 134*fig.*, 137, 145, 146*fig.* *See also* rockfish (*Sebastes*)
Cordilleran ice sheet, 13
Corps of Engineers. *See* US Army Corps of Engineers
Cowichan, 55
Cowlitz River, 38
Crim, Ryan (PSRF), 180
culling, 195
cultch, 166, 169
Curtis, Edward, 48
Cymathaere triplicata: as biofuel, 93

D

Dalrymple, Alexander, 32
dam: alteration to hydrology by, 12; logging and, 43; removal of, 190–91, 196
Darwin, Charles (*The Voyage of the Beagle*), 104
Davidson, George (US Coast and Geodetic Survey), 104
DDT (dichlorodiphenyltricloroethan), 126–27, 131
Decatur Island homeowners group, 66
Deception Pass, 61; current in, 72

haptera, 91
harbors of refuge, 58
Harmon, Alexandra, 39, 46, 55
Haro Strait, 33
Harris, Cole (University of British Columbia), 30–31, 43
harvesting: of bivalves, 159–60; of fish, 122–24; of geoduck, 164, 168, 176–78; of oyster, 161; of salmon, 187–88, 188*fig.*; of wild-stock, 176
hatchery system, 190–93
Hat Island Community Association, 66
Haupt, Lyanda Lynn, 110–12
HBC. *See* Hudson's Bay Company (HBC)
head binding, 213n10
headhunting, 49
heads on poles, 48
Heckman, Hazel (*Island in the Sound*), 79
heer (army), 114
hemlock, 10, 94, 96, 117
Hemphill, Henry, 156, 163, 222n4
herring: as consumer, 110–18; diversity of, 125–27; eggs of, 112–13, 114*fig.*, 117, 215n11; as energy flow gatekeeper, 130–31; fisheries for, 120–32, 121*fig.*; as food, 115; food for, 215n3; larvae of, 114; oil of, 120; rake for, 117; spawning of, 111–12, 215n7; stocks for, 128*fig.* *See also* Pacific herring; red herring
herring, pickled, 216n23
Herring's House (Tohl-ahl-too), 117, 216n19
Hershberger, Paul (USGS), 131
hide boat, 68
Hilborn, Ray (University of Washington), 171, 179
Hitz, Bob, 135
HMS *Bounty*, 34
HMS *Chatham*, 34
HMS *Discovery*, 34–35
Hodgson, Brian, 167
holdfast, 91–94, 97, 101
Holmes Harbor, 122
homebody, 183
Homeowners Association of Herron Island, 66

homewaters: Puget Sound as, xi
Hood Canal: flow patterns of, 14–16, 15*fig.*; historical place names in, 16; lookouts on, 50; nuclear submarines in, 108; oyster hatchery in, 173; sill at, 13; Tswana names and, 30*fig.*, 40
Howe Sound, 103
huckleberry, red, 10
Hudson's Bay Company (HBC), 37–39, 206n33, 206n37; slave raids and, 53
Hunter, Rosa, 155
hydrology, 12
hypoxia, 15–16

I

Incardona, John (NOAA), 129–30, 218n38, 218n39
Indigenous people, 21, 22–24, 27–29, 33–36
industrial pollution, 224n28, 224n29; oyster harvest and, 161–62, 161*fig.*
Industrial Revolution, 36
Inslee, Jay, Governor, 131, 197
intertidal community, 171
Island in the Sound (Heckman), 79
isostatic rebound, 22, 27

J

J57, orca, ix
Jackson, Dick (Squaxin Island tribe), 158
Jamestown S'Klallam tribe, 155
Japanese immigrant, 162–63
Japanese oyster (*Crassostrea gigas*), 162
jellyfish, 122, 174
Jesup North Pacific Expedition, 158
Jetty Island, 65
jig dart lure, 145, 146, 148
J. J. Brenner Oyster Company, 175*fig.*
Johns, Tyler (Squaxin Island tribe), 158
Johnson, Craig, 101
Johnson, James (Department of Fisheries), 141
Journal of Occurrences, HBC, 54–55
Juan de Fuca (Apostolos Valerianos), 31–32. *See also* Strait of Juan de Fuca

ABOUT THE AUTHOR

David B. Williams is an author, naturalist, and tour guide whose award-winning book *Too High and Too Steep: Reshaping Seattle's Topography* explores the unprecedented engineering projects that shaped Seattle during the early part of the twentieth century. He is also author of *Seattle Walks: Discovering History and Nature in the City* and *Stories in Stone: Travels through Urban Geology*, and coauthor of *Waterway: The Story of Seattle's Locks and Ship Canal*. Williams is a curatorial associate at the Burke Museum. Find him on Twitter at @geologywriter.